Crossing the Driftless

Terrace Books, a trade imprint of the University of Wisconsin Press, takes its name from the Memorial Union Terrace, located at the University of Wisconsin–Madison. Since its inception in 1907, the Wisconsin Union has provided a venue for students, faculty, staff, and alumni to debate art, music, politics, and the issues of the day. It is a place where theater, music, drama, literature, dance, outdoor activities, and major speakers are made available to the campus and the community. To learn more about the Union, visit www.union.wisc.edu.

Crossing the Driftless

A Canoe Trip through a Midwestern Landscape

Lynne Diebel

Illustrated by

Robert Diebel

Terrace Books
A trade imprint of the University of Wisconsin Press

Terrace Books
A trade imprint of the University of Wisconsin Press
1930 Monroe Street, 3rd Floor
Madison, Wisconsin 53711-2059
uwpress.wisc.edu

3 Henrietta Street, Covent Garden
London WC2E 8LU, United Kingdom
eurospanbookstore.com

Printed in the United States of America

Library of Congress Cataloging-in-Publication Data

Diebel, Lynne Smith, author.
Crossing the Driftless: a canoe trip through a Midwestern landscape / Lynne Diebel;
illustrated by Robert Diebel.
        pages   cm
Includes bibliographical references and index.
ISBN 978-0-299-30294-8 (pbk.: alk. paper)
ISBN 978-0-299-30293-1 (e-book)
    1. Diebel, Lynne Smith—Travel—Driftless Area.
        2. Canoes and canoeing—Driftless Area.
    3. Rivers—Driftless Area.   4. Driftless Area.
    I. Diebel, Robert, illustrator.   II. Title.
        GV776.W6D54   2015
            797.1220977—dc23
                2014030800

To
Bob,
always

Contents

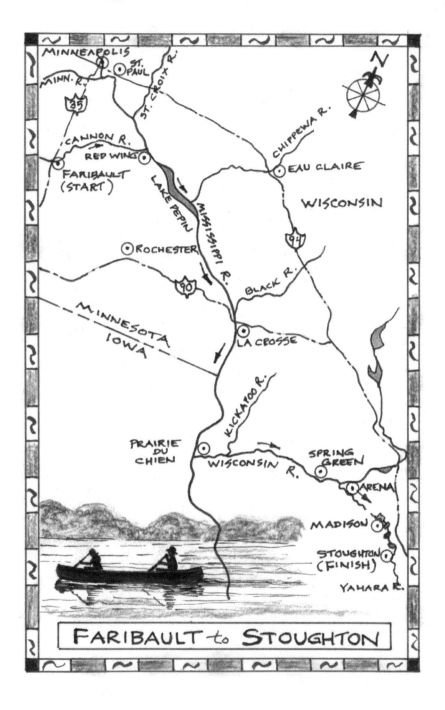

FARIBAULT to STOUGHTON

Preface

This project began on a canoe trip with my husband, Bob. As we always do, we passed those long midsummer days of paddling with talk about rivers and their ways, people we met on the river, questions we couldn't answer. Near the end of this particular riverine adventure, Bob said, "You know, you could write a book about this. Not a guidebook. A book about the rivers of the Driftless." And so this account of our journey evolved, in the way that writing tracks life, a journey across a landscape that has captured my imagination in its rugged grasp, between the two places that hold my heart.

The distinctively beautiful landscape of the Driftless Area spreads over southwestern Wisconsin and edges into the northwestern corner of Illinois. Until I started writing this book, I thought the Driftless Area covered southeast Minnesota and northeast Iowa as well. I was wrong. "No part of Minnesota escaped glaciation," said Carrie Jennings, glacial geologist with the Minnesota Department of Natural Resources. "Driftless" tells us that geologists have found no evidence of glacial "drift," a nineteenth-century term for the glacier's calling cards: deposits of sand, gravel, and rock carried in by the glacier from elsewhere and left behind when it melted. Geologists today call this material glacial till or sediment. Maps of the Driftless Area often include what is called the Blufflands region of southeastern Minnesota and northeastern Iowa, in part because glaciers did not cover these areas during the Wisconsin Glaciation, the most recent ice age that ended about eleven thousand years ago—though the ice sheet lingered longer in northern Wisconsin—and in part because the Blufflands look so similar to the true Driftless land of southwestern Wisconsin, though softer and more undulating. I believe it is the commonalities in the two landscapes—the Driftless and the Blufflands—that lead people like me who are not geologists to consider them as one alluring whole.

To me, it is all the Driftless, a rugged landscape of forested hills, deep coulees, bedrock outcrops, and bluffs; of caves, sinkholes, springs, and disappearing streams; of effigy mounds and geologic mounds; of bottomland and blufftop farms. And flowing down the many coulees and valleys is an intricate network of streams: countless narrow, fast-moving trout streams and quick-to-flood rivers like the Root and the Whitewater in Minnesota and the Kickapoo and the Pecatonica in Wisconsin. Some flow into the broad Lower Wisconsin with its ever-shifting sandbars, others into the Upper Mississippi, which has carved itself a wide valley flanked by bluffs almost six hundred feet high. This valley forms the western boundary of Wisconsin's Driftless Area and the eastern boundary of the younger Minnesota and Iowa Blufflands. In both topographies, the ancient Paleozoic Plateau, once a vast seabed, was dissected, sculpted, and scoured by the erosive power of rivers with millennia to do their patient work.

I grew up along two of those rivers. The South Fork of the Zumbro begins in Minnesota prairie farmland just off the northwest edge of the Blufflands. The Cannon heads up in the same landscape, a bit farther north. Like their companion rivers the Root and the Whitewater, they flow east through the Blufflands to the Mississippi. Many years, the Zumbro floods, sometimes spectacularly, causing no end of trouble for the cities and towns in its valley. The floods aren't as frequent or as disastrous now as they were in the early twentieth century, but when the water rises, everyone thinks about the river.

My favorite place to think about rivers is in a canoe. We have lived in Wisconsin for many years now, in a small town just off the eastern edge of the Driftless, where our home is about a block from another river, the Yahara, which was the last leg of our canoe trip across the Driftless. Over the years, Bob and I have paddled many other rivers of the Driftless. We have talked with people who know about these rivers, and with scientists far more knowledgeable about rivers and their landscapes than we are, about the ways that people affect and are affected by those rivers. Drawing from these conversations and from my own understanding and experience, I have tried to portray these rivers as they are now: the twenty-first century relationship between these rivers and their people; the efforts to repair the damages we humans have wrought on the rivers; the challenges, such as phosphorus and invasive species, that rivers and people face together.

Before the Clean Water Act of 1972 dramatically changed the ways we relate to rivers, farming and industrialization had already inflicted significant damage on the delicate balance of these river ecosystems and changed the hydrology—or movement of water in relation to the land— of each river's watershed, which is the land from which all surface water flows into that river. I try to address the question of whether the rivers of this region are better off now than one hundred years ago, when human abuse seemed to have done its worst, and the related question of whether river restoration is possible and practical.

The way we understand our physical surroundings is influenced by how we travel across the landscape. As recently as the nineteenth century, the traveler routinely journeyed on this river network and understood its ways by necessity. In our world of concrete, it is easy to be oblivious of rivers. When Bob and I paddle Minnehaha Creek through the middle of Minneapolis, for example, slipping under almost a hundred urban bridges along the way, it is the creek that we see and feel and work with, not the eight-lane highway and the traffic overhead. If we were to switch places with one of those drivers above us and cruise along the middle of the wide bridge, we might not even notice that a small creek flows beneath us. On the creek, though, our reality is that intensely natural world, the more primitive layer. We respect its power, watch for its secretive denizens, understand its habits just a little better each time we go there. In the same way, the hiker on the Appalachian Trail sees the mountain terrain more intimately and connects to the landscape differently from the motorist on the Blue Ridge Parkway. When we get out of our motorized vehicles our perspective shifts, in ways that we only gradually understand. To me, seeking to understand the world at river level is essential.

Crossing the Driftless by river highway yielded that sense of connection and knowledge I was after; it also raised many questions that I could not answer. In part, this book is a record of my attempts, through the perspectives of others, to understand more deeply this landscape and its beautiful and vulnerable rivers.

As in Wallace Stegner's novel *Crossing to Safety*, this story is set in part in Madison, Wisconsin. Also as in Stegner's book, evoking a sense of place is not just about communicating what it's like to inhabit that place, but also expressing what it's like to cross out of and into that place. And often, going home means not just crossing to safety but also experiencing the familiar anew. This book tells the story of traveling from home to home, and of seeing things differently.

Acknowledgments

I feel privileged to have the University of Wisconsin Press publish this book, and I thank Raphael Kadushin for creating this opportunity and for his thoughtful help with the subtitle question, Matthew Cosby for his invaluable assistance, and Adam Mehring and Ann Klefstad for their careful and skillful copyediting.

Thomas F. Waters was professor of fisheries at the University of Minnesota, a fly fisherman, an environmentalist, a canoeist, and a tireless advocate for rivers. He was the author of the classic river book *The Streams and Rivers of Minnesota*, among other books. Bob and I met Tom in 2003 while we were working on our Minnesota paddling guides, *Paddling Northern Minnesota* and *Paddling Southern Minnesota*, and over the years, he taught me a great deal about rivers. Tom agreed with Bob's idea that I should write a book about the trip and about the Driftless. I knew that he had long planned to write a book about the Driftless himself and had gathered all sorts of materials—books, pamphlets, research papers, maps. He gave me as much of his massive collection as I was willing to carry away, along with his encouragement. Tom died in October of 2012, while the manuscript was still in its infancy, so he never knew that I had finished it. I will always be grateful to have had his friendship and guidance.

Many thanks go to Carrie Jennings for her excellent tutelage in basic Driftless geology, to John Sullivan for helping me understand more deeply the importance of the Mississippi and its backwaters, and to both for their close readings and knowledgeable comments. I thank Beth Kallestad for helping me better understand the Cannon, Jim Patterson and Bruce Ause for their canoeing tales, Cara Grisim for that ride to Reads Landing, Denny Caneff for always knowing who I should ask, Helen Sarakinos and Rochelle Weiss for explaining thermal discharge regulation, David Aslakson and Gary Birch for helping create the Lower Wisconsin Riverway and for sharing their stories, Jordan Weeks for his enthusiasm about Driftless trout streams, Bob Hansis for the great tour of his stream restoration project, Dave Hopper for helping me understand trout just a little, Pete Jopke for his deep knowledge of Black Earth Creek, and Pat Dillon for that ride.

In addition, thanks go to Mike Davis, Duane Hager, Jon Hendrickson, Mary Stefanski, Steve Zigler, Ann Runstrom, Rich Biske, Jeff Janvrin, Ann Muirhead, Tom Caya, Marian Havlik, Mark Cupp, Abbie Church, Brad Hutnik, Ryan Schmudlach, Scott Teuber, David Heath, Joel Block, Jeff Maxted, and Sara Lubinski for interesting and informative conversations about the rivers we all love. Michelle and Kevin, Brandy and Steve, your generosity to strangers on the river was wonderful.

Most of all, I thank my family. Many thanks to Julie Quinn and her daughter Hannah for kindly and generously launching us on our voyage, to Corrie and Luke Brekke for the camera errand, and to brother Bob Smith for unraveling the mysteries of freight train routes. I thank our son Matt, who answered my endless questions about all things riverine, encouraged me to make the book truly about the rivers, suggested new ways of thinking about the subjects, connected me with other scientists, and explained river science in ways I could understand. He read the whole manuscript, twice, and he gave us that ride, in the middle of a working day. I thank his wife Rebecca for her enthusiasm about this project and for always saying yes when we invite them to go canoeing, even when she was six months pregnant with their daughter Cora, whose arrival we celebrated before the copyediting began. I'm grateful to our daughter Anne, ever-perceptive and astute reader, for her careful reading and inspired suggestions and for taking on this project right at the beginning of a semester of teaching, and to Anne's friend Rafil Kroll-Zaidi for his sage advice on the subtitle. Our son Greg has my gratitude for being our travel concierge on the river and for joining us on many paddling adventures. I thank son James and his wife Devon for their long-distance encouragement; their son Henry was born a month before I finished writing, and our excitement about Henry's arrival gave me the surge I needed to finish the manuscript.

Bob is not only my all-time favorite paddling partner, he had the idea for the journey that led to this book and the idea that shaped the book, and as he has with all my book projects, he encouraged and supported me every step of the way, with only occasional and understandable moments of crabbiness. Bob drew the book's wonderful maps, surprising and delighting me with each whimsical drawing. An engineer by profession, Bob is also an artist who sees the world with amusement, and thus the maps are both precise and playful. I can never thank him enough.

It was a great journey.

Crossing the Driftless

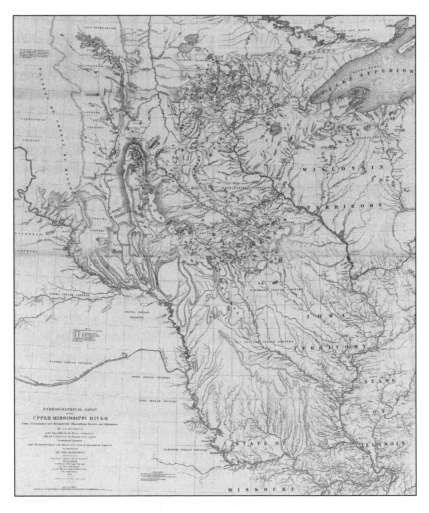

Joseph N. Nicollet's map *Hydrographical Basin of the Upper Mississippi River, 1843*
(Wisconsin Historical Society, WHi-73129)

Prologue

It was in a small history center in Minnesota that we first thought of traveling back to our Wisconsin home by canoe. The center stands near Traverse des Sioux, a shallow river crossing on the Lower Minnesota River. *Traverse des Sioux* evokes the cultural alliance between nomadic Native American tribes who were the territory's first inhabitants and the peripatetic French fur traders who had lived in this land since the early seventeenth century, those who left their cultural footprints by naming many of Minnesota's and Wisconsin's places and by bequeathing their own surnames to their many descendants, names such as LaCanne, LeMieux, LaDuc, LaRoche, Larpenteur. Traverse des Sioux references both the ancient crossing and its eponymous trading post and town, gone now for over a century and a half. And it was a Frenchman who drew the map that so intrigued us that hot summer day.

Astronomer and cartographer Joseph N. Nicollet came to the territory of Minnesota in the 1830s, fleeing from his debts in France, and died in Washington, D.C., soon after he finished charting the northern wilderness. The land Nicollet found enthralled him, and he wrote about southern Minnesota in terms both loving and poetic. The young John C. Frémont, later famous for his 1840s Rocky Mountain expeditions, assisted him, as did German botanist Charles Geyer and Dakota guide Manza Ostag Mani. As they traveled the rivers and prairies by canoe and by oxcart, Nicollet determined the locations of river confluences and heights of land with sextant, compass, chronometer, and barometer. Historian William H. Goetzmann writes that Nicollet took over ninety thousand readings, with remarkable accuracy, and that he was one of the first in the world to use the technique of drawing hachured contour lines—series of parallel lines that follow the direction of the land's slope to create a relief map. An astute observer of the natural and cultural worlds, Nicollet filled his journals with descriptions of the land and people, particularly the various tribal groups of the Dakota people, whom he understood would be displaced by settlers, and his journals and map are the only reliable record of original American Indian place names in the area. From these journals, historian Martha Coleman Bray has written several books chronicling Nicollet's expeditions. Using existing surveys of the territory of southern Wisconsin and explorers' charts of the plains, Nicollet was able to expand the map he drew of the Mississippi River Basin beyond the scope of his wide-ranging expeditions.

The War Department, through its newly created U.S. Army Corps of Topographical Engineers, commissioned Nicollet to chart the territory and determine if the land was fertile and suitable for settlement. The map was complete in 1841, but because the first printing in 1842 lacked his important hachure lines and was thus a deep disappointment to Nicollet, the Army Corps agreed to try again. In 1843, the U.S. House of Representatives authorized a smaller—hachured—version of the map and had it printed and distributed. After the 1851 Treaties of Traverse des Sioux and Mendota, thousands of settlers followed the map into southern Minnesota territory. A series of small but increasingly violent conflicts between these new arrivals and the Dakota tribes displaced by the treaties culminated in the tragic and bloody U.S.-Dakota War of 1862.

That summer day at Traverse des Sioux, Nicollet's map spoke to us not of war, but of river travel and adventure. Bob and I have canoed together on nearly sixty of Minnesota's rivers: long challenging trips, but always downstream. Now here was a map that reminded us of a reality that we had often discussed as we paddled, that rivers are two-way roads for canoes, highways for getting places by water if you don't mind paddling upstream. We had long talked of doing a river journey from place to place, using the river as a travel route, paddling upstream as needed, traveling to get somewhere, not just to float downstream.

Nicollet's graphically beautiful and compelling map, titled *Hydrographical Basin of the Upper Mississippi River*, includes the rivers of what are today the Dakotas, Minnesota, Iowa, Wisconsin, Illinois, Nebraska, and Missouri: a vast web of spidery interconnected river lines, filled in by short, closely spaced hachure lines that portray the land's rounded rises, the degree and direction of the slopes. There are no roads on this map. And the network of river lines called to us.

With his fingertip, Bob traced the river route to our home in Wisconsin.

"Upstream on the Wisconsin?" I said.

"Sure, we can do it," he replied. "The Indians and traders paddled upstream all the time. So can we."

"What about getting from Black Earth Creek to Lake Mendota?"

"Portage wheels. On the back roads."

The idea obsessed us for several years, an obsession that included the desire to have a copy of that map. Like many things possessed by government, the 1843 plates used to print the map were archived and forgotten, for over 120 years; in more recent times, governments have misplaced moon rocks given to states by the Apollo program. In 1964, Alan Woolworth of the Minnesota Historical Society tracked down the original engraved copper plates for Nicollet's map at the Army Corps of Engineers Lakes Survey in Detroit, Michigan, and in 1965, the Historical Society press reprinted the map from those original plates. We bought our copy for fifteen dollars, had it framed—for a lot more than that—and hung it on a wall at home, where it still resides. Bob's handwritten "You are

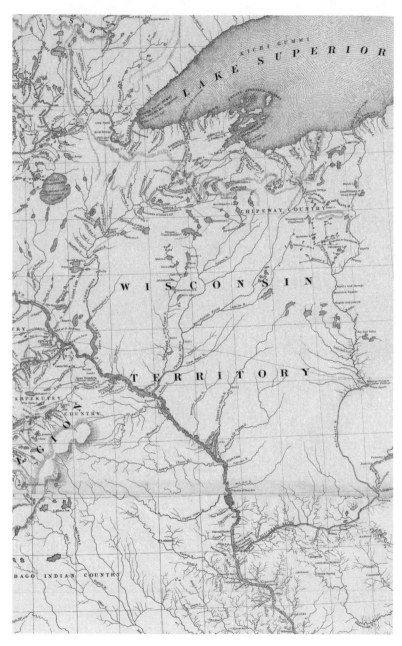

Nicollet's map, cropped to show the area traveled

here" sticky note is still on the glass at the eastern edge of the map, right over our Wisconsin home.

We had our map, and long talks followed about logistics and water level fluctuation patterns, about which canoe was best suited to the wide range of river conditions we would face. Still, three years passed before we decided the time was right. And when we finally launched, it was not from Traverse des Sioux, but from the city of Faribault, Minnesota. I spent all my childhood summers on a lake just outside Faribault, in a farmhouse my great-grandparents bought in 1883, and Bob and I have spent time there with our children every summer.

We loved the idea of traveling from this beloved summer home in Minnesota to our home in Wisconsin. As we first planned it, the journey was about 376 river miles, about 100 of those miles upstream. But low water led us to shorten the route to 359 river miles, and when we encountered impassable debris dams near the end of the trip we portaged 24 of those upstream miles. Cedar Lake is drained by Devils Creek, a little stream that flows into the Cannon River, and the Cannon flows through Faribault and on to the Mississippi, 70 more miles downstream, north of the old river town of Red Wing. Down the Mississippi 164 miles, at Wisconsin's Wyalusing State Park, we would head up the Wisconsin for 78 miles to its confluence with Blue Mounds Creek. We would follow Blue Mounds and then its tributary, narrow Black Earth Creek, upstream for about 24 miles to Cross Plains. Crossing into the Yahara watershed would mean a long portage, towing our canoe strapped onto portage wheels along about 10 miles of county roads to Pheasant Branch, a wetland creek that flows into Lake Mendota in Middleton. From the lake, it is an easy and familiar route, about 23 miles downstream on the Yahara to our home in Stoughton.

But as it is with some journeys, this one wasn't easy. And it didn't always go as we planned.

The river route we chose traverses the hilly Driftless region from its northwestern corner in Minnesota to its southeastern corner in Wisconsin. I've spent my life crossing this land. When I was a child, we drove on U.S. Highway 14 across the heart of the Driftless, headed for my Kentucky grandmother's house. I would be so excited when the hills of the Driftless appeared, thinking, in my childish way, without any sense of how little time had passed, that we had already reached the hills of eastern Kentucky. In the late 1960s, going off to college in Illinois, I drove on newly minted Interstate 90, which roughly parallels what we called Old 14 but skims along the northeastern boundary of the Driftless instead of crossing its heart. Often I made that journey by train, riding the Milwaukee Road passenger line from Winona, Minnesota, to Chicago, crossing the Driftless by yet another route.

When Bob and I made our home near Madison, Wisconsin, a new era of I-90 road trips began, with four energetic children who begged to stop at Castle Rock to climb its Cambrian sandstone tower — geologically alluring, though not in the Driftless — and at the Mississippi River overlook on the Minnesota side to watch a river barge tow lock through the dam at Dresbach.

On each iteration of each route I too am drawn to the same familiar landforms — the Baraboo Hills, the Wisconsin River sandbars, the view west to the Mississippi valley from the upland rise by Limekiln Hill, a certain bluff along the Mississippi where spring water seeping from the limestone face becomes an aqua-tinted icefall in winter, the bend in the river road on the Minnesota side where the highway curves west as it swoops up out of the wooded Mississippi valley to the open fields of the plateau high above. It's a landscape that I'm deeply connected to, in the way that terrain can imprint on our subconscious and become part of our souls. The physical course of the road is in memory after so many trips, almost to the point of recalling it mile by mile. But what of the other older route: miles of river road burnt into the memories of travelers hundreds of years ago? The landscape begs for deeper exploration, this time by river.

Rivers reveal only their narrow slice of the land's breadth, but that slice is telling. Where the river has incised deeply, the land's geologic bones are laid bare. The diversity of riverine ecosystems is often greater than that of the surrounding landscape. Rare plants sometimes survive on the steep slopes of river valleys because the farmer cannot plow there. Alas, invasive species often spread along rivers. The blue heron stalks the river but not the farmer's field. The eagle watches both fish and paddler from his perch but rarely ventures into town. Secretive animals like the coyote, the fox, and the raccoon go to the river to drink. Others, the otter and the muskrat, burrow in its banks. The beaver builds his organic dam to create the deep pool he needs. Wooded river corridors provide textural relief from the monocultures that are modern agriculture and the hardness that is manmade landscape. Only when we strip the bold highway lines from our twenty-first-century maps do we truly see the thin blue lines of rivers, the original highways that served for centuries as the best way to get from one point to another. The river is a more primitive layer underlying the debris of modern life.

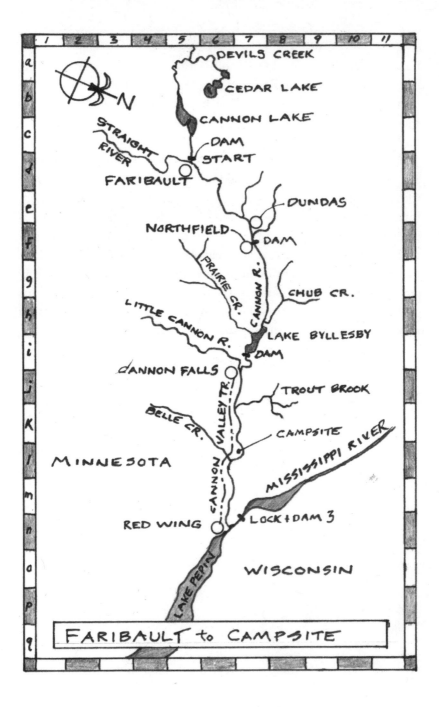

FARIBAULT to CAMPSITE

Down the Cannon

June the twenty-fourth. Stoughton, Wisconsin. Getting ready for a long canoe trip is a familiar ritual. Bob checks the canoe from bow to stern, inspects our paddles and life jackets, collects the camping gear from the jumbled storage bins in the basement, and makes a trip to the hardware store for the fuel that our little camp stove burns. I plan meals for two weeks, gather provisions, mix muesli and trail mix, sort the food into meals, each sealed in a ziplock bag. Packing clothes is easy: we wear the same thing every day and occasionally wash it out. We pile everything but the canoe on the dining room table and floor. One of us asks, "Where are the maps?," remembering the time years before when we were almost an hour up the interstate for a three-week paddling trip in northern Minnesota before we realized that our river maps were still at home. Several times a day, I go to the website that tracks river water levels, fruitlessly hoping that rain has fallen on southern Minnesota, bringing the water level up so we can start our trip at Cedar Lake. We load the truck, strap the canoe to the roof rack, and head northwest on Interstate 90.

June the twenty-sixth. Cedar Lake, near Faribault, Minnesota. The day dawns hot and dry, like all days for weeks now. Yesterday, on our scouting trip, we were dismayed but not surprised to find that the little creek that normally drains Cedar Lake into the Cannon River is not much more than a damp grassy ditch, victim of a primitive board dam at the lake's outlet and several years of drought. Downstream of the two big dams in Faribault, the Cannon itself is low. A period of high winds is forecast on the Mississippi River's Lake Pepin, which we will reach in less than two days, and paddling our open canoe in the high waves on that long, wide expanse of water will be dangerous.

But we're packed and eager to go. As we stand in the kitchen talking, my grandniece Hannah assesses my paddling clothes—loose khaki pants, loose long-sleeved white sun shirt, shapeless hat—with the critical eye of a teenaged girl.

"You look like a beekeeper, Aunt Lynne."

"Thank you, sweetie."

Her mother Julie drives us the five miles to Faribault and a river access point just downstream of the Woolen Mill Dam. Two weeks earlier, after 144 years of weaving woolen blankets, the owners of the Faribault Woolen Mill Company had given up their financial struggle and shut down the looms, they thought for good. At the mill's shuttered outlet store, we cross an empty parking lot, already sprouting weeds, to reach the river. I think sad thoughts of the soft woolen blankets they will no longer weave, blankets that have been an enduring theme in my domestic life, not knowing that the mill will reopen two years from now under new owners Chuck and Paul Mooty, to thrive, brilliantly in fact, perhaps auguring a similar future for the rivers of this beautiful corner of the world. Just upstream is the dam, a relic of the era when river power drove mills. It's been over a century since it last generated power, but the impoundment behind it became the centerpiece of a city park years ago and dams like that are tenacious.

Others aren't. During settlement times, everyone and his brother built a dam on the Cannon, a lively river with plenty of flow to power gristmills, and local fields provided a steady supply of hard spring wheat to grind in those mills: the mighty power of commerce reshaping the natural world. Local historians say at least seventeen gristmills operated on the Cannon and Straight in the nineteenth century, and Alexander

Faribault, the part French, part Dakota founder of the city, owned one of them, the Straight River Mill. When wheat crops began to fail in the 1870s, the mills began to close and most dams were eventually removed. A few mill dams remain, and a hydropower dam was built at Cannon Falls in 1910. But the river is considerably less shackled than a century ago.

While dams are hard on fish, limiting their freedom to migrate up and down the river in order to spawn and thrive, an epidemic of dams can be cured. The more insidious problem of pollution developed more gradually and seems more difficult to reverse. In the 1930s, widespread fish kills began happening on the Cannon, and the river's formerly excellent smallmouth bass fishery faded away. In 1958, the Minnesota Department of Natural Resources (Minnesota DNR) deemed the Cannon uninhabitable for fish, because towns along the river were dumping raw sewage and industrial pollution into the Cannon. Some of the most egregious incidents involved sulfuric acid, dye, fermented corn silage, pumpkin waste, and turkey blood and parts. By the 1960s, most of these same communities had built proper wastewater treatment facilities, though sewage still found its way into the river throughout the 1980s: the small town of Hope, upstream of Owatonna, illegally discharged raw sewage into the Straight River until 2008. It took time, political will, and taxpayer money for these unsavory practices to end, but they did. And the bass are coming back. Walleye, northern, bluegill too, and many other species now swim in the Cannon again, and trout still hide in cold spring-fed tributaries.

Mussels, often called clams, are staging a less certain comeback. The river mussel is an unremarkable-looking creature, at least on the exterior. Most species have a dark oval shell, ranging from one to seven inches long, with narrow concentric growth ridges and sometimes-knobby protuberances, and this rock-like exterior helps the mussel blend into the gravel-covered river bottom that is its preferred habitat. The mussel's secret is that its drab shell is lined with shimmering pearlescent nacre, coveted for years by button makers. Residents of the Cannon Falls area remember the river being "paved with clams" in the 1920s, according to accounts given to the Cannon River Watershed Partnership (CRWP), enough mussels to support businesses that shipped the shells to button manufacturers. But after over a century of overharvesting, habitat destruction, and dams that blocked the movements of the fish they depend on as migratory larval hosts, mussel populations dropped so low that in the 1940s it was hard to find a live mussel in the Cannon. In 1987, a mussel census by Mike Davis of the Minnesota DNR turned up fifteen species in the watershed, an encouraging sign. During a subsequent census in 2012, Davis found sixteen species and said that eight of those species appear to be rebounding. To river scientists, the mussel is the canary in the coalmine, a key indicator of the river's health. Whether you are a mussel or a human being who wants cleaner rivers, Davis's results are good news. Davis calls this the Clean Water Act at work: when we improve wastewater treatment, we get cleaner water. Mussels depend on clean water and free-flowing rivers to survive, and these sensitive yet hardworking little bottom feeders return the favor by further filtering and cleaning the water themselves.

Beth Kallestad, executive director of CRWP, told me that in one sense the Cannon is cleaner now than in the early nineteenth century, because we no long discharge raw sewage and industrial pollution. But because the river now carries pharmaceuticals, household chemicals, water softener salt from wastewater, and road salt from storm water—inputs that are not monitored and whose potential impacts are not known—it is hard to say whether the water is cleaner. And it is increasingly clear that difficult-to-reverse changes in watershed hydrology—channel straightening, wetland ditching and tiling, the wholesale destruction of the flood plain—continue to degrade the river with sediment lost from agricultural fields along the river's tributaries, the branches of the riverine tree that shapes the Cannon watershed.

Watershed is a term worth further description. The watershed of the Cannon is the land on which all surface water—rainfall and smaller streams—flows downhill into the Cannon. Watersheds are divided by ridges or high points in the landscape; thus to move from the river of one watershed into another often requires a portage over these land boundaries. However, the Cannon and the Zumbro and other river watersheds nest into the larger Upper Mississippi River watershed, making it possible to move from one of these watersheds to the other by following the Mississippi from one confluence to the next. It's all about networking.

We stand with Julie on the heavily shaded riverbank, at the confluence with the Straight River, the big tributary that flows into the Cannon from the south, quietly muscling its way into this locus of river union directly across from our launch point. Flowing in from our right is the Cannon itself. The dam upstream aerates its waters and thin strands of bubbles on its dark surface trace the line of flow as it moves past the muddy bank where we stand talking. I like confluences. At these points where rivers join, I feel the physical reality of a riverine system: its connectedness, its overarching goal of gathering waters for the downstream journey that ultimately ends at the sea.

At many confluences, the smaller river is called the tributary and the larger, the main stem. This is the hierarchy of a dendritic river system, so named because its pattern is like that of a tree, with a main stem or trunk, and branches or tributaries. But here in Faribault the classification seems confusing. At their confluence, the Straight is larger than the Cannon, yet once they join, the main stem is called the Cannon: an apparently arbitrary decision made back when people started charting the river highways.

And as it is with some human labels for the natural world, river names can be fluid over time. The name Straight is alleged to be from the Dakota word *owatonna*, loosely translated as "honest trader," but some say the river was named for the fact that it runs straight north. The Dakota called the Cannon River In-Yan Bo-Sda-Ta Wa-Kpa in reference to a striking sandstone spire; Nicollet noted this landmark on his map as "Inyan bosndata" (natural obelisk). It is said that the modern name Cannon is an Anglicized pronunciation of the name given by early French traders, La Rivière aux Canots—River of Canoes. Yet in 1838, Nicollet instead named the river the Lahonton, in tribute to a travel account written by another Frenchman, Baron Louis Lahonton, on a river he presumed was the Cannon. Somewhat as an afterthought, it seems, Nicollet added (The Cannon) to his map as well. A scientist with a poetic sensibility, Nicollet also named southeastern Minnesota the Undine Region, German for water spirit. In the late nineteenth century, the main stem was called the Great Cannon to distinguish it from another tributary, the Little Cannon. Weapons of war played no part in the naming.

On the water. There is a moment just after we push our canoe away from the bank when the boat goes with the pull of the current and we take our first paddle strokes. There's so much promise in that moment, even on a familiar river. We settle into our paddling rhythm and head down the Cannon toward our home in Wisconsin, now 359 river miles, seven Mississippi River locks, and six portages away.

I love canoeing the Cannon. This reach follows the ice margin of the most recent glacier. A string of lakes—Tetonka, Sakatah, and Cannon—that are wide places in the Cannon upstream of Faribault are thought by glacial geologist Carrie Jennings to lie in a broad trench, the remains of a tunnel valley that formed briefly under the melting glacial ice when the glacier was pushed up against the massive bedrock escarpment, or cliff, that is here where our journey begins, the escarpment that defines the channel of the Straight as it flows into Faribault from the south. Meltwater streamed out of the tunnel valley at high velocity, spraying forcefully against the escarpment and over its top, its powerful torrent like a fountain, eroding a number of channels in the high land to the northeast, one of which became Prairie Creek, which flows from Nerstrand Woods into the Cannon, and another became Crystal Lake. An ice-marginal stream channeling meltwater along the edge of the retreating glacier formed the Cannon valley downstream of the escarpment.

Our modern Cannon flows alongside tall bluffs, layer cakes of St. Peter sandstone spread with a hint of Glenwood shale and capped off with a frosting of hard Platteville limestone, all weathered smooth and stained by organic compounds in the spring water that weeps and drizzles down the bluff face. Over millennia, the river has dug itself deep into the surrounding landscape, exposing the land's geologic history to river travelers. If it were spring, the softness of wildflowers—hepatica, bloodroot, wild ginger, dwarf trout lily—would carpet its forested banks. In the stream, shadows of fish dart away from our boat, too quickly for us to learn their names, and the water exudes its indefinable and irresistible river aroma. The wooded corridor is a soothing green refuge from the modern world.

The river chatters over gravel bars and occasionally we feel our Kevlar hull graze a shallow spot. *Ouch.* Three waterproof portage packs and a beat-up Coleman cooler fill the center of the boat to capacity. On top of the load, held tight by the tie-down straps, ride an extra paddle and the portage wheels. Our canoe's hull—long and narrow with no rocker, or curvature, from bow to stern—is designed to go straight and fast. This shape makes it difficult to maneuver around trees that have fallen into the channel, midstream boulders, gravel bars, and river bends; the weight of our gear renders it even less cooperative.

River scientists call the continuous line of the deepest part of the river the thalweg. I suppose I could just call it the channel, but I like the word *thalweg*, its Germanic sound and its meaning, denoting the downhill force of the water and the deepest depths of the river, the river doing what it is meant to do. Following the thalweg grants us enough forward momentum and water depth to outfox our canoe, which stubbornly insists on going straight ahead rather than pivoting agilely around obstacles. We chose this boat for the trip because it will be easier to paddle up the Wisconsin River than our highly maneuverable, but tubbier, river canoe. We won't know if it's a good tradeoff until the trip is over. Meanwhile, we're just happy to be on the water.

17

Cannon River

As the heat of the day intensifies, we're grateful for the dappled shade of riverside trees. Through the leafy veil, I spot what I've been watching for, a bas-relief carving on a bluff face. Sculpted into the sandstone, the improbable image of Shiva—Hindu god of destruction and creation—has watched the Cannon rush by since 1986: not exactly what one would expect to see on a midwestern river. It's at the former site of Scott's Mill where the remains of dry-laid limestone dam abutments along the banks are all that's left of that old structure. Shiva was carved by Jim Langford, a student at St. Olaf College in Northfield who designed a decidedly offbeat senior project merging Eastern religion and art and chose this remote Cannon River cliff to execute his sculpture. He reportedly worked on it for months, with help from his friend Paul Monson, completing just in time to graduate. Ever since, Shiva has

18

been a source of amusement for paddlers and defacement opportunities for kids.

Quite soon, it seems, we float into the Cannon River Wilderness Area, five miles of river bisecting over 850 acres of land, most of which was purchased some years ago by Rice County. The county acquired the property from thirteen landowners, including a hermit named Henry Fisk, who lived for thirty years in a shack in the woods, next to a bubbling cold-water spring. When Henry grew too feeble for life in a shack and went to live in a nursing home, the county decided that the value of his land should pay for his nursing care.

It may be a stretch to call the park through which we travel a wilderness, as the land was logged over at least twice. More accurately, perhaps, it is an important restoration of a remnant of the historic ecosystem called the Big Woods, once a vast dense sugar maple and basswood forest with oak savanna openings, and the remnant is a quiet retreat for hikers and paddlers. CRWP plans to set aside even more land between Faribault and Cannon Falls along this reach of the river known as the Middle Cannon. Their vision of a Middle Cannon River Green Corridor promises benefits beyond the aesthetic. We paddle past third-growth descendants of the forest that help absorb floodwaters and buffer the river from farmland runoff and the paddler from the sun. The return of the forest understory and the regrowth of vegetation on the banks has healed gullies and slowed erosion. Home to rare plants like dwarf trout lily and other relict species, as well as over fifty species of nesting birds, the area is also an important stopover for many migratory birds, some of them neo-tropical visitors.

As we tie up our canoe at the footbridge, the clear call of a white-throated sparrow floats out of the woods. A kingfisher rushes past, noisily objecting to our intrusion into his territory. We climb the bank and from the bridge we spot a great blue heron fishing downstream.

Herons are a constant on our river journeys. The heron fishes the shallows alone, standing on one leg, one eye alert to intruders like us and the other eye on the fish he hopes to eat. As we approach from upstream, the heron waits silent and motionless. When we reach a point that only the heron can define, he abruptly raises his broad wings and lifts off, flapping slowly downstream, legs trailing, toes pointed, neck folded back in a tight S, and disappears around the next river bend. When we round that bend, he is there in the shallows, fishing and watching as before. It must irritate the heron no end to have his solitary fishing expeditions interrupted so often.

It is the same with eagles, though the eagle perches in a tree to fish rather than standing in the shallows. The same ritual: the silent watching, the waiting, the flight around the next bend, and so on down the river. When I was growing up in southeastern Minnesota in the 1950s and '60s, bald eagle sightings were so rare that they made the news and people exclaimed over the event. I never did see an eagle during those years and saw none at all until I had lived in Wisconsin for many years. The eagles are back now. On nearly all of the many rivers we have paddled in Minnesota, we met at least one eagle, often several, some immature. Occasionally we spotted a huge and absurdly messy nest high in a white pine. We watched eagles soar over the Mississippi in downtown Minneapolis.

At Dundas, the current is still brisk as we slip past the limestone building that once was the Archibald Mill. Father Denny Dempsey of St. Dominic's parish in Northfield, an experienced paddler, often kayaks to the ruins of old gristmills along the Cannon and has photographed this mill and the remains of others, including the Cannon River Grange Mill at Waterford and the Randolph Mill, both further downstream. He likes the connection to history and nature that he feels on the river and enjoys imagining what the Cannon was like for the Indians and the settlers.

We almost miss the confluence with Spring Brook Creek. A sandy micro-delta on the left bank is the only sign of the creek's entry. Known formally and on maps as Rice Creek, it is Spring Brook Creek to locals. The creek is Rice County's only trout stream and, most notably, one that supports naturally reproducing native brook trout. Kathleen Doran-Norton, Bridgewater Township supervisor and volunteer for the award-winning Rice Creek Concerned Citizens Group, said that there are more trout in that creek—population 2,000—than there are people in Dundas—population 1,367. Preparing for their first fish count, the group had estimated that two hundred radio frequency identification microchips would be enough to tag all the trout in less than two miles of stream. A little ways into the count they went back for three hundred more and still didn't have enough for all the brookies they found hiding in the little creek—the secret lives of trout.

Because development could change that fish-to-people demographic ratio, the group hopes to establish protective stream buffers. "To drastically change the land use in this watershed would be the death of this creek," said Doran-Norton. The Middle Cannon is designated as a Wild and Scenic River by the state of Minnesota, which gives the township some tools in the form of zoning regulations governing setbacks and subdividing. CRWP works with farmers to reduce nitrate and *E. coli*-laden runoff through a program called Farmwise, which promotes voluntary conservation but has had only a lukewarm reception in the farming community.

Soon the river slows, like a train coming into the station. This is Northfield, our first portage. We take out at Riverside Park, just upstream of the Malt-O-Meal dam, where the Cannon drops ten feet over the concrete structure that once diverted the river's flow into the adjoining historic Ames Mill. Happily, the Friday morning farmers' market is in full swing in the park. We strap the canoe onto its slightly wobbly wheels and wade into the crowd in search of food. As we nibble gratefully on mini spinach quiches and grapes, two genial drunks approach.

"Oh, grapes!" says the taller one. "I'm from Alaska and haven't had grapes in years. Where are you going with that canoe?"

We share our grapes and our story with the inebriated Alaskans and listen to their opinions about canoeing and about the dam. Northfield

Northfield, Minnesota

citizens have argued politely for years about the Malt-O-Meal dam. Traditionalists hold that it is a symbol of Northfield's historic and present identity as a mill town—MOM Brands still produces Malt-O-Meal cereal in Northfield—and thus deserves to stay forever. Others want the river to run freely. Kayakers suggest replacing it with a whitewater race-course. Biologists have worried that if the dam were not removed properly, downstream mussel populations would be buried and extinguished by the released sediment. Every year, students at Carleton and St. Olaf colleges in Northfield study the dam issue and write research papers about it. In recent years, as the dam structure deteriorates, the Minnesota DNR has had its say as well. In the end, though, the dam's fate belongs to its owner, MOM Brands. According to CRWP, MOM Brands has a plan, tentatively approved by the DNR, to replace the dam with a series of rocky drops. But MOM Brands told CRWP that because the DNR isn't pressuring them, they wouldn't implement the plan until they have to. That's a lot of acronyms but not much action. Some dams are tenacious indeed.

When a community owns the dam, citizens do make the decisions, and the way a city treats its river shows how it feels about its river. Architect Witold Rybczynski writes that a "city with an attractive river . . . not too large and not too small—gains not only river walks. Crossing a bridge in a city feels like a temporary natural reprieve. That's why lovers meet on bridges . . . the cities with beautiful natural settings will always have a leg up." A lovely tribute to the successful intersection of cultural and natural landscapes, this assessment also raises a question: What is an attractive river? Even as the world increasingly understands that the best river is a healthy free-flowing river, river health is rarely the highest goal of city planners. Communities with historic dams that no longer serve their original purpose sometimes cling to their identity as a dam town. Dam preservationists often feel that an undammed river is somehow a lesser river and describe their vision of a post-dam river as "shrinking to a trickle." Some anglers argue to keep a dam because they find the best fishing just downstream of a dam, even though it is known that fish populations grow in number and diversity throughout the river reach when a dam is removed. A free-flowing river is dynamic. Though a dam may satisfy the human desire for control of nature, as conservationist Wendell Berry wrote in *The Unforeseen Wilderness*, "Men may dam it and say that they have made a lake, but it will still be a river. It will keep its nature and bide its time, like a caged animal alert for the slightest opening. In time, it will have its way; the dam, like the ancient cliffs, will be carried away piecemeal in the currents."

We may accept the degradation that a dam inflicts on our river, but when the water we drink is threatened, we take action. Northfield's drinking water comes from deep aquifer wells, safe from the pollution problems that plague surface water such as rivers. But because karst topography—limestone bedrock riddled with horizontal and vertical fractures and fissures, caves and sinkholes, where groundwater can move rapidly—is common throughout southeastern Minnesota and southwestern Wisconsin, a water supply in karst territory is never completely safe. Though the existence of karst underpinnings in the Northfield area is speculative and probably not severe, the problems karst has caused in other areas are well documented. Northwest of Welch, a tiny community along the lower Cannon, karst is common and aquifers there are extremely high in nitrogen that percolates down into the karst from agricultural fields and reemerges in well water. Three different municipal sewage lagoons in southeastern Minnesota have collapsed into the bedrock since 1976, and each time, millions of gallons of sewage drained into the underground drinking water aquifer. Manure ponds can do the same. Understanding, mapping, and respecting the ways of karst aquifers is essential in order to preempt such catastrophes.

In Minneapolis and other cities on the Upper Mississippi, where the river itself is the city's sole source of drinking water, ensuring the best possible water quality becomes the goal of urban riverbank planning and storm water management. But this task is complicated by the fact that most cities on a river discharge their treated wastewater and untreated nutrient-laden storm water into the river, where it flows downstream to the next city. Of the six counties in the Cannon watershed, only the Dakota County Soil and Water Conservation District publicly states that water quality is a top priority, according to Beth Kallestad. It's all about priorities, and somebody is always downstream.

We head downstream as well, following three young women in kayaks. They paddle hard and quickly leave us in their wakes. The riparian buffer shrinks to a narrow margin of trees between the river and the surrounding agricultural monoculture and the Cannon flows more slowly. As does the time.

Approaching the old Waterford Iron Bridge, we perk up at the sight of several official-looking men in waders, up to their chests in the current.

"Hey, I bet you brought lunch!" calls one as we draw near. We all laugh.

"Is that a metal detector?" asks Bob, pointing to equipment the other men are operating. He doesn't answer.

"There's a scuba diver down there," he says solemnly, and we're instantly curious. *They look like law enforcement, not DNR.*

"What are you looking for?"

But they won't say any more and return to their serious work. For several miles we concoct stories: they can't tell us anything because they're federal agents and a murderer threw his gun in the river, or there's a gun and a body down there, or maybe a gun, a body, and a metal box full of cash. I make a mental note to ferret out the rest of the story. But everyone knows that rivers keep their secrets, and I never will find the truth.

Voices and laughter ahead interrupt our conspiracy theorizing. Around the next bend, two middle-aged women float downstream in large inner tubes, their cooler bobbing along behind in its own inner tube, tethered to them by a nylon rope which one woman is drawing toward her. "We do this every Friday, but only for three hours," laughs one, "and only if it's not raining."

By the time we near Lake Byllesby, the pleasant effect of their contagious good humor has dissipated and we're tired. It's time for a shore break at the confluence with Chub Creek, next to the State Highway 56 bridge. In mid-September of 1838, on his way overland to explore the Minnesota River valley, Joseph Nicollet and his team camped along the Cannon. On his sketch map, he marked the campsite as just upstream of this confluence. After the group forded, his companion, biologist Charles Geyer, wrote in his botany journal, "the river is about 60 yards wide, 3 feet water & has a very Swift current."

The river is still about sixty yards wide and three feet deep, but because the river is impounded downstream of here in order to generate hydropower, there is very little current now. In the next 4.6 river miles, the Cannon riverbed drops sixty feet, the height of the dam that we will portage in a few hours, but the river itself is a flat lake. Which means the gradient is just over thirteen feet per mile, an impressive drop. It's intriguing to think about what the river with the "Swift current" looked like when Nicollet was here, and how beautiful the series of rocky drops and falls must have been, no doubt even lovelier than Little Cannon Falls on the tributary that joins the Cannon downstream of the dam. But we will never see it. This dam isn't leaving.

Under the intense midday sun, the three-mile slog across Lake Byllesby feels endless, especially at the beginning. If we could fly over Byllesby, we would see that the upper end of the impoundment is a delta, a broad fan of former topsoil washed down from tiled farm fields and eroded gullies along upstream tributaries. But we don't need to fly to know that it's shallow here, and our canoe, like us, drags its tail. At the end of the slog, the second and hardest portage of the day awaits.

At the downstream end of Byllesby, we float quietly for a moment to watch laughing, shouting teenagers jump from a bluff into the water far below, and then we land to portage. Once again, the canoe makes the overland journey on its wheels, which wobble ominously across the parking lot and stubbornly refuse to roll when we reach the grass.

A few years ago, Bob tried to sell these portage wheels on Craigslist. He was asking fifteen dollars. A young man drove twenty-five miles to look at them and offered ten dollars. Bob was adamant about his price. The young man wouldn't budge either, and he drove away without buying. Which is why we don't have a better set of portage wheels today.

We unload and trek everything: cooler, Duluth packs, portage wheels, paddles, and canoe, one by one, sixty feet down a treacherously steep dirt trail crisscrossed by slippery tree roots and studded with rocks. At the bottom, a dozen or so anglers quietly fish the swift outflow of the dam. On the last trip, as I reach the final five-foot drop to the water's edge, one angler takes my load. I jump to the rocky shore and thank him.

Portage complete. Bob takes a picture of me standing in the shallows, grinning victoriously, and then we're back in the boat. The Cannon is shallow here—the result of several years of drought and pressure to keep water levels up in the impoundment—and we paddle to the opposite shore to find a good flow line down the boulder-strewn channel. We turn the canoe downstream and take a few strokes. Then, in a quick and careless moment, the canoe rolls suddenly to the right. We both roll out, landing up to our chins in the river. *Oh no, the camera!* It's in the zippered mesh pocket of Bob's life jacket, not in the little waterproof Otter box he keeps tethered to the thwart! But getting back in the boat comes first. Dragging the canoe to the shallows, we climb back in and wave sheepishly to the watching anglers, who kindly do not laugh. We are soggy but fine, our gear is secure, and surprisingly little water flowed into the canoe. Predictably, though, the camera refuses to work. The last time we capsized was five years earlier, running a small waterfall on a northern river. A camera was a character in that story too.

Soon the little town of Cannon Falls is behind us and we're floating into the Blufflands, down a valley that snakes between high rounded hills covered in hardwood trees. Paddling alongside a mossy limestone cliff face adds a vertical dimension to the riverscape, and the world of the river becomes sculptural. Three big turtles, the largest at least a foot and a half across, look like boulders on the sand shore. A pair of anglers stands quietly in the shallows, slightly apart from one another, casting and watching. The river winds and riffles, a red-tailed hawk hovers overhead, our spirits lift.

A river terrace, set far back from the river edge, is up to thirty feet higher than water level. Jennings says terraces are glacial outwash sediment which once formed the river's floodplain when water levels in the Mississippi and its tributaries were higher. And much wider. My imagination fills this wide valley with a powerful torrent of glacial meltwater, carving the land and depositing sediment along its margins. At the River Terrace Prairie Scientific and Natural Area, this glacial sediment is laced down firmly by the grass roots of a restored prairie and stays out of the river. But sediment from the mostly cultivated land along two upstream tributaries, the Little Cannon and Belle Creek, clouds the water. Jennings says that the hills north of the river are covered with highly erodible loess soil, deposited there by glacial winds. Putting slopes like this under plow sends topsoil down the river.

At the confluence with Trout Brook, we stop to walk up the trail that follows the tributary stream. An owl watches us from a big oak tree, its head slowly swiveling as we pass. Upstream landowners are working with the Dakota Soil and Water Conservation District (SWCD) to reduce erosion on their properties and Dakota SWCD monitors the trout stream to see if their strategies are working. Right now the stream looks good, as the drought means even less runoff than usual. Back at the confluence, where the clear shallow water ripples into the more turbid Cannon, a father and his two teenaged daughters are fishing. The older girl has just landed a smallmouth bass. "I don't want to touch it!" she squeals to her amused father.

A passing hiker tells us that canoeists sometimes camp on the wide sandy bank just across the river, so we cross over. As we land on said sandy bank, two pickups roll in from the gravel road that follows the river on this side. Three black labs jump down from one of the truck beds and several men unload coolers and lawn chairs. We wave and move on down the river, hoping to find our own piece of riverbank.

Around the next bend, a glimpse of several bicyclists reminds me that the Cannon Valley Trail runs along the river too, on an old rail line between Cannon Falls and Red Wing, and I remember that there's another trail in the works. The Mill Towns Trail will run between Cannon Falls and Faribault, linking the Cannon Valley Trail with the Sakatah Singing Hills trail. Bicyclists will be able to ride from the Mississippi River at Red Wing along the Cannon River to Faribault and continue on the Sakatah trail from Faribault to Mankato, the city where the southeast-flowing Minnesota River makes its big bend to the north. *River to river, just like we're doing.*

A slight movement on a long low branch that shades a quiet eddy: a green heron, his rust-colored neck and long bill outstretched, crouches now motionless on his perch, waiting for the intruders to pass so he can give his full attention to fishing.

It's nearly dusk now and we still haven't found a place to camp. We overtake two boys floating in huge inner tubes and ask how far it is to Hidden Valley Campground, but they've been smoking weed as they drift along and their answers are vague and confusing. Another mile brings a group of teenagers in a flotilla of inner tubes, floating coolers in tow, laughing and splashing. From downriver comes a booming bass beat, the music of Snoop Dogg. *The campground!* At the landing, a boy of no more than sixteen wades in the shallows, mumbling earnestly, "I have to pick up the cans. We're good kids, just want to have fun." A young couple—Michelle and Kevin—befriend us and we talk rivers together into the evening. Friday night on the Cannon, 44.1 miles downstream.

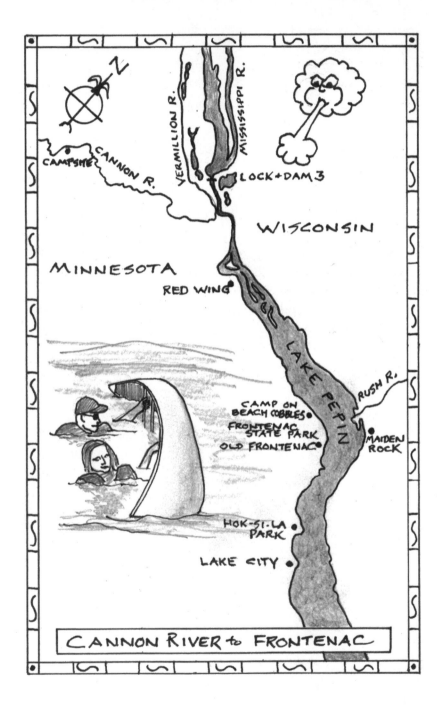

CANNON RIVER to FRONTENAC

On the Upper Mississippi

June the twenty-seventh. Mornings on the river begin with a quiet dawn ritual. One of us boils water to make muesli and coffee; the other packs the gear. We're grateful that last night's party ended before eleven; they are indeed good kids. This particular morning dawns in a muted fashion, a lovely mist hovering over the river. Even the birds are hushed. As we float under the Cannon Bottoms road, I recall the year that flooding had piled a small mountain of debris against the bridge pilings, leaving no space for even a canoe to slip through. Our quiet journey continues, curving through the gentle meanders, past the sandbars of the Cannon River Turtle Preserve Scientific and Natural Area, where the rare wood turtle is sometimes found. But not today.

The sun has almost burned off the fog as we reach the Cannon bottomland, where the river wanders through miles of marsh, splits into several channels and later regroups. This broad delta was built with sediment from upstream farmland, loess soil blown over the land by glacial winds. Jennings said, "When I canoe the lower Cannon—Welch to Red Wing—what I see is the thick, black organic soils once present on the long sloping hills of the lower Cannon tributary watersheds—this dust blanket that had an extra hundred thousand years to develop into a soil, that was so eagerly put under plow when settlers arrived—that now clogs the floodplains of the lower Cannon. I see a squandered resource."

31

A wood duck takes flight as we glide round a bend, and a male merganser swims warily ahead of us, then flies off as well. We've met many a merganser on the rivers, often a female followed by an obedient string of fluffy young ducklings. When the mother spots us, she quickly herds her brood into the shelter of shoreline grasses and then distracts us from her babies by pretending to have a broken wing, flapping and squawking dramatically downstream, apparently hoping that the predators in the canoe will see her as more tempting prey than her now hidden babies. Once she judges that we are far enough from the chicks, she abandons the broken wing act and flies back upstream to her brood. Although it's comical to watch, all merganser mothers seem to do this, so it must work.

The current is almost imperceptible and the marsh grasses are so high that we can't see what lies beyond, so we follow a compass heading. *Are we on the right channel?* The Cannon Bottoms are a marshy maze, a malleable wetland where a spring freshet or a drought will rearrange the river's flow patterns, rendering any previous map useless. It was here in this intricate network of quiet waterways that Native Americans once hid the canoes that they used to travel up the Cannon toward the vast bison hunting grounds that lay to the west. Which is why French traders named it La Rivière aux Canots.

We pass what Bob thinks is the confluence with the Vermillion River, a quiet channel emerging from the woods, sluggishly flowing into the Cannon from the northwest. A turkey vulture cruising overhead seems vaguely sinister, and as if on cue, a horrifyingly loud shriek pierces the still air, then another and another. *Wild dogs or coyotes running deer?* More shrieks. *Is that a human scream? No, it has to be a deer. Deer sometimes scream, right?* Another piercing cry hits a high note and then trails off. As abruptly as it began, the frightful noise ends. But there's no time to talk about the haunting shrieks and we'll probably never know for sure what they were. Minutes later we emerge from the Cannon Bottoms and paddle around a bobbing green can buoy into the main channel of the country's biggest river.

We're just downstream of Lock & Dam 3. Traffic is light this morning, but the weekend has begun and the motorboats are on the move. We stay alert, feeling our way into the rhythm of this riverine interstate highway. The Cannon was all about maneuvering through riffles, drifting with the current, peering into the clear water to spy on fish, spotting denizens of the riparian zone. On the big river, motor craft preclude that kind of leisurely paddling. Surprisingly, the deep-keeled pleasure boats throw bigger wakes than the much larger but less frequent barge tows, and our canoe rocks and rolls each time. As each boat passes, we turn to meet its wake, pointing our bow into the closely spaced waves to keep from taking on water. We follow the edge of the main channel, defined by red and green buoys gently bobbing in the current. Red on our left, green on our right. On the edge we can be agile, ready to dart aside. But we want the speed the channel offers. In the deep main channel is the river's flow, its power. It's a delicate dance: the motorboats lead and we follow.

A Mississippi channel that is reliably deep enough for river commerce is a modern construct. Between Minneapolis and St. Louis, a series of twenty-nine locks and dams impounds the river into a string of what are called "pools," which form a stairway down the river's gradient. More like lakes with a current than a river, these pools are deep enough for commercial river traffic to navigate.

A river is a dynamic system, however, and maintaining the depth necessary for navigation is a Sisyphean task. Huge dredging rigs work up and down the river, sucking up the riverbed's ever-shifting sands to maintain the depth necessary for fully loaded vessels to travel and spitting these massive amounts of sand onto the banks, mounded in startlingly high dunes. They must do this for as long as the river is used for commerce; if dredging were to stop, the river would fill the channel with sand again. Along the channel's shorelines are long narrow wing dams, composed of willow branch mattresses weighted down with stone and mostly submerged and invisible but for the slight disturbance their presence causes on the surface of the water. Like long fingers pointing into the channel, they were built before the lock and dam system to help to divert the flow from the banks into the center, where it scours and dredges. Closing dams partially block water from leaving the channel, leaving the river's extensive floodplain and wetlands and their inhabitants disconnected from the river itself.

Impoundment, dredging, flow diversion: these are radical changes to the river's flow regime and thus to the Mississippi's complex ecosystem. In its 2010 report, *Big Price—Little Benefit*, the Nicollet Island Coalition alleges "documented environmental degradation to river ecosystems resulting from barge navigation," concluding that damming the river is the root of its problems. The Upper Mississippi serves the transportation sector at the expense of its own health.

Or perhaps more accurately, the river serves the Army Corps of Engineers (the Corps), the Inland Waterways Trust Fund (IWTF), and the Inland Waterway Users Board, an industry advisory board that decides how to spend both the IWTF fuel tax revenue and U.S. taxpayer money. The Nicollet Island Coalition report indicates that despite the declining economic value of river transportation, the Corps continues to propose expansion of the lock and dam system. According to the Izaak Walton League, IWTF currently receives about 90 percent of its funding from taxpayers and only 10 percent from taxing its corporate participants, and taxpayers are fully responsible for new construction. A new dam? No problem, the taxpayers will fund it. The Izaak Walton League calls barge transportation "an unprofitable industry," citing studies that compare barge and train costs, and labels this subsidy a "corporate bailout." A 2011 report to Congress estimates that on the Upper Mississippi taxpayers pay six times the amount of revenue generated by the fuel tax for maintenance alone. Because so much of the tax money is spent on maintenance and new construction, there's less left over for restoration of the river's struggling ecosystem.

The project of remodeling the river to meet the needs of commerce began early in the nineteenth century. Before the makeover, the Upper

Mississippi was a braided stream of shifting sandbars, thousands of heavily wooded islands and hidden snags, sometimes deep and sometimes shallow, ever changing. Easily navigated in the canoes of the Native Americans and pirogues of the French traders, the river was inhospitable and unpredictable to larger craft. In the 1930s, after over a century of small changes, the Nine-Foot Navigation Channel Project was launched. Within less than a decade, the Corps transformed the free-flowing Upper Mississippi into a riverine interstate highway, fully navigable by barges from Minneapolis to St. Louis, a very different creature than it had been for over twelve thousand years. This is the river we paddle today.

Soon we're at ease with the traffic and enjoying the ride. Bob and I like paddling together. Though we talk about all sorts of things as we travel rivers, we rarely find reasons to talk about the job of moving the boat along. Sometimes, when people learn how many miles we've canoed together, they ask how married people like us can get along in a canoe when many couples get fighting mad at their paddling partners, especially if they're married. I think it's because after so many miles of paddling downstream together, we both know what the other is doing without talking about it very much. I'm always in the bow and Bob is in the stern. We know that theoretically we should switch, because the bow paddler is the power source and Bob is a foot taller than I am and much stronger, but after this many years we're just going to leave it as is.

In those rare and silly moments when we tried to switch places, the fighting always began immediately. "Why did you do *that?*" So we stay in our places, specialists, so to speak. Up there in the bow, I see things before Bob does—submerged rocks, logs, shallows—and react with a corrective stroke. Sometimes it's a simple draw stroke, which pulls the bow sideways, though my favorite is called a crossbow draw, which I prefer because it has more power than a simple draw. For those of you noncanoeists, I'll explain. Say I'm paddling on the left and I spot a big, slightly submerged rock dead ahead. Without switching my hand positions on the paddle shaft, I swing the paddle over to the right side of the bow, lean out as far as possible, and draw the paddle blade through the water toward the bow, as fast and hard as I can. This immediately pulls the bow to the right, away from the onrushing rock. When Bob sees me do this, he instantly does whatever it is he does back there to draw the stern of the boat to the right as well. He doesn't ask me what I'm doing, just follows my lead. If we're quick enough, we skim past that pesky rock without a scrape. Bob, as stern paddler, is the steersman, so if I sense that he is doing a corrective stroke back there, I act accordingly, without asking. We can paddle a Class II rapid without much talk other than to first agree on the approximate line we will follow as we weave through the maze of obstacles ahead. And to those who ask about what all this canoeing together does to our relationship, I just say that after over five thousand miles of canoeing together, we're still married.

My thoughts wander to the river itself. It's deep and dark, laden with sediment from its tributary the Minnesota River, a big-volume river that flows across Minnesota's southern agricultural land—run-off country—and pours its load into the Mississippi at Minneapolis. I'm struck by the uniform appearance of the banks, thickly wooded in silver maple trees, right down to the water.

At a break in the forest, a sandy beach appears on river right, marked as the Red Wing Wildlife League's private landing. The League owns considerable Cannon bottomland—twenty-eight hundred managed acres shelter waterfowl and other wetland creatures—and the group's goal is to return the land to its 1930s condition, the way the floodplain was before the lock and dam system arrived. The last time we paddled down the Cannon was several years ago, when instead of heading directly to the Mississippi, we dove further into the bottomland to explore a bit and quickly got lost. Wandering the maze of narrow intertwined channels and dead-end sloughs, we met a fisherman in a flat-bottomed boat who kindly showed us the way. He led us down the Vermillion Slough, around the downstream end of Diamond Island, over a closing dam that was submerged under high water that day, into the channel. Along the way, we glimpsed only a small sample of the vast bottoms, which also includes Minnesota's Espen Island State Wildlife Management Area.

From the opening of a cut leading into those small off-channel sloughs and lakes, it's less than a mile to the town of Red Wing. This old river town was built on a high glacial outwash terrace that follows the outside of a channel meander dominated by a huge riverside bluff known as Barn Bluff. Ancient burial mounds attest to this bluff's importance to prehistoric Oneota peoples. The Mdewakanton Dakota who built a village at its base used it as a lookout. All the early explorers mentioned it in their journals. Henry David Thoreau, in one of his rare travels outside of Massachusetts, in fact on the last journey of his life, visited the Mississippi valley. He traveled here on the advice of his doctor, who felt the clean air would be good for him. As part of his Mississippi tour, Thoreau climbed Barn Bluff to "botanize," taking extensive notes on the flora, and traveled by steamboat down the river to Prairie du Chien. From there he headed back east, crossing the Driftless by train.

At about the same time we spot Barn Bluff looming further downstream, hunger makes us pull into the first landing we find, Ole Miss Marina, and unpack lunch supplies.

"I'll have the usual," Bob says dryly. That would be gouda cheese, which travels wrapped in a red wax jacket, a crispbread called Wasabrod, oranges, and dried apricots. Bob adds a handful of trail mix laced with M&Ms because he's hungrier than usual. From the picnic table, we watch the river traffic, but no canoes pass.

Some local people say they are afraid of the river—the muddy water, the currents, the pollution, the barges. Others embrace it. I talked with kayaker Jim Patterson, who lives in Red Wing close enough to the Mississippi to see it out his front window and likes paddling the stretch between Baypoint Park and Colvill Park, a short trip just right for a Saturday afternoon.

"Just past the bridge, there's a cut into the back channel, and then you're in no man's land," he said, "and you can immerse yourself in nature in just a short time."

Though he finds the Mississippi a convenient paddling destination, Patterson prefers smaller rivers, like the lower Cannon, where he often spots groups of eagles, and the Rush River that flows into the Mississippi at Maiden Rock, Wisconsin. "On a summer day, it's cool there under the overhanging trees, paddling the clear shallow water. Lots of down trees to walk around, you have to be experienced to get down the Rush," Patterson said. "I don't see many other paddlers on any of the rivers. From time to time we do see people on makeshift rafts— college-age kids, usually. They strap together barrels, add a wood platform, build a little house on top, and float down the river. One pair had a chair on top of their house and they rowed from up there, using super long oars."

For several years, he and his wife have been paddling segments of the river route from their cabin in Cable, Wisconsin, back to their home in Red Wing. The route is down the Namekagon, down the St. Croix, down the Mississippi. Bit by bit. So far, they've made it as far as the end of the Namekagon. Someday they'll finish, just not right away. "It weaves a nice tale. It's anti-epic," he said with a chuckle.

And through Patterson I learned about Bruce Ause, longtime director of the Red Wing Environmental Learning Center, now retired, who for years led groups of area kids on all sorts of canoeing adventures. The kids canoed the Cannon all the way from Waterville, which is upstream of Faribault, down to Red Wing. They canoed and kayaked on Lake Pepin and down the St. Croix. And they canoed the Mississippi Headwaters, all the way from Lake Itasca to Red Wing, a 527-mile journey that they broke into five segments, one each year, an amazing adventure for young canoeists. "The big thing for me," said Ause, "was that Red Wing Shoe has been driving this program, for forty-three years now. They're very modest about it, but the thing is that kids just couldn't afford these programs otherwise. It's a wonderful chance to instill love and respect for the environment." Ause said he still paddles the Mississippi backwaters a lot, in his Folbot kayak or Old Town canoe, always with the double-bladed paddle that he prefers. "In the spring, at high water," he said, "you can get anywhere you want to in the backwaters around Red Wing." And Ause still hears from the grownup kids who he taught to canoe on the big river, thirty years ago.

Still trying to replace the defunct camera, I dial niece Julie, who lives and works in Red Wing. Using a cell phone in a canoe amuses me; it's a concession to our thoroughly modern natures. Though I know we don't need a phone, it's an undeniably comforting connection to the way we're accustomed to being. But Julie doesn't answer.

Leaving the marina, we pass three young men milling about on a pier.

"Need any gas?" calls one.

We just smile.

"Ice and a coke?"

"How about a cold beer?" Bob replies.

"Now you're talking!" he cheers.

Along the riverfront downstream, Barn Bluff stands alone, a ponderous presence lording it over the town. In the distant geologic past, the mountain-like rise was an island in Glacial River Warren, cut off from surrounding uplands by an earlier course of the river, and the pavement of Highway 61 now covers the old riverbed where that version of the river once flowed. At the base of the bluff, barges are moored along the levee, and on shore, the railroad line and Levee Road run past worn-out industrial buildings. Past the bluff, as we draw closer to Lake Pepin, we pass a scattering of little riverside cabins.

A low rumble makes me look back: a barge tow is following us, slowly. It'll be a while before it overtakes us. There's a no-wake zone in Red Wing, and we're happy that the cruisers have to move slowly here too. Wakes are a problem for canoeists, but they cause trouble in another

Barn Bluff

way, far more insidious and lasting. According to research done by Scott Johnson of the Minnesota DNR, high-energy wakes from motorboats can greatly accelerate natural erosion, eroding the banks by as much as two feet per year on the inside of a river bend and up to fourteen feet on the outside of the river bend over a three-year period, destroying shore-land and washing more sediment in the river. The study, conducted here in the Red Wing area, considered only the specific effects of recreational boating, not commercial barge traffic, and Johnson found that erosion was most common when the river was at least three feet above normal low water level. "In concert with the higher water levels from impound-ment, and land use that makes shorelines more vulnerable, wakes are capable of accelerating erosion," said Matt Diebel of the Wisconsin DNR. Ironically, too much sediment renders the river less attractive to those who enjoy using it for recreation, some of whom are driving the wake-generating boats. It's a cycle that affects more than weekend boaters. The increased sediment also damages fish and wildlife habitat and increases the need for channel dredging, which is funded by tax-payer dollars.

From a pier, a uniformed sheriff's deputy waves us over.

"Hi there. Where are you headed?"

"Hok-Si-La Park, down by Lake City."

"You better be off the lake by tomorrow. The wind's coming up."

"What's the forecast?"

"Twenty to thirty miles per hour, for four days or more."

Worse than we had thought. Paddling through the delta toward the lake, we can already feel the tailwind pushing hard. We have over twenty miles of wide-open lake to paddle, and with all that open water the wind will quickly pick up speed and build big breakers soon after we're past the lee of the delta. Our open canoe doesn't have the freeboard (or hull height above water) to ride waves like that without swamping. Skimming close to the land would feel safer but take considerably longer, and as the sheriff said, we need to be off the lake soon. We won't make it to Hok-Si-La.

Quickly, we resolve to take a straight course instead, crossing the series of shallow open bays from point to point—Presbyterian Point, Friedrich Point, Greene Point—hoping to round the final curve of Point No-Point, the massive three-mile-long bluff of Minnesota's Frontenac State Park that creates the optical illusion of a point, before the wind rises further. We aim for distant Frontenac and paddle hard. No more sightseeing.

Lake Pepin is a naturally wide reach of the Mississippi, twenty-one miles long and, in places, three miles wide. After the last ice age, Wisconsin's Chippewa River, flowing with a torrent of sediment-laden meltwater from the Laurentide ice sheet, deposited its load at its confluence with the Mississippi, which couldn't carry the sediment away as fast as the Chippewa delivered it. The sand and gravel settled in a broad alluvial fan that extended far into the Mississippi, forming a natural dam on the big river that partially blocked its channel just upstream of the Minnesota town of Wabasha, well known as the setting of the movie *Grumpy Old Men*. (Remember the backwater scenes? They were actually filmed on Lake Rebecca, northwest of the Twin Cities, not in Wabasha.)

Pepin wasn't always the lake that it is now. According to research by geologist Dylan J. Blumentritt, sediment cores reveal that when the lake first began forming over ten thousand years ago, it went through various permutations. In addition to the large Chippewa fan, there were two smaller tributary fans, at the mouths of the Cannon River and its nearby upstream neighbor the Vermillion. These three natural dams divided the flow in the big river channel into a chain of riverine lakes. Because the Chippewa fan grew faster than the others, the water level gradually rose and submerged the other fans, and Lake Pepin became one body of water, extending all the way upriver to where St. Paul is now. Until settlers began farming the Minnesota River valley, the Mississippi delta grew at a moderate pace, slowly filling in the upper end of Lake Pepin.

The lake is now shrinking at a rate ten times that of presettlement times, and the upper end of Pepin has moved sixty miles downstream of St. Paul.

The biggest villain in this very modern story is intensive agriculture along the Minnesota River, where fields are extensively tile-drained. Water that falls onto a tiled field quickly drains into a network of drainage ditches that empty into tributaries of the Minnesota, taking a swath of topsoil along with it. Overloaded with water that once infiltrated the land gradually but now pours into their channels, the rivers rise precipitously after a rainfall and erode their own banks as well, increasing the sediment load of the Minnesota even more. Runoff from the Minnesota fills Lake Pepin with sediment, shrouding the lake's ecosystem.

When we paddled tributaries of the Upper Minnesota River—like the Blue Earth, the Le Sueur, the Cottonwood, and the Chippewa—in the spring or after a rain, the water was often a sediment soup. What happens in the Minnesota River doesn't stay in the Minnesota River; eventually it ends up in Lake Pepin: all that wasted prairie dirt.

Runoff was already a major problem when the federal government mandated that gasoline contain at least 10 percent ethanol. Now data from the U.S. Department of Agriculture Economic Research Service show that farmers responded by planting even more acres of corn on land they had previously left fallow to help the environment. When corn prices soared, Dan Charles of National Public Radio reported that the federal Conservation Reserve Program had removed 1.6 million acres of land from the program nationwide, acres that were then planted in corn instead of grasses, in part because the federal government reduced the Conservation Reserve Program, in part because ethanol production had driven up the price of corn. Soil from fields where row crops like corn are planted erodes at rates far greater than from fallow fields, chemical runoff adds insult to injury, and the resulting nasty effect on the river environment is predictable. Production of the biofuel that was supposed to save the environment is instead furthering its destruction. That's a sad irony, the effects of which may never be addressed, given the persistent nature of federal laws and unsustainable farm policies.

But out past the shallows of the delta, we're not thinking about erosion. Or the scenery, though the view from the upper end of Lake Pepin is nothing less than spectacular. Five-hundred-foot-high forested bluffs march along both sides of the river's vast valley, the line of their ridges defining an undulating boundary between midsummer green and deep blue sky. Distant sailboats move swiftly and soundlessly through the tableau.

For over all this beauty, the wind roars, drowning out our voices and almost every other sound, and the waves grow. We surf each following wave and rock in the crisscross chop from powerboat wakes as we head down the shallow bay. My knuckles are white on the paddle grip. We really don't want to swamp out here.

Over the din of the wind, Bob yells, "Just stay on the right; don't switch sides." I nod my assent without turning around. The waves come in groups, three or four average-sized ones followed by a big surge. With little adjustments in speed, we find we're able to ride the crests. When I turn my head, cautiously, after one set of three, looking to see whether the big one will soon follow, I notice that the barge tow has crept closer.

Though we haven't taken on much water yet, the wind is rising steadily. We resist the growing urge to paddle harder, which only sends our bow diving into the troughs of the waves, and try to stay with the rhythm of the waves. But we angle instead a little closer to shore. It feels safer there.

Three miles down the lake, the barge tow pulls even with us. We're far enough off his starboard bow that his wake doesn't cause us any trouble, though I suspect that the tugboat captain thinks we are fools to be out here. We've passed the third point of land and left the tempting safety of the sandy beaches behind us. To our right, the enormous wooded limestone-capped bluff of Frontenac, three miles long and 430 feet high, rises straight up from a narrow pebble beach. It looks like a medieval fortress. We're hoping to reach the sandy landing at Old Frontenac, a least a mile further beyond this forbidding cliff. I'm still tense but not terrified. The water's warm, we're strong swimmers, and we're not far from shore, such as it is.

A sudden shove from one of those big waves and we take on more water. And we edge even closer to shore. Bad idea. A breaking wave catches us and in a flash we are over, struggling to right the boat in the shallows. Paddles in hand, we wade through the breakers, muscling the thrashing canoe onto shore.

"You okay?"

"I'm fine. You?"

"Just wet."

Our waterproof packs are still safely lashed in the canoe, and the brief dramatic interlude concludes with a comic denouement: a red-coated gouda cheese, small escapee from the cooler, floats away.

We stand side by side on the wet pebbles, staring out at the lake, uncertain at first what to do next, as though there must always be something to do next. The waves are pounding hard on the shore, too rough to launch again. On this narrow stony beach, there is just enough room to stay out of the water. The bluff is too high and too steep to climb.

"We just have to wait for the wind to die," says Bob after a pause.

The unfettered wind on big Pepin often holds paddlers captive on shore, and the wise traveler waits it out rather than risk a deep-water capsize. Windbound on Pepin is a familiar tale in the annals of Mississippi River paddling. Referencing an 1830s canoe journey with his friend Robert Serril Wood, George Catlin, the artist of Indian life, wrote in *Letters and Notes*, "We were stranded upon the Eastern shore of Lake Pepin, where head-winds held us three days; and, like solitary Malays or Zealand penguins, we stalked along and about its pebbly shores til we were tired, before we could, with security, lay our little trough upon its troubled surface."

In solidarity with these long-ago castaways, we secure our canoe and stalk our own pebbly shore, following the undulating foot of the bluff to find if we can spot Old Frontenac, talking about how perhaps we could tow our canoe along the shallows to that friendly landing. And though we walk a quarter mile, Old Frontenac is still out of sight, and we return upwind to the canoe to wait out the blow. There's still nothing to do, so I walk the shore again, looking for shells and shiny stones.

There was a time when mussel shells would have littered this shore. Until the late nineteenth century, vast numbers and varieties of mussels lived in the Mississippi, along the entire length of the river, filtering the water and feeding mussel eaters like raccoons, muskrats, otters, and people. After a raccoon had finished his mussel meal and departed, a midden of empty shells on the shore would tell the tale.

Then mussel shells became the raw material of the button industry. A century ago, clammers, not raccoons, would have been hard at work along this very shore, harvesting mussels with crowfoot bars, forks, rakes, diggers, scoops, basket rakes, tongs, and by hand while wading the shallows. The *Annual Report of the Commissioner of Fisheries to the Secretary of Commerce for the Fiscal Year 1916* documents the Mississippi mussel's economic lure to those living on Lake Pepin: "Probably the most productive portion of the river in 1914 was in the vicinity of Frontenac, Minnesota, where, within a few miles, the 45 men engaged caught 645 tons of shells, valued at $10,570 and $2,100 worth of pearls and slugs. Lake Pepin as a whole produced 1,932 tons of shells, valued at $31,486 and $11,820 worth of pearls." Across Lake Pepin in Maiden Rock, Wisconsin, the commissioner reported that crews harvested 390 tons. In today's dollars, those are tidy sums. By 1914, the pearl button industry was still profitable and the river was still rich with mussels, but the harvest was only half of what it had been in 1911. By 1929, according to the United States Fish and Wildlife Service (FWS), "the mussel beds were literally wiped out."

As it was with the vast herds of buffalo up the Cannon River on the plains, and as it was with the endless stands of white pine up the Chippewa River in Wisconsin's north woods pineries, after twenty-five years of relentless harvest by newcomers, the seemingly limitless supply of mussels, a supply that formerly sustained both humans and animals on the Mississippi River, disappeared. A mussel bed still exists back at Friedrich Point, and another at Maiden Rock. But as I walk the shore today, only pebbles and cobbles pave the place where clammers once shoveled up 645 tons of mussels. Not even an empty shell.

It's a beautiful summer afternoon, though, and the powerboats are still out on the water, roaring up and down the lake. One smallish boat passes close to shore, headed upstream and upwind. As the broad prow of the boat slams each oncoming wave, the water's force pushes the hull up to about forty-five degrees. Then the boat drops precipitously into the trough, slamming the water's surface. I can't see the faces of the driver and his passenger—invisible behind the curved windshield—but I'm willing to bet they love this struggle against the power of wind and wave, or they wouldn't be out there.

It's clear that we are stuck on our stony beach until the wind lets up, at least a bit. We cook up some dinner—fried spam, onions, green peppers, garlic and mushrooms over rice, and an orange apiece for dessert—and we wait, restlessly. It's a beautiful summer afternoon, and across the lake the Wisconsin bluffs shimmer green in the late afternoon sun. Our water bottles are almost empty. And we're windbound.

At dusk it is clear that the wind has no intention of abating. At least the persistent gusting has blown away the bugs and we have no need of a tent tonight. Spreading our foam pads and sleeping bags on the stones, we lie down but can't sleep, anxious with the knowledge that the wind may not let up at all.

"If it does quiet later tonight, we could paddle at least a little ways down the shore, maybe reach a landing where there's drinking water," I say. Bob doesn't reply. Either he's asleep or he's weighing the risks. I resist the urge to say more. We can always drink boiled river water.

As the sky darkens, I slowly sense someone or something watching us, but see nothing at first. Then a slight movement shakes the branches of a stunted tree growing straight out of the bluff. A masked face peers out of the leaves, shining eyes unreadable. It is a raccoon, perched on a branch about twenty feet above us, meditatively licking his long front fingers, watching us closely. *The gouda, he must have found the gouda.* I nudge Bob. We silently watch the raccoon get comfortable, adjust his position on the branch, scratch his ear with his hind paw in a relaxed fashion, watching us thoughtfully all the while.

"I think he's waiting for us to go to sleep so he can rummage through our cooler," I finally say with a sigh. "I hope he has red wax stuck in his fingernails."

Reluctantly, we pitch the tent and drag all the gear inside with us. As dark finally comes, the raccoon descends from the tree to circle our thin-walled refuge, hissing from time to time. When I shine the flashlight through the screen, his eyes are red and malevolent in the beam, and he growls. He circles again and again, toenails clicking an erratic tattoo on the stones, but can't figure out how to get in. The scent of orange drifts into the tent and I realize that he must have found an orange peel we carelessly left outside.

After he finally gives up and leaves, silence descends, broken only by the rhythmic shush of waves on the stony shore and the ever-present sound of the wind. Then a distant train whistle on the other side of the river reverberates against the bluffs, and I fall asleep.

A low heavy sound slowly intrudes into my semi-conscious mind and I feel the stones under my sleeping pad begin to vibrate slightly, in tempo with the rumble. A moment later, a sudden beam of intensely bright light flashes over the tent, jolting us both wide-awake.

"What the hell is that?" hisses Bob.

The light comes from the river. Against the charcoal velvet of the midsummer night sky looms an undecipherable shape—massive, black, ominous, as though the starship Enterprise has just landed on Pepin. The light sweeps us again and then stops, like an interrogator's beam, right on our little green tent. I'm ready to confess, or to be beamed up, or both. At the same moment, Bob tells me it is a triple-wide barge tow, the largest allowed on the Upper Mississippi. *How does he know that?* Moving up river in the dark of night. The crew scans the river with a searchlight to spot obstacles and channel markers, not marooned canoe-ists. Though the lake is wide here, the tow runs surprisingly close to our shore. Rumbling ponderously past, it looks now like an enormous lighted floating factory and, magnified by our sense of threat, seems to take up more than its share of the river. Even after the light has past, the beast's low departing growl keeps us awake for what feels like a long time. Finally, the only sounds left are again the wind soughing in the trees and waves hitting the shore. Theoretically we should start paddling now, while the lake rests a bit. But the slender crescent moon has been swallowed by high black bluffs across the river, and neither of us has any desire to share the dark river with a giant starship.

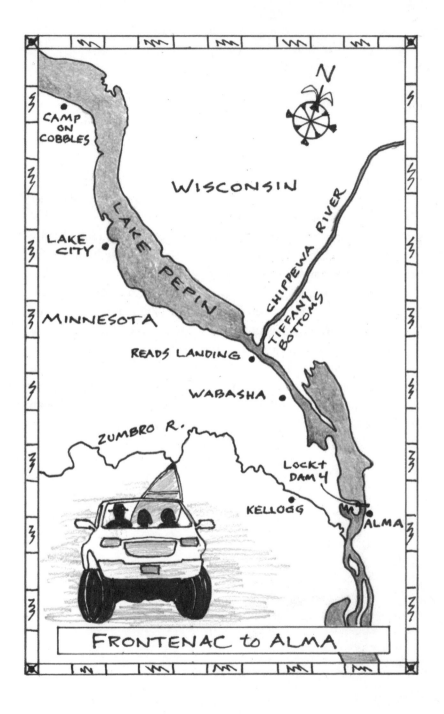

CAMP ON COBBLES

WISCONSIN

CHIPPEWA RIVER

LAKE PEPIN

LAKE CITY

MINNESOTA

TIFFANY BOTTOMS

READS LANDING

WABASHA

ZUMBRO R.

LOCK+ DAM 4

KELLOGG

ALMA

FRONTENAC to ALMA

Windbound on Pepin

June the twenty-eighth. Launching before dawn, we paddle furiously to clear the breaking waves, to get back into the shipping lane. The wind is still gusting some, the waves, still cresting, but not nearly as much as yesterday and there are no boats about to hash the water into confusing patterns. We paddle on, soon finding the rhythm of the water, but with a sense of trepidation about what our tailwind has planned for the day. "The lake seems both idyllic and menacing this morning," muses Bob.

The formerly elusive shore of Old Frontenac is behind us when the sun rises from the dark bluffs of Wisconsin. We pass Long Point, where white pelicans waddle along the narrow sand spit, edging nervously away from us, beaks luminous gold in the soft dawn light.

As the wooded point of Hok-si-la Park appears on the starboard bow, our tailwind has become even friskier, urging us down the lake. Though there is no lee to be found, at least we're not taking on any water, yet. We sail on past the park's sandy beach, and by breakfast time we're landing at Lake City, Ohuta Park. It's the last day of Water Ski Days and volunteers from a local church are selling pancakes in the park. Canoe in tow, we get in line.

Pulling a canoe around on wheels is an open invitation to strangers, who love to ask us questions and tell us their own stories. An elderly man in line with us says that as a boy he swam the mile and a half from

Lake City to the Wisconsin side, along with four of his friends. No boat to accompany them, he tells us, shaking his head and chuckling, just five boys swimming across that big stretch of rough water. And their parents didn't know a thing about it until they got there. From Pepin, he phoned his dad, who drove downriver, crossed the river at Wabasha, and drove up the Wisconsin side to fetch the boys. His dad was not pleased.

"In the car," the man says, "it was 'Yadda, yadda, yadda,' and 'Yeah, yeah, yeah.'" But then he chuckles again and tells us that he and his friends quickly forgot the parental firestorm. "We swam it again later that summer."

An elderly dairy farmer tells us he lived for seventy-five years on the land his immigrant German grandfather had settled, high on the bluff, watching the river flow by. "I was born there on the farm," he says, "and I milked seventy-five head of cattle until I retired." Now he helps his son, an electrician, who milks fifty in his spare time. He smiles, "The cows don't talk back to me. And I love looking at the lake."

With the farmer are two women, both curious about our journey, both eagerly studying our maps. One tells us she spent her life raising beef cattle near Plum Creek, Wisconsin, and now lives in a condo on the bluff above Lake City, overlooking Pepin. The other says she used to own a golf course. Both women tell me they long for adventure.

Another man, who grew up on the dry Great Plains of North Dakota, with no chance to learn how to swim or canoe, says that as a boy he had an opportunity to go to Boy Scout camp along the border with Canada. In preparation for the adventure, his scout leader showed the boys how to canoe. They sat in canoes lined up in the middle of a street in their North Dakota town, and the leader handed out paddles and demonstrated the paddle strokes. The next thing the boy knew, they were all up at the farthest tip of northern Minnesota, crossing Lake of the Woods to Oak Island on a steamer, canoes strapped to the deck of the boat.

"Two miles out, the steamer ran into trouble and caught fire. The scout leader and the boat's captain just loaded us and our gear into the canoes. As we paddled away, canoeing on real water for the very first time, the burning boat sank behind us. I still don't know how to swim," he concludes with a grin.

Cara Grisim, one of the event organizers and a local businesswoman, is seated at a picnic table with her dad, Jerry, and they invite us to join them. By the time we're halfway through the pancakes and sausage, she insists on driving us in her pickup truck the nine miles to the bottom of the lake.

"This wind's just going to get worse, for three more days," she says, "and there's no place at all to get off Pepin until you get to Reads Landing. The tracks run right next to the water and it's a long steep drop straight down to the water's edge. If you get into trouble in the waves, you're out of luck. I'll give you a ride."

We have choices. We could be purists, camping in Lake City until the wind dies, probably in three days. We could tow the canoe on its rickety wheels for nine miles along the shoulder of U.S. Highway 61 to Reads Landing. Or we could take the ride. We're both a bit impatient, one of us more so than the other, so we don't even have to discuss it.

"That'd be wonderful!" I say. "Are you sure you want to do this?"

"Of course I'm sure! I just need to run home and get the truck," she replies.

By the time we reach Reads Landing, we have shared so many stories about our lives that we feel like old friends, and Bob and I are no longer windbound.

Back in the day, Reads Landing was a bigger town, with a multitude of warehouses, twenty-seven hotels, twenty-one saloons, fifteen stores, one church, and one school. That was before the railroad arrived, during the time that the Mississippi's confluence with the Chippewa was a bustling hub for logging drives and riverboat travel, and many loggers wintered in the town's hotels. The town even made a bid to be

Minnesota's capital. Reads Landing is now a village of about two hundred people, and the historic red brick schoolhouse is now the Wabasha County museum.

Across the river from the landing, low tree-covered banks frame the confluence with the Chippewa, emerging from the huge delta that formed from the alluvial fan at this confluence, the land that transforms the Mississippi River into a lake. When the Chippewa lobe of the Laurentide ice sheet melted, it drained through the Chippewa, scouring a deep wide canyon, creating a braided meltwater stream. The modern Chippewa, the Mississippi's largest tributary between Lake Pepin and the Wisconsin River, flows within a broad sandy outwash plain deposited by that glacial stream. For thousands of years, the Chippewa carried in sand and gravel from the Central Sands region, lining the riverbed of the Lower Chippewa and spilling out into the channel of the Mississippi. And the river's sand just keeps building. Heavily wooded and laced with wetlands, with countless beaver dams creating intricate networks of ponds and sloughs, this ever-growing delta is the downstream end of Tiffany Bottoms, the most extensive contiguous floodplain forest in Wisconsin.

Thousands of acres of state-owned land—floodplain forest and interior swamps, upland forests and savannas—lie along both sides of the river between the towns of Nelson and Durand, extending fifteen miles up the Chippewa from the confluence. According to the Wisconsin DNR, this wild area attracts nearly every species of bird found in Wisconsin, including species like whip-poor-will, redheaded woodpecker, pileated woodpecker, yellow-headed blackbird, red-shouldered hawk, great egret, cerulean warbler, prothonotory warbler, great blue heron, and blue-gray gnatcatcher. Flycatchers, night herons, and bitterns inhabit the interior swamps. That's just a starter list. One group of bird watchers counted seventy-six species in one outing. In the warm months, groups arrange trips with the Chippewa Valley Motor Car Association, an organization that operates a train of little yellow track-maintenance cars along ten miles of railroad track that once carried train cars loaded with logs. The bird watchers ride the slowly chugging mini-train into the heart of an otherwise roadless wildlife area. And year-round, anyone can hike the tracks to explore the depths of the reserve.

The Chippewa River originates in far northern Wisconsin, in two headwater forks. When Europeans arrived, Native Americans had long traveled between Lake Superior and the Mississippi by paddling up the Bad River, then down the West Fork of the Chippewa and the Chippewa, and though the Bad was said to be rough going, with many portages, the newcomers adopted this river highway as well. The Chippewa was a famous logging river during the nineteenth century, as the Chippewa watershed was the source of about a third of the logs from north woods pineries. I have never paddled the river and must confess that my most vivid—though imaginary—images of the Chippewa come from fourth-grade regional history lessons and from listening as a teenager in the '60s to Joan Baez's version of the traditional American ballad "The River in the Pines." Originally collected in *Ballads and Songs of the Shanty-Boy* by Franz Rickaby, who got it from a fellow in Eau Claire, Wisconsin, it tells the sad tale of a young woman and her lover, a young log driver who met his end in the "fatal rapids" of the Chippewa. Baez's version ends with these words:

> Now every raft of lumber
> That comes down the Chipeway,
> There's a lonely grave that's
> Visited by drivers on their way
> They plant wild flowers upon it
> In the morning fair and fine.
> 'Tis the grave of two young lovers
> From the river in the pines.

Hearing these lyrics evokes in me elementary school memories of old photographs depicting tiny figures of log drivers standing atop enormous log jams, and of vivid tales about how log blockades were released by those daring fellows, men who often lost their lives when the jam suddenly broke and a wild rush of pine logs surged and tumbled downriver, through the "fatal rapids."

It's interesting to note that Nicollet knew the river as the Chipeway, which it was called for many years, and that spelling does rhyme better in these lyrics than does Chippewa. As folk songs are wont to do, the mournful ballad portrays the river as a scene of tragedy, and though I didn't learn this in elementary school, the pineries were indeed the scene of an ecological tragedy, with the river playing its part in the drama by carrying the logs downstream. The good news is that, according to Mike Svob in his guidebook *Paddling Southern Wisconsin*, the Chippewa is actually quite a good canoeing river, especially from Eau Claire to the confluence where the journey ends in the wild, remote bottomland.

Our companion the tailwind is in a ferocious mood today, and fortunately the Mississippi is riverine once again, buffered from the wind by wooded islands, waves manageable. Having left much of its sediment behind on the bottom of Lake Pepin, the formerly murky Mississippi now runs almost clear, with a lovely copper tint, apparently unchanged at least in color since Zebulon Pike passed this way, headed upstream on his unsuccessful expedition to find the river's source. "The water of the Mississippi, since we passed Lake Pepin, has been remarkably red; and where it is deep, appears as black as ink," wrote Pike on September 21, 1805.

We push off from the landing, and through the copper-tinted lens I watch the sandy bottom moving beneath us. Eelgrasses sway gently in the current and a water snake whips past. *Or could it be an eel?* Gone too quickly to tell.

If it is indeed an American eel, this fast-moving creature is one of the Mississippi's greatest long-distance travelers. The eel's life story weaves an epic tale. The larva hatches in the Sargasso Sea between the West Indies and the Azores and slowly drifts, a tiny transparent leaf-like creature called a glass eel, into coastal waters, metamorphosing over several years, first into a rounder darker being called an elver and then into a yellow eel. Adapted now to both brackish and fresh water, the yellow eel swims in the estuary of a coastal river like the Mississippi. Only the female ventures upstream as far as the Upper Mississippi, scaling dams and bypassing rapids by crawling overland on mud and wet grass. Her journey may take years. When she is sexually mature, she returns to the Mississippi estuary, where the males are waiting. They morph once again into saltwater fish and swim—together, one would hope—back to the Sargasso to spawn and die.

Here at the foot of Lake Pepin, we're also at the northernmost tip of the Upper Mississippi River National Wildlife and Fish Refuge, which extends south along 261 miles of river and covers 240,000 acres of land, from the mouth of the Chippewa to Rock Island, Illinois.

The efforts and influence of a Chicago businessman named Will Dilg and his newly organized Izaak Walton League led Congress in 1924 to authorize the Refuge, to save the river from what they feared was the brink of a collapse. "The Ikes," as they are known, were named after the well-known English author of *The Compleat Angler*. They pushed to end the destruction of the river's floodplain by farming and draining and fought pollution of the river. "Will Dilg and the Izaak Walton League," writes John Anfinson in *The River We Have Wrought*, "challenged agricultural and commercial interests as to the primary values of the river and its floodplains." Though this remarkable legislative action came six years before the Corps, authorized by Congress in 1930, began to impound and dredge the upper river, the pressure to build the lock and dam system was already building as the Refuge was born. The irony of these conflicting Congressional acts is inescapable, and the debate between agriculture, commerce, and the Corps on the one hand, and conservationists like the Ikes on the other, still rages. As does the dredging. As Anfinson wrote, "Apparently, Americans are unwilling to accept either the loss of the river's ecosystem or the loss of the river as a transportation artery, since Congress has mandated that it be managed for both." My father was a hunter and a fisherman, a member of the Ikes who took the side of the Refuge. Though I had no idea what the organization was about when I was growing up, I remember glancing at issues of the League's magazine *Outdoor America* when they arrived in the mail, wondering briefly what it meant to him but never asking. Now I wish I could.

Today, we stare at an enormous pile of dredged river sand, a pale yellow vertical desert towering over the channel across from Reads Landing, just downstream of the confluence. Down the face of one high dune runs a long sheet of plastic and atop the dune is a hose connected to a riverside pump that pours a stream of river water back down the plastic. It's a homemade water park. This sand pile is a mere fraction of the sand dredged from the shipping channel. The Corps built a sediment trap in 1984 near the mouth of the Chippewa to capture inflowing sand, and the Corps pumps sand into an old gravel pit near Wabasha, piles sand in fields and along the riverbanks, and builds new islands from this excess of sand. It's an endless job, and all for the benefit of the barge traffic.

A short paddle brings us to the town of Wabasha, where we float under the bridge, admiring the elegant steel truss structure built in 1988, replacing one that had been there since the 1930s. This bridge is the first crossing since we left Red Wing. Which, of course, is why the grumpy father of the swimmer with whom we talked in Lake City had to drive so far to retrieve those adventurous and headstrong boys.

When the previous bridge was built, people apparently didn't think much of the river, or at least the way in which it carried the highway into Wabasha's riverfront reflected a certain disdain. As the old bridge reached the Wabasha shoreline, the elevated descent ramp made a right turn and traveled for some distance along a shabby riverfront, effectively blocking the view of the river. Wabasha no longer turns its back on the water: the 1988 bridge has a straight approach road, and the town, which has remodeled and landscaped the riverfront, seems now to have made friends with the Mississippi.

Just behind the fountain, the terraces, the trees, and the statues that line the riverfront, a big new building houses the National Eagle Center. Here you can learn about the lives of eagles, attend programs starring live eagles, and generally celebrate the robust resurgence of our national bird in the Upper Mississippi River Valley, where hundreds of the birds now fish, nest, and thrive. In 1972, there was only one eagle's nest in the Refuge; now the Fish and Wildlife Service reports well over three hundred active nests.

What brought about this remarkable change? According to a recent FWS study, the eagles are successfully nesting here in part because of dramatically improved water quality: since the late 1980s, concentrations of polychlorinated biphenyls (PCBs) and mercury have dropped 60 percent and levels of other contaminants have been reduced as well. But there's more to the eagle saga than PCBs and mercury.

From 1782, the year that Congress named the eagle our national bird, until the passage of the Bald Eagle Protection Act of 1940, the eagle was persecuted almost to the point of extinction, with impunity. Benjamin Franklin maligned the eagle by calling it "a bird of low moral character . . . and a rank coward." Hunters, ranchers, and farmers who saw the eagle as a predator of game animals and livestock, a bird with no redeeming value, routinely shot every eagle they saw and destroyed the eggs and the huge nests as well. Alaska had a bounty on the eagle. Not everyone who killed eagles was driven by scorn or hatred: Native Americans had long hunted eagles for the feathers, which they prized. But regardless of motivation, the result was the same for the eagle.

Even after the killings were outlawed, the decline continued for many reasons documented by the FWS: contaminated water, electrocution by power lines, and lead poisoning from eating carrion containing lead birdshot. Rachel Carson asserted in her 1962 book *Silent Spring* that the eggshell-thinning chemical DDE, a breakdown product of the insecticide DDT, is the primary cause of eagles' declining populations. In 1921, however, W. V. Van Name had written in the journal of the Ecological Society of America that bald eagles were close to extinction then, twenty-five years before DDT was used in the United States, and a 1937 Smithsonian bulletin reported that the bald eagle had vanished from New England. These reports, which were used to support passage of the Bald Eagle Protection Act of 1940, suggest that DDE was probably only one factor.

It also became more difficult for eagles to find enough food as the population of human hunters and fishermen spread in the Upper Mississippi River valley. But in an interesting irony, the lock and dam system that has inflicted so much damage on the river has inadvertently helped the eagle at dinnertime. The turbulent waters below a dam stun and kill fish, offering the piscivorous bird an easy meal, year-round. Some believe the most important reason for the raptor's resurgence is that our citizens now value the eagle and act accordingly, as evidenced by the creation of the National Eagle Center in Wabasha, with its mission of education and protection.

As I am thinking warm and fuzzy thoughts about Wabasha, I notice three small boys standing along the riverfront railing, smiling and waving. I smile and wave back, and they hurl a barrage of small stones, which fortunately fall short. I am the mother of three sons, so I don't take it personally.

"Little hooligans," chuckles Bob.

Downstream from the town, Pool 5 is a frenzy of fast boats and jet skis, at least in the main channel. Bob suggests that we escape through a quiet backwater channel to Robinson Lake, to avoid all the cross-chop. In that quiet place our bow carves a dark path across the sluggish water's duckweed carpet and tiny emerald duckweed leaves cling to our paddle blades. As my paddle snags the tough anchor line of a pond lily, the edge of its leaf pad flips up to show off the purple underside. A single lily flower blooms in the wide green bed. Canoeing the back channels is slow but peaceful work, a meditative respite from the intensity of the weekend boat traffic. In the backwaters, the river is once again somewhat natural, no longer a highway. Though the flow is gone and the water stagnant, here the river has a quiet, intricately detailed beauty that draws us in and passively resists our desire for a fast downstream pace. *There is more to life than simply increasing its speed.*

Wandering through the duckweed, we talk about where we'll sleep tonight, debating whether to camp on an island or try for a room in the little river town of Alma, Wisconsin, five more miles down river. We decide that finding an island campsite on this busy weekend night seems unlikely and camping there could be noisy and unappealing. Which are really just excuses. I pull out the cell phone and dial up our son Greg, who agrees to look online for a place. He calls back to say we can stay at the Alma Hotel. Our cell phone connection is marginal. "She said it's a sort of 'hostel,'" he adds in a dubious tone, "I think it's . . ." and the call fails.

As we traverse the shallow open water between Robinson Lake and the channel, swarms of jet ski riders buzz our canoe as though we are not there, darting across our path, turning suddenly to create the craft's signature rooster tail wake, generating inordinate amounts of irritating noise. Once past Teepeeota Point, we cross the equally busy main channel to the Wisconsin side, buffeted all the way by the chaos born of tailwind and wakes. It is a strenuous Sunday afternoon.

We follow the Wisconsin shoreline berm, crowned with railroad tracks. Behind the berm, invisible to us out here in the channel, the confluence with the Buffalo River hides in the backwater called Beef Slough. Before emptying into the slough, the Buffalo flows through wetlands and shallow Riecks Lake. Tundra swans long depended on the lake for a rest stop during migration, but the Buffalo, one of the Upper Mississippi's more ecologically challenged tributaries, has filled the lake with silt. A native plant called bur reed, a species that thrives in shallow water, gradually replaced the wild celery and arrowhead that the birds once fed on, and thick beds of bur reed choked the open water runways that the birds need for takeoff. Most migrators have been landing elsewhere to rest and feed, and though the lake has recently been dredged in a vain attempt to restore its appeal to migrators, the swans go where the food is.

Landing at Alma involves a ladder and a rope, mysteriously yet conveniently hanging down the ten-foot-high, sheer bank, and then a quick hop across the tracks. It's nice to be out of the riverine madhouse. We're at the northern end of long narrow Alma. Like many little towns on the Upper Mississippi, Alma is stretched thin along a glacial outwash terrace, and this particular stretch of terrace is only wide enough for two streets, one perched diagonally above the other, the upper street wedged snugly into the base of steep towering bluffs. The town's commercial buildings, mostly dating from the nineteenth century, have elegant bones but somewhat worn exteriors. Winter on the Upper Mississippi dramatically reduces the stream of tourists along the river road, and many businesses in Alma struggle to survive. Others, like The Commercial, a classy art gallery in a restored brick building on South Main Street, have been there for years. Wings Over Alma draws visitors to watch eagles year-round and especially in the winter. The warm water discharged by a power plant makes eagles' winter fishing expeditions more profitable, as does the open water in the tailrace of a dam, where the birds find stunned and dead fish. Thus the winter abundance of eagles on the river at Alma, with both a dam and a power plant. During the spring and fall migrations, bird enthusiasts watch from Wings Over Alma's riverside spotting deck as many thousands of swans, cranes, geese, pelicans, and ducks pass through, traveling the Mississippi flyway.

Halfway down Main Street to our night's lodging, and soon after we drop the canoe rig over a steep curb cut, our portage wheels begin wobbling in a dramatically new fashion: not a good thing. At the Alma Hotel, we park the canoe on the sidewalk. Still wearing his lifejacket, Bob walks up to the bar, where five patrons in various stages of Sunday afternoon inebriation are seated on barstools.

"Our son called about us getting a room tonight," Bob says to the barkeep.

"You don't need a lifejacket in here," offers one of the patrons.

"I don't know about that, our canoe's right outside on the side-walk."

"Oh!"

Everyone, including the barkeep, hurries out the door to see the canoe.

"You ought to get a motor," suggests one thoughtfully, adding that he works on a dredging rig. We chat for a bit about the hazards of canoeing the big river.

"So, about the room?" Bob asks the barkeep.

"You should probably see it first."

Up the stairs from the bar, we see why she said that, as the place is being renovated. There's no light in the upstairs hall, paint is peeling from the walls, and there's one shared bathroom. But the room and the bed are clean and comfortable. Our window overlooks Main Street, where groups of motorcyclists gather, revving their engines, not too loudly. We say yes and follow her downstairs to the bar.

"How much do we owe you for the room?" I ask.

"Oh, it's very expensive, about . . ."

"Two hundred ninety-seven dollars," interjects the dredger.

"Twenty-two dollars and sixteen cents; that includes the tax," the barkeep concludes with a grin. "It's just a sleeping room."

When we lock the canoe to the dumpster behind the hotel, Bob in-spects the recalcitrant portage wheels. One metal support has buckled so much that another bounce down a curb will render the wheels useless and the other support is twisted.

"So what'll we do about the portage from Black Earth Creek?" I ask.

"We'll figure that out when we get there. Let's get dinner."

On our evening walking tour of Alma, we have a tasty meal at Kate and Gracie's, a session at the laundromat, and a trip to the pier down-stream of the dam to scout tomorrow's exit route. As an afterthought, we carry the wheels to a municipal trashcan and drop them in. He should have taken the ten dollars.

LOCK + DAM 4
ALMA

WEAVER

BUFFALO CITY

WISCONSIN

WHITEWATER R.

MINNEISKA

LOCK + DAM 5
WHITMAN BOTTOMS

MISSISSIPPI R.

TREMPEALEAU RIVER

LOCK + DAM 5A

PERROT STATE PARK

TREMPEALEAU NATIONAL WILDLIFE AREA

TREMPEALEAU

MINNESOTA

LOCK + DAM 6

ALMA to TREMPEALEAU

Locking Through

Five o'clock Monday morning. Though the barkeep assured us that the cook would be fixing breakfast by now, we knock and knock on the kitchen door, in vain. Sans breakfast, we carry our gear up the street and over the tracks to the town pier, happily downstream of Lock & Dam 4. As we hustle past, a barge tow pushed by an Archer Daniels Midland tugboat is locking through. The tow isn't moving, and the captain too sits motionless in the wheelhouse, staring straight ahead. *Is he asleep or just concentrating?*

Below the dam, the river temporarily ceases being a carefully managed navigational pool, a caged animal, and surges like it isn't chained up, like it's a natural river. And in the pearlescent gray light of early dawn, we are alone on the water, swept along by the swift current and the tailwind that never sleeps, traveling right down the middle of the main channel, masters of the Mississippi.

Then, for only a moment, I am distracted by a massive structure on our left. At Dairyland Power's Alma Station, a steady stream of coal rides a conveyor belt into the plant. *From the barge?* That's a question for another time.

I turn away and search the opposite bank of the channel instead. Along this reach, the Zumbro flows in from Minnesota, and I'm watching for the confluence. Though Nicollet labeled the river on his map by the Dakota name of Wazi-Oju, or Place of Pines, the French had long called it "La Rivière des Embarrass," which translates to "River of Difficulties," in reference to the many snags and deadfalls that block its lower reaches. Des Embarrass, pronounced by the French as day-zahm'-bah-rah,' gradually deteriorated into Zumbro.

As a child, I lived along a tributary of the South Fork of the Zumbro, close to their confluence, and I want to see the confluence of my old home river with the Mississippi. Upstream of the tiny Bluffland town of Zumbro Falls, the three forks of the Zumbro become one river, and this main stem rambles eastward for forty-four miles into the Kruger Unit of the Richard J. Dorer Memorial Hardwood Forest, meandering through a beautiful narrow valley flanked by high bluffs covered in hardwood forest. By canoe or kayak, it's a wonderful stretch of river, swift flowing, often punctuated by gravel bar riffles and light rapids. This reach is especially scenic in the fall, when the forested hills blaze with color. After it passes the Kruger Unit, the river drops deeper into the Mississippi valley, runs through a short channelized stretch northeast of the little town of Kellogg, then meanders through the woods to its confluence with the Mississippi. We always ended our paddles down the Zumbro at the Kruger Unit, so the river's final reach is a mystery to me.

Duane Hager farms near Kellogg, and the Zumbro runs through his land. "Rivers and farming are interrelated as far as I'm concerned," said Hager. "The soil on my farm doesn't erode into the river much at all. Ever since right after high school, when I went on to school and took a Farm Management course from a teacher who looked at things differently from most, I've made a lifelong commitment to building the life in the soil. It's just like your livestock, you've got to feed it." Hager raises a rotation of small grains, such as oats, and alfalfa and corn. He pastures beef and dairy cattle. He said he doesn't go after organic certification; the calcium and trace minerals he adds and his tillage practices make the difference that he believes in. "The life in the soil—fungi, bacteria, and invertebrates—makes it more crumbly, stickier, and much less prone to runoff," he added, "and healthy soil reduces my dependence on inputs, the things that you have to add to the soil if you don't keep it healthy—fertilizers, herbicides, pesticides. I don't know how much our environment and the people themselves can tolerate." Though he personally resists the pressure to grow big, Hager laments the economics that often rule the farmer. "I'm almost the Lone Ranger around here. It's too bad the numbers don't favor stewardship more." Hager's stewardship—conservation tillage and well-fed soil that soaks up the rainfall—offers a way to address the sedimentation problem.

The elusive juncture with the Zumbro that I seek seems indistinguishable from the entry to a slough, a backwater, or a side channel. So many islands, so many choices! On the chart, it looks as though the opening we're passing must be the mouth. *Or is this West Newton Chute, the opening to a side channel?* I had heard that the Zumbro once joined the Mississippi farther north, closer to Wabasha, and further south, near the Weaver Bottoms. *Where is it now?*

Before the last glacier, the Zumbro flowed directly into the Mississippi, but glacial meltwater plugged the mouth of the river with a sand terrace that is now ten miles long and three miles wide. To get around the terrace, where sand prairie, savanna, and woodland communities now grow, the Zumbro had carved two more channels—one to the north and one to the south, and the land along the Mississippi east of the terrace and along the Zumbro to its west is now wetlands: open water marshes, wet meadows, and floodplain forests. This complex confluence was altered again in the 1970s, when a manmade channel was dug through the terrace and the Zumbro once again had a direct route to the Mississippi. It was a big project, one that Duane Hager remembers well. A straight shot to the Mississippi now means that when the Zumbro floods, the water runs off the fields faster because the water ahead of it flows downstream faster, a good thing in terms of short-term flood control but bad in terms of loading the Mississippi with more sediment.

Modern Mississippi River floodplains are the sediment that is continually deposited by the impounded river. Tributaries like the Zumbro carve their own paths across this floodplain, their channels splitting and rejoining in wide meandering curves, and continue the endless task of moving their sediment loads into the big river, ever rebuilding their deltas for dredgers to remove. "Sediment transport by rivers is a natural process, but easily thrown out of balance by human activities, and sometimes in ways that are not intuitive. For example, when a river goes over a dam, it drops its sediment upstream of the dam, and downstream, the water will be relatively free of sediment, which may seem like a good thing. But in order to transport the amount of sediment it is capable of carrying, the water will then start to erode new sediment from the downstream riverbed, incising and changing the channel with its energy," explained Wisconsin DNR aquatic ecologist Matt Diebel. "The health of a stream depends on a balance between the water supply and the sediment load." Duane Hager is doing his part.

If you drive north on Highway 61 from the town of Kellogg toward Wabasha, along that stretch of highway you see small watery bits of abandoned channel and then a slough on the right that connects to the Mississippi in the middle of town, probably the route of the old northern channel. South of the modern Zumbro channel, Minnesota's Kellogg-Weaver Dunes Scientific and Natural Area and the Nature Conservancy's Weaver Dunes Preserve protect species like Blanding's turtle. And five miles south of Kellogg along Highway 61, where the southern channel once emptied into the Mississippi, is Weaver Bottoms, now fed by the Whitewater River.

We sweep past the presumed mouth of the Zumbro, silent in our morning solitude and personal musings, enjoying the ease of being alone on the river. And soon we float along the eastern edge of Weaver Bottoms, a wide, shallow, windswept backwater of mostly open water at the confluence with the Whitewater, partly concealed from those of us in the channel by a long line of low islands. The river's name references the milk-pale sediment that washes from its banks when it is in flood, as there are no whitewater rapids on this river, only one short boulder-filled drop created by an old rock weir.

We talk about a canoe trip we took a few years ago in Whitewater State Park, paddling from the tiny town of Elba, Minnesota, downstream for about ten miles. In many ways, the Whitewater is a lovely river. The frequent riffles, the broad sandbars, the sense of isolation and glimpses of distant bluffs all make for a good day of paddling. That warm sunlit spring afternoon, the valley was filled with the song of the warbler, the loud insistent call of the flicker, the whistle of the oriole. Sandpipers and killdeer skittered across the sandbars, swallows built nests in the clay banks, and wild turkeys roamed the high grass on the banks.

Yet amid the beauty, erosion is the darker story of the Whitewater. On the reach we paddled, the channel was often burrowed so deep in the earth that we felt as though we were in a roofless tunnel. This sad tale began in the late nineteenth century. Over a period of forty years, farming practices in the Whitewater valley led to catastrophic erosion. By the 1930s so much soil had poured off the surrounding hills that it lay twelve feet deep in the valley, building steep-sided riverbanks now sometimes fifteen feet high. Records say the flood of soil buried the riverside community of Beaver up to the chimney caps, and much more washed downstream to the Mississippi. Now, every time it rains and the river rises, more soil from these high banks crumbles into the river and washes downstream. Because the floodplain lies deep under the soil, disconnected from the river, flood water has no place to go but downstream, and the edge of the channel is no longer home to the plants and animals that make up a healthy, dynamic floodplain.

Erosion in the Whitewater uplands has largely been corrected by changing the way people farm and where they farm. And the land in this valley is part of over a million acres of land that lie between the Zumbro River and the Root River valleys, land that has been designated as Minnesota's Richard J. Dorer Memorial Hardwood State Forest, named in honor of the man who helped inspire the changes and who is buried in the historic Beaver Cemetery. In his classic book *The Streams and Rivers of Minnesota*, Thomas F. Waters tells Dorer's story:

> He respected all wildlife, the native plants, the soil and rivers, and all the natural elements of what we now call an ecosystem working in harmony. And he saw man as a part of the ecosystem—hunting, fishing, learning, planting, and modifying his own impact on the system. Concentrating on the Whitewater Valley, Dorer (Minnesota Department of Conservation) led the fight for restoration of the eroding slopes. Trees, shrubs, and grasses were replanted, gullies were blocked and filled, grazing stopped, improved cultivation practices were encouraged. . . . Dorer was an environmentalist before the word was coined; Minnesota is fortunate to have had him. The restored river valleys of the southeast are today living monuments to his stewardship.

Yet the legacy of what happened, the altered shape of the land, is still there. The relationship between the water table and the surface of the ground was changed back then, and there is a new equilibrium. Ever since the damage was done, the Whitewater has been dumping too much sediment into the Weaver Bottoms. On the wide-open expanse of water at the confluence, wind-driven waves keep the sediment in suspension and uproot vegetation that tries to grow. In *Immortal River*, his book about the Mississippi River, biologist and ecologist Calvin Fremling tells the story of the demise of the Weaver Bottoms that once was. In 1940s and '50s, during the first decades after the river was impounded, the wetland was so rich with vegetation and muskrat mounds and migratory waterfowl that great numbers of hunters flocked there every hunting season. But as the sediment poured in, the once verdant wetland deteriorated steadily, eventually becoming a shallow lake almost devoid of plants and wildlife.

Because the lock and dam system keeps water levels pretty much the same, the river no longer follows its natural cycle of a high spring pulse giving way to low water by late summer, when the soil in the bottoms dries and compacts enough for aquatic plants to germinate, root, and thrive. The tall grasses, smartweed, cattails, duck potatoes, bulrushes, and other species that once filled the bottoms no longer had a chance and had all but disappeared by the late 1960s. With them went the swan and the mallard and all the other waterfowl. And the wind and waves were free to persist in their erosive habits.

In the mid-1980s, as part of the Environmental Management Program (EMP) for the Upper Mississippi, the Corps built Swan and Mallard islands as windbreaks and planted vegetation, the first attempt at reversing the destruction. Unable to root in the constantly flooded conditions, however, the plants died. In 2005 and 2006, the Corps reduced water levels of Pool 5 during the growing season, but most plantings still died. Drawdowns help consolidate the sediment, giving vegetation a chance to root, but their use was limited by the need to maintain the nine-foot channel, thus they were only done when flow was high. In addition, the effect of a drawdown is greatest at the downstream end of the pool, and Weaver Bottoms is only about halfway down Pool 5.

After all that work, Weaver Bottoms still looked pretty bad and many people said as much. One river scientist says in retrospect that the agencies in charge were over-optimistic about the results and consequently the public had unrealistic expectations and that the Corps just wanted to get rid of a lot of sand.

Corps hydraulic engineer Jon Hendrickson, on the other hand, said that the Weaver Bottoms project that some judged a failure was actually not, that the decline in vegetation during that time was generally true all along the Upper Mississippi. "And Weaver Bottoms was an incomplete project," added Hendrickson. Swan and Mallard islands, sand islands that look as though they were drawn with a draftsman's French curve, did reduce wind fetch, but these two islands were not enough. For years, swans and mallards just flew on by.

Island building is back in favor now, yet Congress chronically underfunds the EMP, by half. And, as Anfinson writes, "Critics of the EMP contend that its solutions are too local and too insignificant to make much difference." The Ikes would like to see Congress authorize restoration of the bluff tops and the tributary deltas, to go to the source of the problem.

Despite the slow pace at which Weaver Bottoms is returning, FWS Winona district manager Mary Stefanski said migratory waterfowl are coming back. "A wild rice bed is filling Weaver Bottoms," said Stefanski, "and we've had a great recovery during fall migration." She credits both those drawdowns—which reproduced the river's natural low-water cycle—and improved water clarity for the rice's return. FWS aerial surveys over the past decade find increasing numbers of migratory waterfowl resting and feeding in the bottoms during fall migration. Though numbers certainly haven't reached the levels seen in the 1950s, the swan and the mallard—not to mention the blue-winged and green-winged teal, gadwall, widgeon, scaup, pintail, northern shoveler, canvasback, goldeneye, bufflehead, merganser, and my favorite, the little coot—have returned to Weaver Bottoms to feast on wild rice.

Just past the bottoms, I look up the riverbank toward the Minnesota village of Minneiska, a seemingly unremarkable small town when we have driven through on Highway 61. From down here on the river, though, Bob comments that it looks like a perfect little European village, nestled in the lap of the high green bluff, a cluster of bright rooftops and steeples pointing skyward from the trees. On his map, Nicollet labeled the nearby Whitewater River as Miniskah River, and though the river's name was later translated to English, the modern name of the village evolved from this Native American word for white water.

Now the main channel narrows, bounded on the Minnesota shore by a railroad berm and on the Wisconsin side by a long straight dike all the way to the dam that lies downstream. Behind the dike, disconnected from the river except for two culverts that allow oxygen-rich river water to flow through, is the north end of Whitman Bottoms. When the river was impounded, the dike protected this maze of narrow channels and small lakes from the wind and waves that changed Weaver Bottoms, preserving habitat that hosts visiting waterfowl during spring and fall migrations.

We're closing in on Lock & Dam 5. Bob turns on his marine radio and clicks to channel fourteen. He has been rehearsing this.

"Lock and dam number five. Southbound white canoe requesting permission to lock through. Over."

A pause, filled with static, then a brisk voice replies, "Just give me ten minutes to fill it up. Over."

I swivel around to look at him, and we both grin.

Red traffic light turns to green. Massive double doors creak open, we paddle in, doors creak closed behind us. We're all alone in the huge lock—large enough to hold a tugboat and eight barges—until the lock-master leans over the side to greet us and to remind me to hold the mooring line that hangs down the concrete wall, but not to grip it or tie up. She asks where we're headed and wants to hear all about the journey. All the while, river water is quietly flowing out of the lock chamber. Ever so slowly, the wall of the lock slides by and the line slips through my hand as we drop with the water, chatting with her as she slowly rises higher and higher above us. It's an odd, rather disconcerting feeling, like being in an invisible elevator. The distance we drop, six feet, is the dam's head, the difference between the water elevation above and below the dam, a measurement that varies with changes in the river's flow.

Downstream doors swing open, light changes from red to green, whistle toots, and we paddle out through the slight turbulence of the tailwaters, waving goodbye without looking back. No matter how many times I lock through in a canoe, I will always feel that the dam exerts only illusory control over the immense power of the waterway that Fremling calls Immortal River. The knowledge that a six-foot-high wall of water lies behind those doors is deeply unsettling. Only long after we leave the dam behind does my hand relax on the paddle grip.

On the Wisconsin side of Pool 5A is the undiked lower half of Whitman Bottoms, a huge backwater hardwood forest with a complex ecosystem, about six thousand acres of bottomland swamp. It's a maze of waterways that floods when the water is high, as is the natural relationship between a river and its floodplain. Waumandee Creek flows through the bottoms to the Mississippi. In some upland areas groves of gnarly swamp white oak grow, a tree that was once more prevalent in bottomland throughout the river valley but has slowly died out since impoundment. Slowly is the right word—these trees can live to be over three hundred years old. To help reverse the losses, John Sullivan, retired Wisconsin DNR water quality specialist, raises swamp white oak and American elm seedlings as a hobby for the Corps and FWS to plant along the river.

The whole of Whitman Bottoms is the preferred hangout of a real live river rat named Kenny Salwey. Though Salwey lives in the hills north of Alma, for most of his life he has hunted and fished, guided hunters and fishermen, run a trap line, dug ginseng, and otherwise eked out an independent living in the undeveloped land along the river, a way of life once followed by many others, in the early twentieth century. Selway spends his days, and often his nights, in the Whitman Bottoms, where he has built several small shacks for overnight accommodation. Encouraged by the local conservation warden to share his experiences, Salwey now talks to kids, speaks on public radio, writes books, and tells stories, about his life, about the Upper Mississippi River valley, about respect for the environment. And he has found an eager audience for his storytelling and his downhome writing in books like *Muskrat for Supper.* The BBC filmed a documentary about Selway's life, titled *Mississippi—*

Tales of the Last River Rat. Salwey and Whitman Bottoms are relics of what the river once was.

Floating down Pool 5A, we pass the opening to a side channel at the bottom of Island No. 52. *A path into the bottoms?* The chart says yes, but it looks shallow and impassable, and there's a better way into the backwaters downriver and off the channel, at Merrick State Park near Fountain City.

Pool 5A. The name makes the impoundment sound like a bureaucratic afterthought. But, then again, you will find on the navigation charts that there is no Pool 23 in between Pool 22 and Poll 24. Clearly, the Corps didn't have their numbering act together when they labeled the dams. It's the government approach to natural resource management, no doubt, but I often think about names, how they change our perception of a place. For example, compare the impersonal utilitarian "Pool 5A" to the evocative names of its backwaters—Haddock Slough, Horseshoe Bend, Pickerel Run, Pap Slough, Polander Lake, Betsy Slough. The last gravel state highway in Minnesota, the one that follows the Whitewater River, is mentioned on local radio broadcasts in the spring, as in "the Beaver to Weaver Road is closed again due to flooding," referencing the places that the road connects—ghost town of Beaver and live town of Weaver—in a homespun, inadvertently poetic fashion. Every name has its stories.

Yet there are many who do not care whether it's a name or a number. Mike Chicanowski, the founder and president of Wenonah Canoe in Winona, said that Pool 5A is his favorite place to paddle on the Upper Mississippi, that when Europeans visit, he takes them canoeing on Pool 5A, where they are invariably amazed by the vast and beautiful world of the Refuge, especially the backwaters of this very impoundment. "They tell me there's nothing like it back in Europe," he said. "Nothing."

A few years back, we took his advice and paddled the Straight Slough Canoe Trail, from just below Lock & Dam 5 to the Verchota landing near Minnesota City. In contrast to the sometimes boring and even sterile uniformity of the main channel, the bottomland world can be a fascinating tangle of vegetation. Here is where the birds hang out—white egrets, blue and green herons, bald eagles, turkey vultures, ducks of every stripe and color, songbirds everywhere. A riot of swamp willow thickets, beds of rushes, the round leaf pads and yellow blossoms of American lotus, arrowhead plants, and flowering wild iris edge the wooded banks of the slough.

The birds are here in the backwaters because this is where the food is. On the hot June day that we were there, a small gang of common mergansers floated on the dark water, bottoms up, searching for minnows or whatever other little fish they could find. One dove, with a slight leap, and disappeared; the others immediately followed. Anglers of the human variety sat quietly in flat-bottom johnboats drifting with the current.

We had heard that the improbable-looking longnose gar—a long narrow relic of the Cretaceous, armor-clad in shiny diamond-shaped scales and sporting a long beak—lives in these sloughs, as it has for millennia, patrolling the water column for minnows and carp, aggressively grasping prey with rows of needle-sharp teeth and swallowing it whole. Though the gar is known to sometimes migrate—and even to shoot right through a dam gate that's open at high water—the usual habit of the gar is to live and fish in quiet pools. Anglers have no luck catching them unless they have the patience to allow the gar to swallow the hook. And we saw no trace of the ancient river denizen, though I looked.

Another layer of the river's history hides deeper, under the bottom of the slough, unseen except by mussel scientists. Wisconsin DNR biologist David Heath told me that beds of empty mussel shells, the remains of mussels buried by the river's impoundment, lie preserved under the sediment, and when biologists dig deep enough, they find excellent clues to the historic fauna, the astonishing numbers and varieties of mussels that once lived in the Upper Mississippi. Mussels still live on the bottom of the Mississippi, but only in areas where silt hasn't coated the gravel and stone substrate that they need for their living quarters. According to Heath, one of the noteworthy mussel sites remaining on the Upper Mississippi lies back upriver in Pool 5, somewhere in Pomme de Terre Slough, also known as Belvidere Slough. When we took the Straight Slough canoe trail, we paddled slowly through Straight, Burleigh, and then Crooked sloughs. The fast-moving interstate highway of the main channel seemed miles away on that trip.

Today, unwilling to be patient, we make only a brief exploratory foray into the slough and then return to our downstream voyage. Still remarkably alone on the river—except for a motionless figure in a hooded jacket hunched over in his fishing boat, who seems to be trying to shut out the rest of the world—we follow the red nun buoys to the Wisconsin side, floating past the town of Fountain City, another riverine beauty crowned with two slim tapered steeples. Just as I suggest that we stop for lunch at the Monarch Tavern, a shrill whistle echoes off the bluffs and a freight train rumbles through town, headed south. It's a long, long freight and we'd have to wait for it to pass before we could land. Ever restless, we move on.

Each day, about sixty-five trains travel both sides of the valley. A handful of Amtrak trains carry passengers. The rest carry freight, bulk commodities such as grain, fertilizer, taconite, frac sand, coal from Wyoming, and shale oil from North Dakota. The Burlington Northern & Santa Fe and Canadian Pacific freight lines are major iron strands in the big transport braid that is the modern Mississippi River valley. Inns on the river generally offer their guests earplugs.

Locking through at Dam 5A, we're on our own. Though Bob's radio alert works fine again, this time there's no friendly lockmaster waiting in the lock, hanging over the wall to chat, just a flat, detached voice through a speaker, like an automated lock-through, a letdown after the good time we had at the first lock. A quiet drop in the lock and we're in the Winona pool.

Winona is a town I thought I knew well. All through the late 1960s, on my way back to college, it was in Winona that I caught the Milwaukee Road, riding the train to Chicago on what is now Amtrak's Empire Builder line. And I often visited high school friends who had moved to Winona. But I didn't know then about the town's interesting geological past.

In *Immortal River*, Fremling explains that after the level of Glacial River Warren dropped, the river bottom was much deeper than it is now. Sediment carried by the river's many tributaries gradually refilled the scoured-out gorge. Because the river itself was now much smaller than Warren, it no longer filled the wide valley. Instead, interwoven strands of flow carved smaller channels in the sandy sediment, leaving sandbars between the strands. One watery strand of this braided channel system flowed along the base of the bluffs behind what is now Winona. Sediment from small tributaries—Burns Creek, Gilmore Creek, and Garvin Brook—built deltas that blocked this side channel, forming the small lakes, Lake Winona and Boller Lake, that now lie between those bluffs and the huge sandbar that is their eastern shore, and the city's site. Down here at river level, this arrangement is far less obvious than from bluff-top Garvin Heights Park, where there's a panoramic view of the sandbar city.

Winona's founder built his city on sand. And the geological past, both ancient and relatively recent, explains the present. Not only is Winona built on sand, its sandbar foundation is in the river's floodplain. Unlike Red Wing, Wabasha, Minnesota City, Trempealeau, La Crosse, and Prairie du Chien, all of which are built on sand terraces that are higher than the floodplain, logical places for both prehistoric and historic inhabitants to build their settlements, Winona is right down at river level. Flooding probably wasn't a big problem for the Dakota who had long had a prosperous village on the sandbar, as their dwellings were easy enough to move when floodwaters threatened. But European-style buildings are less portable.

In 1851, right after the treaties of Traverse des Sioux and Mendota opened Minnesota for development, Orin Smith, a longtime steamboat captain, quickly claimed the land and platted the town. He must have known that a town on the Mississippi in the new territory would become a center of commerce, which it did; but he was a river man and should also have realized that flooding would be a big problem for a city built on a floodplain.

Winona now has eleven miles of levees to protect it from the Mississippi's rampages, and massive pumps remove water that does manage to get in. But back in April of 1965, when the Upper Mississippi was building up to its biggest deluge in collective local memory, the city had just started constructing those levee walls. They knew the flood was coming. As Fremling writes: "For almost a month, the city was like a war zone, with trucks, heavy machinery, and hundreds of people working twenty-four hours a day. Volunteers and contractors saved the city . . . by building a temporary levee over twenty feet high." Busloads of high school students from towns as far away as Rochester, Minnesota, came to help fill and pile sandbags. The river crested at 20.77 feet.

Winona will be paying for Orrin Smith's city planning for a long time.

Of course the Mississippi levee dilemma is much larger than just Winona. Hydrologists have documented that the more levees that are built along the Mississippi, the higher the river will rise during a flood, ever more tightly constricted as it will be by levee walls that separate the floodwater from the floodplain, which is where the river wants to go and needs to go. But because levees create a false sense of security about building on the floodplain, more building occurs on the Mississippi River floodplain every year, particularly down around St. Louis. The federal government has encouraged this unwise practice by subsidizing levee construction and now, when the levees fail, by bailing out the communities with taxpayer-supported relief.

And it's not just cities that build levees. Bottomland has rich soil, and floodplain farmers protect their fields with levees. Not so much on the Upper Mississippi, however. According to the United States Geological Survey, only 3 percent of the relatively narrow floodplain along Upper Mississippi River Navigational Pools 1–13, the reach that extends from Minneapolis to Clinton, Iowa, is currently behind agricultural levees. This is small potatoes compared with the reach between Clinton, Iowa, and St. Louis, where 53 percent of the agricultural floodplain is behind levees, and the reach downstream of the confluence with the Ohio, where up to 82 percent of the floodplain is behind agricultural levees. The difference here along the Upper Mississippi River is that the great majority of bottomlands in the Refuge are publicly owned wildlife areas, where new levees will not be built.

In the early days of attempting to manage the river, the engineers on the Corps River Commission held firm to the idea that levees were the only answer to flood protection. In 1883, Mark Twain wrote in *Life on the Mississippi*: "One who knows the Mississippi will promptly aver—not aloud, but to himself—that ten thousand River Commissions, with the mines of the world at their back, cannot tame that lawless stream, cannot curb it or confine it, cannot say to it, Go here, or Go there, and make it obey; cannot save a shore which it has sentenced; cannot bar its path with an obstruction which it will not tear down, dance over, and laugh at." It has taken over a hundred years for the River Commission to admit defeat, but Twain would probably be gratified to learn that the Corps is finally wising up and slowly rethinking the "levees only" policy.

As we float around the bend at the head of Latsch Island, I look back into the dead end slough on the right, where at least a dozen empty barges are moored along the shore. From this angle, I glimpse the new museum that has come to Winona, the Minnesota Maritime Art Museum. Their online newsletter just advertised a new exhibit titled *The Art of the Canoe*, so we stopped there on the drive to Faribault, and found an intriguing collection of canoes, mostly historic. But I was entranced with what the museum's designers had done with the site, transforming a tired and ugly industrial waterfront with a vast swath of flowering native prairie plants that blankets the land around the new Prairie-style building. Along the waterfront levee wall, a feature that in the site's former life projected the ugly nature of the urban riverbank, the designers have transformed the scene by the simple act of adding an attractive iron railing and tables and chairs that face and embrace the river. It's almost as if the long rows of rusting, empty barges across the backwater, formerly the grimy reality of the river scene, are now a serendipitous floating art installation.

Dead ahead, the road between Minnesota and Wisconsin crosses the main channel on a cantilever through-truss bridge that soars over a small sandy beach on Latsch Island, where we stop for lunch. Refueled, and recalling the suggestion of our Winona friend Sue, we decide to visit the other side of the island, Latsch's alter ego. To get there, we will paddle upstream on the channel that flows between the island and the woods of Wisconsin.

And around the tip of the island's tail is another art installation. A continuous string of houseboats, or boathouses as Latsch Islanders call them, one hundred quirky residences, all moored along the island's back channel. A few are simply boathouses, that is, houses for boats. But I discovered that about a quarter of them are fulltime dwellings for people. Several are two stories high. Many are gussied up with sundecks, container gardens, clotheslines, and solar panels. One sports a roof made of sheet metal pieces arranged into a crude patchwork resembling a geodesic dome. The houses float on wooden platforms built over dozens of fifty-gallon barrels. Though they have no electricity, no cable television, no internet, and no plumbing, they do have a neighborhood alliance— the Winona Boathouse Association. It looks like a good life.

Cruising along the Wisconsin shore, where a berm topped with railroad tracks forms another riverbank dike, we come to Trempealeau

Mountain, the cone-shaped, forested knob that stands haughtily aloof from the nearest community of bluffs. Before we began our journey, I read various accounts about traveling the Upper Mississippi in centuries past. One writer who paid particular attention to Trempealeau Mountain was George Featherstonhaugh (Brits pronounce it "Fanshaw"), who in 1835, just a few years before Nicollet began his mapping expeditions, journeyed down the Wisconsin, up the Mississippi, and up the Minnesota.

In *A Canoe Voyage Up the Minnay Sotor*, Featherstonhaugh relates his encounter with this puzzling geographical anomaly and his subsequent conversation with the Yankton Sioux with whom he shared supper:

> At 2 p.m. we reached Trombalo, and as this rock had attracted a good deal of notice, I determined to examine it carefully. It is not an island, as it has been supposed to be, but is an outlier of the sandstone and limestone bluffs, running nearly a mile and a half east and west, being separated from the west bank of the Mississippi, and not from the east bank, as some travellers have supposed . . . From this outlier, or part of the bluff; thus standing as it were in the water the early French travellers called it "La Montagne qui trempe à l'Eau," which is now corrupted to Trombalo . . . I then asked them the name of the mountain at the base of which we were, and they answered "Minnay Chon ka hah," — literally, as I afterwards found, "Bluff in the Water," — than which nothing could be more descriptive . . . and *Ompaytoo Wakee*, or Daylight, brother to Wabeshaw, a celebrated chief . . . (said that) *Minnay Chon ka hah*, the outlier we had visited in the afternoon, was in fact, he said, a sort of island, as there was an obscure passage round it . . . (and) it was the custom of his band to go to the top of *Minnay Chon ka hah*, at the season for hunting wild geese, and that they made offerings to Mangwah Wakon ("wild goose god"), that he might be favourable to them in their hunting.

As Ompaytoo told Featherstonhaugh, there is water behind the mountain. When Nicollet passed this way, the peripatetic Frenchman referred to the Trempealeau as Mountain Island River and inscribed this name on his map, interestingly without any mention of the river's French appellation.

But the open water of those days is no more. According to Fremling, railroad construction in the early twentieth century diverted the Trempealeau River to flow between the outlier and the bluffs of Perrot State Park, and the railroad built a berm along the channel. The Trempealeau River's heavy sediment load subsequently filled in what is still euphemistically called Trempealeau Bay, creating a wetland that is now a wildlife refuge. And the mountain is no longer an island.

The Trempealeau, which according to the Wisconsin DNR has the highest phosphorus levels of any river in Wisconsin, delivers a lot of unwanted nutrients with its sediment, though the approximately three thousand acres of wetlands at the confluence help recycle the nutrients rather than send them all down the Mississippi. "Most wetlands only temporarily detain phosphorus; plants take it up, but then release it when they die. Any permanent 'removal' from the river isn't sustainable, as it happens through sedimentation, which will eventually fill up the wetland. Wetlands can, however, permanently remove nitrogen by denitrification, which sends it back to the atmosphere as N_2 gas," explained Matt Diebel, Wisconsin DNR aquatic ecologist. "Denitrification" is the breakdown by anaerobic bacteria of nitrates in the sediment into molecular nitrogen.

This wetland ecosystem took a big hit during the flood of April 1965, when the berm of the Burlington & Green Bay Railroad that separates the wetland from the river gave way. The entire wetland was inundated and the river dropped eight inches. In his 1994 article in *Big River* magazine, Rob Drieslein recalls the aftermath of the break: "The flooded waters overrunning the area had deposited tons of thick, muddy silt into the backwater area. The silt provides a poor substrate for aquatic vegetation, an important food source for wildlife. Refuge personnel blamed the poor substrate, in part, for the failed attempts to establish wild celery in the refuge during the mid-1980s." According to Drieslein, some residents still believe that certain individuals used dynamite to break the berm and save Winona from flooding, but this has never been proven.

Three thousand acres of savanna and bottomland forest, the balance of Trempealeau National Wildlife Refuge's acreage, shelter both nesting and migrating birds, thousands of ducks, geese, and swans. The Tremp's confluence is a lovely place, embraced as it is by the refuge and by Perrot State Park and the bluffs. Several hiking trails in the park lead to the top of Brady's Bluff. From this 520-foot bluff, which looks down on Trempealeau Mountain, the hiker looks across the confluence to the outlier and beyond, if the day is clear, up the vast river valley as far as Winona.

Next stop is the town of Trempealeau, Wisconsin, and the eponymous hotel where we will spend the night. We land at the Sunset Bay Marina, where a young man charges us twenty-two dollars to store the canoe for the night, just sixteen cents less than the price of our room at the Alma Hotel, and we walk to the Trempealeau Hotel, a beautiful old establishment a block from the river where an upstairs room with a shared bath costs only thirty-five dollars. The town is hopping tonight, couples strolling, children running, music pouring out of bars, the band warming up at the hotel, the dining room packed. Down by the river, another train hurtles past, its powerful deep-throated voice vibrating everything in town.

After dining on walnut burgers, we walk to the top of the hill to find cell phone reception. Bob calls niece Corrie, who lives in La Crosse, to talk about the camera. She will buy us a new one at Best Buy and her husband Luke will meet us at the La Crosse Marina tomorrow for the handoff.

I call Greg, who sounds amused by our soft new style of canoe travel. He calls back after a few moments to say that he has found us a riverside motel for tomorrow night in Genoa, Wisconsin, only thirty-five miles downstream.

"She said to call an hour ahead to let them know when you'll arrive," he adds.

Thirty-nine miles today. Dance music rocks the barroom downstairs, another freight rattles past down by the river, and the canoe still gently rocks beneath me as I fall asleep.

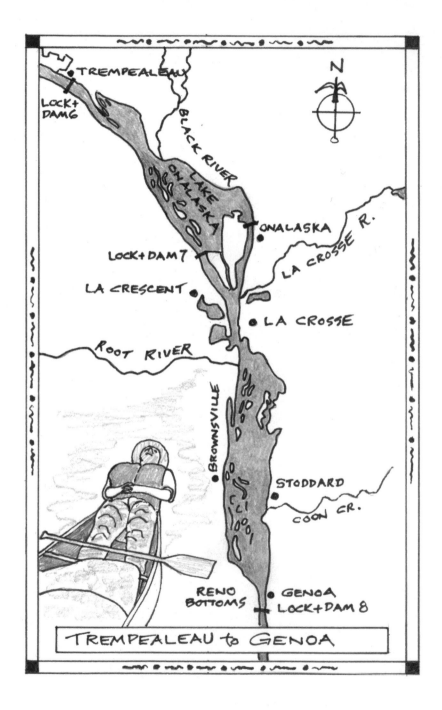

TREMPEALEAU to GENOA

Of Barges and Steamboats

June the thirtieth. At dawn, a cold heavy fog and its accompanying sense of mystery drench the river. Alive with the possibilities of the day, we slide our canoe into the current downstream of Lock & Dam 6. We know that by afternoon boredom will have set in and all the trees will look alike, but for now the river runs through our veins. Once again, we're the only boat on the river, yet we're not alone. Herons and egrets fish the shallows and eagles soar above. The eyes of a big snapping turtle watch us, disappearing swiftly and silently as we get too close.

We follow the channel and the channel follows the Minnesota shore, where a stately line of half-dome bluffs rises over five hundred feet above the river, a precipitously steep wooded array of cliffs, faced in places with rocky outcrops of St. Peter sandstone or of the Prairie du Chien Formation, the rocky layers of ancient seabed that built these bluffs. Across the Mississippi in Wisconsin, the top of a ghostly pointed bluff, twin brother to Trempealeau Mountain, appears to float on the surface of the low-lying mist. We're in the embrace of the bluffs now and I feel the visual power of this familiar landscape in a way that only happens for me on the river. Viewing the river valley from a bridge or an overlook is a snapshot, a static moment. Floating the river is a movie. It's a subtle but telling difference. As we travel down this wide, deep valley, the ebb and flow of shape and form, the ever-evolving view, slide past my eyes in a visual narrative, and the grandeur of the Upper Mississippi builds.

I find a kindred sense in the accounts of early explorers, who at first believed the lines of bluffs were mountain ranges, and in the many accounts of writers who followed. In *Letters and Notes,* George Catlin wrote, "From day to day, the eye is riveted in listless, tireless admiration, upon the thousand bluffs which tower in majesty above the river on either side, and alternate as the river bends, into countless fascinating forms."

The paddler finds that the morning fog shapes a different image than does the late afternoon sun. On every passage down the river, the angle of the light, the hues and textures of water and land change. When Catlin painted the familiar forms of the Mississippi bluffs, many were treeless; today, after centuries of wildfire suppression, most are thickly forested. I recall historic accounts and art as we float, and the images blur into one. We're traveling down a river valley peopled by the ghosts of paddlers past.

But the river is quite real, and very soon, it seems, Pool 7 comes to an end. As we pass Dresbach Island, both the speedboat traffic and our ever-present tailwind begin to rise. A fight ensues between the wakes and the waves and we're caught in the middle of the muddle. We paddle cautiously into Lock & Dam 7 through water that our paddling friend Warren would call "squirrely," a chaos of current, cross-chopped waves, and boat wakes bouncing off the concrete walls that guide the river craft into the lock's inner sanctum.

From within, I look downstream, over top of the lock gates, all the way to the bridge that carries Interstate 90, the bridge I have crossed so many times in my life. I'm about to see it from underneath for the first time. Already I sense how disconnected the bridge is from the river, how foreign its linear shape and concrete materials are in this curvaceous riverine world. When we cross the same bridge in our car, concrete side-walls prevent us from looking down to the river that flows directly below us; only distant water is visible.

My perfect bridge is one built of wood or stone, with see-through railings that afford a clear view of the river, a tacit acknowledgement that the river should be seen, has beauty and importance. A bridge with solid sidewalls one cannot see through is a statement that what lies below is not worth looking at, that all that matters is crossing the river. In the same way, locking through forces us to encounter the river as a human construct rather than a natural flow of water over land.

Beyond the bridge, a glimpse of a distant cluster of moored houseboats—a house on the water has definite allure—alongside scattered sandbar encampments—even better—returns me to an intimate relationship with the river. We're at the upstream end of the long river town of La Crosse and also at the upstream end of an elaborate riverine highway interchange. The Black and the La Crosse both flow into the Mississippi from Wisconsin at this sprawling confluence, and the Root River joins the Mississippi from Minnesota at the downstream end of town.

On his 1843 map, Nicollet called the Black by its Winnebago name: the Sappah, which means Black. He drew a three-pronged set of outlets for the river, labeling them, in downstream order, Old Mouth, Broken Gun Chanl, and New Mouth, which was the widest. In his 1853 Wisconsin Gazetteer, John W. Hunt also refers to the Broken Gun Channel as the middle outlet of the Black River; I have searched for but never found an account of the curious naming of the Broken Gun Channel. Though historic maps are sometimes simplified and thus deceptive, it seems that the delta of the Black now has a more complex network of channels. One of these, known as Tank Creek, is what is known as a distributary, the mirror image of a tributary. Like the Atchafalaya River that departs from the Mississippi at Simmesport, Louisiana, to carve its own route to the Gulf, Tank Creek departs the Black to follow its own path to the Mississippi.

It was on another canoe journey, at another time, that we explored Tank Creek, in the spring when the river was high, so different from this summer's low flows. That day, the rushing dark-tinted waters of the creek, rich with organic aroma as they poured out of the Black, had blocked its narrow channel with debris dams, necessitating several portages. Delicate toothwort flowers carpeted muddy banks and migrating songbirds flitted through barely leafed trees. After one portage, we paddled past the rusted remnants of an iron truss bridge that's no longer in use. The narrow wooded confines of the lively Tank widened as we neared the Mississippi and the creek slowed, sprawling into marshy bottomland where a vigilant pair of eagles watched us pass their nesting tree. Then the Tank emptied into the quiet of Mud Lake, a shallow backwater connected to the big river by narrow outlet channels, small pieces of the intricate bayou-like puzzle of waterways that is the delta. Across the lake, a long straight margin of islands covered with softly greening trees concealed the Mississippi's main channel. Against this green backdrop, a slender white bird dropped from the sky, diving beak-first into the shallow water, again and again. Beyond the trees, across the wide valley, we saw for the first time that day the horizon line of distant dark bluffs rising high above the big river in Minnesota's Great River Bluffs State Park, where the hiker finds a bird's eye view of the Black's delta from five hundred feet up.

When the Corps impounded the Mississippi in the 1930s, the final reach of the Black's main channel, which runs parallel to the Mississippi for about ten miles, disappeared under the waves of Lake Onalaska, the wide shallow expanse of open water behind Lock & Dam 7, separated from the main channel of the Mississippi by a string of low wooded islands. Within the lake, the Black's now amorphous main channel hugs the shoreline, forming again when it slides between the shore and French Island. Downstream of an earthen dam and concrete spillway between the island and Onalaska, and downstream of Lock & Dam 7 and the interstate bridge, the Black reaches its historic and true confluence with the Mississippi, slyly subverting the lock.

Here on the river I feel as though I'm starting to understand this complex confluence, at least a little. These recent chapters in the story of the Black River's relationship with the Mississippi are on record, but I wonder too what permutations the Black went through before written history. Some clues lie upstream. When Bob and I first canoed the Black, it was between the towns of Irving and North Bend, a particularly lovely and remote stretch of river that rambles through the steep hills of the Driftless. The wide gorge, sandy bottom, and frequent sandbars along this reach reflect the lower Black's ancient past as an early outlet for Glacial Lake Wisconsin, and the dark water for which the river was named comes from organic compounds at its headwaters in northeastern Taylor County, a little way south of Timm's Hill, outside the Driftless. After the river crosses into the Driftless at the city of Black River Falls, it traverses the unglaciated area from northeast to southwest. The river valley, carved into the ancient bedrock, grows deeper as it nears the Mississippi River valley, and the underlying geology of the Driftless is visible along this reach. We walked into the mouth of one of its tributaries, Roaring Creek, a small stream with a steep gradient, and up the narrow sandstone canyon that flanks its final drop into the Black, to see a series of small waterfalls drop over sharp-edged hard bedrock ledges. On one tall bluff we paddled next to, the moist Cambrian sandstone bedrock of the sheer cliff face was covered with the small leathery leaves of liverwort plants, anchored by their rhizoids in rock fractures, doing their part to disintegrate this rock face: a very long-term project, and one tiny piece of the Driftless Area's master plan to erode the Paleozoic bedrock.

White pines top the bluffs and the lower banks are densely wooded with hardwood trees and river birch. Because little of the Black's watershed is agricultural and much is forested, phosphorus and other nutrient levels are low compared to the nearby Trempealeau and the water is clear. In the shallows, we spotted live mussels and their tracks in the sand. In deeper water were northern pike, bass, redhorse, and huge schools of minnows. And the many bald eagles that flew over us are further testament to the river's abundant fishery. That day the river was low, only about a third of its usual flow, and we had to follow quite a meandering downriver course, occasionally grounding in the shallows and wading for a bit. The channel split at one point; searching for higher water, we wandered off into an alternate Black River, a channel with more flow and fewer deadfalls.

To the paddler, Driftless rivers seem to be all about change. Water levels rise and fall, sometimes dramatically. When the river floods, whole trees are scoured from the banks and carried downstream to be dumped carelessly on sandbars or in sandy shallows, where their presence helps shape the ever-shifting sandy outlines of the channel. The Black shares its past with the Wisconsin River—both drained Glacial Lake Wisconsin and both were log transport routes from lumber camps to the Mississippi during the logging of the north woods. Though the Black is a smaller river, in the eyes of the paddler they look very similar, as do their sandbars, ever moving and shifting.

Near the city of Onalaska, the Black is home to the paddlefish: fascinating, improbable-looking creatures that the fossil record shows have been around for probably three hundred million years, fish that once swam happily throughout the Mississippi's vast watershed, migrating from north to south as climate change dictated. Imagine the shape of a smallish shark and then attach a long canoe paddle blade to its snout. Though superficially it does resemble a shark, the paddlefish is actually related to the sturgeon family, and is a mild-mannered filter feeder that lives mostly on tiny zooplankton such as daphnia as well as on any edible tidbits like insect larvae and mayfly nymphs that float into its wide-open mouth and get tangled in the comb-like gillrakers at the back. Despite this species' tenacity over the millennia, the paddlefish no longer thrives in this region, and dams are the primary reason. Dams prevent the paddlefish from following its preferred spawning migration routes, and dams have destroyed both its spawning grounds and the backwaters where it feeds and rears its young. Polluted waters and historic over-fishing can also be blamed, at least in part, for the declining fortunes of the paddlefish. The final suspect is the fisherman who illegally catches the fish for its eggs and sells them as caviar that retails for up to twenty-five dollars an ounce; in recent years, illegal harvesting of paddlefish has increased.

Now here is the good part to the paddlefish story. In the early 1990s, Steven Zigler, a scientist at the USGS, decided to find out where paddlefish still live in the Upper Mississippi and what their migration routes look like. Along with Ann Runstrom of FWS and other fisheries biologists, he caught a number of adult fish in the Mississippi, the Chippewa, and the Wisconsin rivers, tagged them with radio transmitters, and released them. From 1994 to 1997, the scientists tracked the movements of the paddlefish, by boat, by plane, and by hovercraft.

They learned that paddlefish like deep slow-moving water, like the final reach of the Black, where groups of the tagged fish congregated in a backwater right next to the interstate bridge I have crossed so many times. Paddlefish also like Pool 5A near Polander Lake, where the eating is good and several deep-water habitats have been dredged out just for them. The team learned that on the Wisconsin River, paddlefish hang out much of the year below the Prairie du Sac dam, where there's plenty to eat, and then migrate to near Arena to spawn. They learned that some paddlefish migrate to spawn as many as 230 miles, often heading downstream, against their instincts, because of upstream dams. And they learned that paddlefish are able to lock through.

In the spring of 1996, when the paddlefish were on the move, one of the tagged fish traveled upstream from Pool 8 to Pool 7. The paddlefish swam into the lock alongside a barge headed upstream and when the light turned green, the paddlefish followed the barge out again. The scientists tracked every move of this enterprising creature: the not-so-secret lives of fish.

Soon after we float under the Interstate 90 bridge, Bob spots the daymark sign at the head of Minnesota Island, and we detour into the East Channel that runs to the east of this long wooded island, passing first a group of houseboats and then the official confluence with the Black River. Much of La Crosse is built along a glacial outwash terrace. On the east side, the city backs up to towering Grandad Bluff, 552 feet above the river, a high point on the wooded ridgeline of the bluffs. Its superior height may be somewhat an illusion, however, created by the fact that as we move downstream, the river digs ever deeper, yet the elevation of the ancient Paleozoic Plateau, that level which determines the potential height of the bluffs, remains essentially the same. To the west, islands and more islands braid the river channel: Taylor Island, Barron Island, Isle La Plume, Hintgen Island, Green Island. Further west, a maze of small unnamed islands outlined by sloughs and backwaters sprawls across the wooded floodplain on the Minnesota side, ending as the land rises up to the Great River Road and the railroad line that run along the eastern edge of the little town of La Crescent.

We float slowly past Barron Island, where the beaches and sand volleyball courts of Pettibone Park are empty on this cool gray June morning. Across the river is a brightly painted riverboat, the *La Crosse Queen VII*, a modern tour boat disguised as a nineteenth-century paddlewheeler. Unlike many replicas, this boat is truly driven by its big paddlewheel, rather than by modern propellers, though its engines are modern diesel rather than wood-fired. Today, empty benches lend the boat an air of abandonment.

There's more, as there always is, and the story began, according to historian Richard Durbin's *The Wisconsin River*, in the early 1850s when many wealthy Europeans and Easterners took the "Fashionable Tour." Tourists, for this is who they were, would board a fancy steamboat, typically in St. Louis, cruise up to St. Paul, and return downriver to Prairie du Chien, admiring the majesty of the river and the bluffs and the picturesque wildness of the land and its inhabitants. From Prairie du Chien, they might return to St. Louis to conclude a round trip journey of about eight or nine days. Or, a smaller steamboat might carry some passengers up the Wisconsin River from Prairie du Chien to Portage, then down the Fox River to Green Bay where they would book passage east through the Great Lakes to the Atlantic coast. Minnesota historian Theodore C. Blegen claims it was George Catlin who in 1835 first proposed this grand concept, as a way for citified people to sample the "Far West," for this midsection of the continent was indeed still wilderness, the front edge of the vast unknown west.

The tour became quite fashionable, and in June of 1854 "The Grand Excursion" was held to celebrate the opening of the first railroad line from Chicago to the Mississippi River, or in the words of the railroad developer, "the nuptials of the Atlantic with the Father of Waters," the railroad link that would allow travelers to go from New York City to the Mississippi in less than two days. After riding two Chicago & Rock Island Railroad trains from Chicago to Rock Island, a group of between 700 and 1,200 (estimates vary considerably) wealthy and influential east coast travelers, among them former president Millard Fillmore with his daughter and son, along with various artists, ministers, and reporters, boarded seven steamboats for a festive sightseeing expedition up the Upper Mississippi to St. Paul and back: Eastern elites meet Wild West.

Back in the day, the Upper Mississippi was a destination. Today, however, on a cloudy cold Tuesday, everyone is at work, and the forlorn tour boat floats quietly, moored near the wooded mouth of the La Crosse River, the city's second confluence, the river known to Nicollet as Prairie à la Crosse R.

I have never paddled the La Crosse, but I do know that the Wisconsin DNR views this river as a great example of the federal Clean Water Act at work. In recent years, wastewater treatment plants along this river have reduced their phosphorus discharge by 90 percent, a dramatic and highly commendable change. This quiet but accomplished river passes through Fort McCoy, Sparta, Rockland, Bangor, and West Salem as it meanders over the wide valley, dammed four times in its sixty-one miles, toward its namesake city and the Mississippi. Below the dam at West Salem that impounds the river in Lake Neshonoc, the river is more turbid and prone to algae blooms. Within the city of La Crosse, a large wetland on the river's floodplain divides North La Crosse and South La Crosse and extends upriver beyond the city limits. When I look at a river, I always wonder what it would be like in a canoe. When DNR fisheries biologist Jordan Weeks looks at the La Crosse upstream of the dam at West Salem, he sees a big trout stream. Downstream of the dam, he says, it is home to muskies: the river seen through the eyes of an angler.

Near the tail of Barron Island, the twin spans of the Mississippi River Bridge are ahead, one bridge built in 1940 and the other in 2004, carrying Highway 14 and Highway 61 across the big river. From this angle their shapes overlap to form an elegant pattern of arched and trussed blue-painted steel. When I was a child journeying east with my family we crossed the older of these two bridges, and I still remember my first glimpse of its iron lacework and graceful curves.

It's late June. And it's cold. It shouldn't be this cold in late June. I'm trying to keep the complaints chorus mostly reined in. But it is cold, and the damp air combined with the wind makes it feel even colder. It's also mayfly season, though, and we should probably be grateful for the cold and the wind, which will delay any hatch that may be pending. *Hexagenia* hatches on the Mississippi are legendary. Vast numbers of nymphs crawl out of the Mississippi mud, morph into their winged adulthood, take flight in great clouds, and land on every surface in sight, all at once and all in one or two days. The fact that they swarm to mate, lay eggs, and die is well-known, but the environmental cue that prompts all the mayfly nymphs on the Mississippi from Iowa to Minnesota to hatch at once is apparently still a mystery. The bulk of the hex hatch often happens at night, and lured by the highway lights to die on a bridge roadway, mayfly bodies will pile in drifts on bridges over the Mississippi, drifts so deep that road crews get their snowplows out of storage to remove the slippery mess. On the Johnson Mayfly Emergence Scale, a hatch of that size would rate five out of five points.

Despite the fact that many find the clouds and piles of smelly bugs a source of incredible irritation, mayflies are ecologically exciting and important. Not only is a hatch an enormous food hit for many creatures, mayflies cannot thrive in an unhealthy river. Though by 1927 the mayfly had pretty much disappeared from the heavily polluted Mississippi, the creature staged a strong comeback after water quality improved in the 1980s. In the words of Kenny Selway, mayflies are "the Mississippi's barometer. A big hatch means a healthy river." Just not today, please.

Here's a note for the tech crowd. The National Weather Service at La Crosse recently began tracking the mayfly hatch every year, using Doppler radar to follow the largest swarms up the river valley from Davenport, Iowa, to the Twin Cities, and posting the results online. Imagine, a cloud of insects large enough to show up on radar!

At the Municipal Harbor on La Plume Island, Luke stands on the pier, our new camera in hand. We are chatting with him about family and about how grateful we are for the camera rescue when the door of his minivan slides open and his two young daughters and their two friends tumble out, all four dressed in various shades of pink. All talking at once, they chatter about tending their 4-H goats and about going to Wabasha this afternoon to see the eagles. Their young energy and enthusiasm is a warm radiator on this chilly damp day.

Leaving La Crosse, we paddle hard and my cold wet feet begin to warm. At least it's not raining. In fact, it hasn't rained once since we left Faribault. Bob clicks on the weather radio and we listen for a while to the National Oceanic and Atmospheric Administration (NOAA) channel describing the weather for everywhere else in the Upper Midwest before finally getting around to the La Crosse area. We learn that it is still only sixty degrees and the north to northwest wind is gusting to almost twenty miles per hour. But I knew that without listening to NOAA. I'm still cold and the wind is briskly herding our little boat down the river. NOAA National Weather Service features synthetic voices in both genders. Today, Donna speaks like the machine that she is, intoning

"These are the eleven a.m. central time conditions on Tuesday, June 30 . . ." with the telltale hypnotic cadence and odd pronunciations of synthetic speech. She does sound better than the former robotic voice of NOAA known as Paul, strange and disconcerting. On past river adventures, when the afternoon doldrums arrived, we would switch on a radio with a windup battery charger, cranking up the volume and singing along when the music was good, and once ran a winding rapids while the radio rollicked with Irish fiddle music. But when the radio broke, we didn't get another. Today as we resort to Donna's pontifications for entertainment, I know it's getting boring on the river.

At the wooded mouth of Minnesota's Root River, I perk up. The Root is one of my favorite paddling streams, though it doesn't look like much at the confluence, where it's just another slow-moving river adding its heavy, brown sediment load to the Mississippi. To confuse the uninitiated, the Mississippi disguises its confluences in wooded backwater tangles, where all the trees seem to be silver maples. Fremling writes that the native silver maple is the floodplain survivor of the impoundment stresses, thriving where other species give up.

The best of the Root begins upstream of the little town of Lanesboro. There it is the quintessential Blufflands river, rambling as it does through the wooded hills, past the tall sandstone cliffs that it has spent thousands of years carving, chattering through gravel bar riffles and occasional light rapids. Cold and secretive little trout streams flow in through the willow thickets that bristle at their mouths. The fishing is good, turtles and otters frequent the banks, and birds are everywhere: eagles, hawks, herons, bank swallows, songbirds, kingfishers. A paddler with some time to spare can spend days canoeing, fishing, and camping along its banks.

Like many Blufflands rivers, however, the Root originates in heavily farmed glacial till land. Its tributaries bring in runoff from the watershed's urban areas as well. "The Root begins in a judicial ditch in Mower County and ends in a judicial ditch in Houston County," said

Rich Biske of The Nature Conservancy (TNC). Since 2006, TNC has been working with soil and water districts in the watershed to target areas with the greatest runoff. Biske said their strategy is to address the problems—both nutrient overload and historic changes in the landscape that affected the stream's hydrology and now exacerbate flooding downstream—at the source, working on prairie streams in Mower County. Near Chatfield, TNC is working with a landowner to restore a floodplain wetland. In the Forestville area, they have worked on restoring contiguous lands.

Starting about five miles before its confluence with the Mississippi, the Root is channelized, the victim of historic flood control and agricultural drainage efforts, and near the town of Hokah an earthen levee follows the channel. Conservation groups continue efforts to restore and manage much of the Lower Root River floodplain, however, and over thirty acres of riparian buffers have been installed along tributaries of the Lower Root. TNC has designed a hybrid concept that allows farmers to use riparian buffers for limited grazing and haying rather than just setting the land aside.

"Right now," Biske said, "less than 3 percent of the watershed is protected. There are such heavy demands on the tillable land. And I don't know how much more that land use can be stretched." He said there are fewer rain events than in the past but these few are more intense, and they need to prepare for those in order to protect the streams from the floods that follow torrential rains. Research by the USGS in eight agricultural watersheds across the river in Wisconsin supports this idea, finding that a small number of rainfall and snowmelt runoff events accounted for the majority of phosphorus and sediment loading to streams.

"Despite all the challenges, these bluffs are still home to more species of greatest conservation need than most other places in the state. It's wonderful to crown a slope and just explore the plant communities that are there, such a diversity of plant and animal species that call this ancient landscape home. We take it for granted, but it's a really cool place," said Biske. Amen to those sentiments.

From the bluffs of Minnesota to the bluffs of Wisconsin, the river's gorge is almost four miles wide now. Back in La Crosse the Mississippi was a braided channel of narrow waterways laced with islands. Now it has broadened to over two miles of open water, a lake-like expanse. We feel quite small out here.

Who lives under these waters? It's definitely too murky for fish spotting. In talks with fisheries people, I have learned the basics about the pool's finny demographics. In a recent EMP fish census, the Number One Fish in Pool 8 was a little minnow called the weed shiner, only a few inches long, a slender, delicate, silvery creature with disproportionately big round eyes. The pumpkin-seed-shaped bluegill, my favorite at a Friday fish fry, ran a distant second. Third was largemouth bass and fourth, emerald shiner, another little guy. And black crappie rounded out the top five. All five species are happier in the relatively sluggish water of an impoundment—an environment described as lentic—than in the swift current of a free-flowing river, and their populations seem to be replacing the riverine species, like white bass and quillback, that were more common twenty years ago. For some species, the fisheries crew caught only one specimen, yet noteworthy on that list were the northern hog sucker and the stonecat, both known to be intolerant of pollution. The fish that didn't make the top five but have relatively stable populations include channel and flathead catfish, northern pike, smallmouth bass, walleye, sauger (close cousin to the walleye), and yellow perch, a favorite food for fish-eating birds and ice fishermen alike.

The survey turned up one of the lowest numbers of common carp in twenty years. Happily, the survey found no Asian carp, which doesn't mean they aren't there, only that they weren't caught for the count by electrofishing or netting. On another cheerful carp note, commercial fishermen in Illinois have found a market for the invasive Asian carp so prevalent in the Illinois reach of the Mississippi. Several companies now freeze the fish and ship them to China, where diners prefer wild caught carp. The Chinese-American business owner of Two Rivers Fishery told the *Wall Street Journal* that carp farm-raised in China taste like mud. It seems fitting to send them home again: Asian carp, the international traveler.

The roster of long-distance travelers in the Upper Mississippi, fish that instinctively migrate to spawn and feed, includes the mythic bewhiskered channel catfish, which in these reaches can grow to over forty pounds and over forty inches long. But if you can believe Mark Twain, that's not so big. In *Life on the Mississippi* he wrote, "I have seen a Mississippi cat-fish that was more than six feet long, and weighed two hundred and fifty pounds." No doubt a blue catfish, rare in these parts and a fish that grows bigger and travels further than the channel catfish. Fishermen go after channel cats at night, for like its mammalian namesake, it sleeps all day and prowls all night. Another big cat, the flathead catfish, is a homebody, rarely traveling more than five miles, and is less tolerant of murky water than the channel cat, preferring the clearer tributaries to the big river.

One of the lesser-known migrators in this region is the lake sturgeon. Steve Zigler of the USGS described a project that will track the movement of the lake sturgeon between Lake St. Croix, the lowest reach of that river, and the Mississippi. They'll take tiny samples of the fin rays of the sturgeon to study the trace element content, hoping to find a trace element "signature" unique to the place where the fish was spawned. Their guess is that the trace element signature in the fin ray of a sturgeon that grew up in Lake St. Croix can be distinguished from that of a sturgeon spawned in the Mississippi. If this is true, the research team will be able to learn where a fish was spawned, where it will spawn again, and where it travels as an adult to eat: the itinerary of its life. It's a bit like the concept of *terroir*, a French word meaning that an organism or food grown in one distinctive area has that unique elemental composition, the signature of the land or river in which it grows.

The lake sturgeon: a fish with a sense of place, and yet a yearning to travel.

A gathering of big birds sails over us, playing on the wind, a vivid white *V* against the grey sky. When I was a child, I thought my mother knew every bird. But apparently she didn't, because many years after, when I was a mother myself, on a summer day at that lake house near Faribault, she and I and the others watched eight big white birds flying in a *V* overhead. And she didn't know what they were. The birds flew upward from the lake in a slow effortless spiral, more or less keeping formation, riding the thermal with amazing grace. They reached the height they wanted, soared off to the northeast, then returned, swooping low enough to show off their distinctive profiles—backward curve of neck, long sturdy wedge of beak, legs trailing behind. As they sailed by on the wind, Mom said, "heron?" but without any conviction, just to satisfy our need to identify, and then they were gone. If I shut my eyes, the picture of them climbing the wind, silhouetted against scattered clouds on blue sky, their white bodies reflecting the light of the sun each time it moved from behind a cloud, is still there in my mind's eye.

We never did look them up in a bird book. Two years after, though, on a visit with our children to a natural history museum in St. Paul, the lingering question of those birds was answered in a strange postscript. The first exhibit hall presented a wall of many drawers, deep glass-topped drawers filled with items like miniature kayaks, arrowhead collections, preserved animal bodies, American Indian jewelry. It was like a game of chance to open a drawer. You didn't know what would be inside because there were no labels on the outside, only numbers. As I slowly opened drawer number five, my first choice, the folded body of a large bird lying flat under the glass gradually appeared. In order to squeeze it into the drawer, the curator had arranged its body, legs, and wings in a position no bird had ever chosen. The poor creature was nearly folded in half, but instantly I recognized the neck and head. The label read:

American White Pelican
Lake of the Woods, 1978
MN DNR ♂
Warroad

We finally knew the name of our dreamlike fliers.

Pelicans on the Lake Pepin sand spit, pelicans soaring over Pool 8 —
it is quite exciting to realize that pelicans are returning to the Upper
Mississippi, after years of scarcity and even absence. In 2006, during
our paddling adventures on the Upper Minnesota River, a more remote
habitat, Bob and I saw hundreds of pelicans, but for years they were
rarely seen on the Mississippi. Refuge scientists say that pelicans now
nest every year on sandy islands in the Mississippi south of here, the first
colonies on the Upper Mississippi since 1909. The nesting season is over
now, so the flock soaring over Pool 8 is more likely to be on summer
vacation than house hunting.

Across the river a dredging rig fills a barge tow with the mountains
of sand they call "dredge spoil." We're in the main channel now, where
the cruiser traffic is light but steady. Whenever we hear the low grumble
of an inboard motor behind us, or see a boat cruising toward us, we
raise our paddles in a joint salute, hoping the driver will see the flash of
the wet blades and slow down to reduce the wake. Some do, most don't.
Those who don't often smile and wave as they roar past, oblivious to
the unpleasant effect their big wakes have on a canoe.

After a lunch break at Wildcat Park landing in Brownsville—gouda
cheese and Wasabrod once again, as we have no imagination when it
comes to the midday meal—we follow the Minnesota side of the river
into leafy green backwater channel beauty, the quiet water where migrating waterfowl feed. Here are stiff and broadleaf arrowhead, also
known as duck potato, and wild celery, also known as eel grass, the
leaves of which move in lovely sinuous patterns on the water's surface.
Both grow underwater tubers that are the favored forage of birds such as

canvasback ducks and tundra swans. Here also are yellow lotus, another source of tasty tubers, and big beds of nutritious wild rice. In the past ten years, these avian greengrocery stores have increased in Pool 8, in part due to restoration efforts. "Some of these rice beds are huge and stalks may reach nine feet in productive beds," said John Sullivan, retired Wisconsin DNR water quality specialist and long-distance paddler who has lived on this reach of the Mississippi for nearly thirty years and loves to explore the backwaters.

In late fall, many thousands of tundra swans, traveling south from the tundra to winter on Chesapeake Bay, and guided along this leg of the journey by the great river valley that is their flyway, rest and feed on the Upper Mississippi backwaters. And they hang out here long enough to attract flocks of people. Along the Great River Road south of Browns-ville, there's an overlook where bird watchers gather in November to take in the magnitude of the migration, a spectacle graced by the con-versations of the resting tundra swans, a sound sometimes described as a mellow murmuring. In recent years, more than 78,000 tundra swans have congregated on the river throughout the Refuge for up to a month, feeding and resting for their long journey, until finally the river froze over and they moved on. Canada geese, eagles, white pelicans, mallards, gadwalls, pintails, widgeons, and other winged migrators join them, numbering in the thousands as well. On the flight north again in the spring, tundra swans don't linger here—only on the fall flight.

These backwater channels are beautiful. John Sullivan says he hopes people will understand that the river is so much more than the main channel. A navigational channel just can't compare to the amazingly diverse aesthetics of the backwaters, the network of life that is the life-blood of the river, the places that Sullivan loves to explore, often standing in his canoe and poling it through the mazes of his favorite backwaters, like the Black River Delta, Whitman Bottoms, Tiffany Bottoms. "These tributary delta areas are very hydraulically complex and offer diverse aquatic plant communities and floodplain forests," said Sullivan, who spends much of his warm-weather free time in his canoe. "They're where the river is most beautiful and interesting."

As we float the backwater channel, I think too of how Featherstone-haugh described the braided channel of this same reach on September 4, 1835: "The valley betwixt the opposite bluffs was here near three miles wide, and I seemed to look down upon an immense forest, growing upon innumerable islands, among which various streams were gliding. Some of the islands were so extensive as to contain ponds of consider-able extent, and large areas of the zizania, already frequented by the wild fowl, which had begun to arrive from the north in immense quantities."

Though the once abundant zizania (wild rice) is returning to the river, when a river becomes a lake, it loses. The intricate web of habitats that the sloughs, the off-channel lakes, the backwaters offer to the rich community of creatures that live on a river such as the Mississippi gradually disappears. Trying to restore the river that once was is a big, ambitious project and one that will never bring the Mississippi back to the way it was before the lock and dam system forced the river to permanently flood much of its former floodplain. Rehabilitating is a better, more realistic word, according to Jeff Janvrin of Wisconsin DNR, who coordinates the Corps habitat projects on the Wisconsin side of the river, such as building new islands. We float past Boomerang Island and Horseshoe Island. Long, low narrow curves of land completed twenty years ago, the islands are now covered with vegetation, and their orientation to the prevailing winds allows beds of tasty greenery to grow in the lee of the curved shorelines. From above their shapes must look artificial, but from down here on the water their wooded shores look as though the river spawned them and they have always been there.

If you were to fly over the Upper Mississippi you would see a pattern in the changes wrought by the lock and dam system. Just downstream of a dam, the river is channelized at first, then the islands and backwaters appear, relatively intact, and the channel becomes riverine and braided rather than lake-like. As you move downstream, the islands gradually disappear and the water spreads across the former floodplain in an open featureless expanse. If you hovered over the next lock and dam you would see the pattern repeat. Though I already knew, at least abstractly, that this is true of the Upper Mississippi, here on the water I feel rather than know the profound changes wrought by impoundment. Downstream of a dam, the river still feels like a living river. Approaching the long straight line of a lock and dam, it becomes a different creature, artificial, confined and controlled.

Aerial photographs taken in 1930 of the river reach that is now the lower end of Pool 8 reveal an intricate braided channel, the river's flow split in half by a wide floodplain forest laced with narrow waterways and small off-channel lakes; that area is now a wide-open lake. For a time after the dam created Pool 8 in 1937, high points of land in the wooded floodplain, formerly only seasonal islands, found a new role as permanent islands. For a time. Within sixty years, however, wave action and current had swept 90 percent of these islands downstream. Today all that is left of that wide floodplain forest is submerged stump fields.

By damming the river, we humans introduced wave action, a force that can destroy river features like islands that were deposited by the glacial flood and protect the river's geomorphology and ecosystems. Divided thus into braided strands, the river flows faster in some strands and slower in others, yielding the varied kinds of living spaces—vegetation-filled backwaters, quiet shallows, deep pools, fast channels—that attract and nurture a wide range of fish and other creatures. Islands deflect the persistent wind that builds the waves that nibble away shorelines and fill the river with suspended sediment, and small islands are where migratory water birds nest and raise their young. "With future sedimentation, the pooled portions will slowly evolve to conditions somewhat similar to what existed prior to the impounded river. This will also mean increased dredging to maintain the navigation channel. The speed of this new resurrection will vary by pool and will likely be influenced by tributary sediment loads and habitat projects such as those constructed in Pool 8," said John Sullivan.

During the early stages of rehabilitating Weaver Bottoms, back upstream in Pool 5, Janvrin said they observed the way some small islands functioned as "sand traps," capturing sand by changing the way the current flowed and deposited its sand load, and they used these lessons to build six islands in the open areas of Pool 8. Charmingly named "seed islands," these small seedlings were simply piles of rock, oriented to capture and hold some of the sediment that the river continuously carries downstream. Though the little creations were expected to grow much larger over time, their actual growth has been slight. Janvrin says the concept was a bit like that of slightly emerged wing dams, which are rocky fingers interwoven with willow mats extending from the shoreline into the channel, angled like wings and designed to capture sediment and divert the scouring flow away from the banks and into the channel. Because the sand captured by the seed island piles only as high as the water, the small island grows slowly, though it does give the river what Janvrin calls "a little bit of sandpaper" to work with.

Island building on the Mississippi isn't new. In the early twentieth century, for example, before impoundment, two long islands were built downstream of Ferryville, Wisconsin, in order to straighten the channel. Today, these islands, like many built in recent years, are indistinguishable from the river's natural islands. When we change the river to meet our cultural needs and desires, the river always adapts, often in ways we later regret. Occasionally the adaptation is for the good, as in the case of the islands.

In *Nature's Metropolis*, historian William Cronon describes the early growth of the city of Chicago as a process by which "natural and cultural landscapes began to shade into and reshape one another." And it seems that this is the story of the Mississippi River valley, which has become what Cronon would call a cultural landscape, not to the extent that Chicago is, of course, but no longer a natural landscape either. We push the river, and the river pushes right back, by flooding our dwellings and our farmland, by no longer being the beautiful, life-filled, swiftly flowing, almost animate being that it once was, the beguiling riverscape that first drew us to settle along its banks. The pushing match continues until a truce of sorts is reached, where we humans grudgingly acknowledge that we cannot continually reshape the river without the risk of losing what we first valued in it. Then we begin our rehabilitation efforts. Perhaps we must not ask whether we can return the river to what it once was, which we cannot, but whether the future changes we plan are worth the price we know the river will make us pay. "The most important question about the river's future is how long it will take the changes we have already made throughout the watershed to work their way through the system. It is like we started pulling at loose threads that we thought were bothersome and are now watching to see how much of the garment unravels," said glacial geologist Carrie Jennings.

When we depart the greenery, it is to cross toward the Wisconsin side through what is labeled on the navigational chart as "stump fields." This is where that low-lying bottomland forest once grew. Despite the chart's seemingly dramatic warnings, we see no stumps, only feel the threat of long-ago decapitated trees lurking below the surface. We cross ever so cautiously, on the diagonal, a downstream ferry so to speak.

Upstream, I can just barely see the houses of Stoddard, Wisconsin, and the green and tan traces of more Corps-built islands. Stoddard is where Coon Creek flows in, the stream that Nicollet called the Raccoon River, the stream made famous in the 1930s when conservation crews began to rebuild the deeply eroded land of Coon Valley, a story told in a later chapter.

A long barge tow is parked along the Wisconsin shore, pointed upstream, the tug engine quiet. Behind the barge, the railroad tracks and the Great River Road run in tandem along the shore, three strands of transportation lined up together. Intrigued by the big beast, which looks far less threatening while at rest, we paddle close and follow the entire length of the tow, studying the rusty riveted sides and speculating about the cargo that weights it down, why it's parked here, going nowhere. Just before we reach the bow of the tug, a disembodied voice booms over a loudspeaker.

Barge tow on the Mississippi

"You! Canoe! You shouldn't come around the front of a tow where we can't see you from the wheelhouse. That's a good way to get killed."

Silence.

Bob calls, "We're really sorry."

Silence. The voice is not accepting our apology.

We paddle downstream, deeply ashamed of being so foolish.

Bob turns to me and says quietly, "I didn't realize the engine was idling, not shut off. He could have started up at any time."

It was pure stupid. Ironically, even though Bob and I pride ourselves on being careful canoeists, we broke one of the cardinal rules of paddling the Mississippi: always stay clear of the barge tows. *That's a good way to get killed.*

Big swells generated by our constant companion the tailwind, but no breakers this time, take us on a long roller-coaster ride toward

Genoa, alongside the straight levee-like shoreline topped with railroad tracks and banked with riprap. The lock and dam appears, a tiny concrete rectangle on the horizon. A long earthen dike stretches from the dam across the river to Minnesota, its straight edge an incongruous shape on the river. Behind that dike is Reno Bottoms, a sprawling labyrinth of backwater sloughs with not a straight edge in sight. A canoe trail has been mapped through the maze with signs to guide the way, and paddlers often travel the sloughs to see the wildlife. Yet it is rumored that some get lost deep in the bottoms, where they find that every little island looks alike and none look like what they see on the map. We'll bypass those bottoms tomorrow.

As we cruise alongside the railroad tracks, I see a small figure far ahead, standing alone atop the riprap, waving what looks like a white flag. As we paddle up, she smiles widely, dishtowel in hand, introduces herself as Anne, our innkeeper, and directs us with her towel toward a low timber railroad bridge. Under the bridge we go. Anne and her husband Jim, along with their friend David, meet us at the concrete ramp on the edge of a duckweed-bedecked pond. As these gracious and generous people help us load our gear into Anne's car, Anne tells their story. Anne Zabolio Muirhead is the descendant of immigrants from Campodolcino, a town in northeastern Italy. Her people settled here on the Mississippi River before the Civil War, about 1850. Many of the Italians who immigrated to Genoa were stonemasons whose skills are evidenced by the fine stone construction of Anne's family's house, and it seems the northern Italians may have been drawn to the rugged terrain of the Driftless, a smaller-scale version of their mountainous home-land, but Anne's ancestors were not stonemasons. They established the Zabolio General Store in Genoa, a business that was in the family for four generations. She and Jim lived in Texas for years and have just moved north to tend to the property.

We carry the canoe across Highway 35—Wisconsin's Great River Road. Just past their 1868 stone inn, the Zaboglio House (Anne's family dropped the *g* that was used in the Italian spelling of the name), we come to the adjoining Genoa Motel, where we will stay. In our large, comfortable room is a sign reminding us not to clean fish in the bathroom.

In the evening, over deep-fried channel catfish and coleslaw at the Big River Inn down the street, we talk about our kind innkeepers, about the easy life of Mississippi River canoeists like us who stay in motels and eat delicious fish dinners in restaurants, about the unexpected Italian heritage of this river town, and about the remarkable early twentieth-century mural of the local riverscape, a wide landscape scene painted on the wall behind the restaurant's bar, long ago, before the lock and dam system was built, in a time when the river was wild and free.

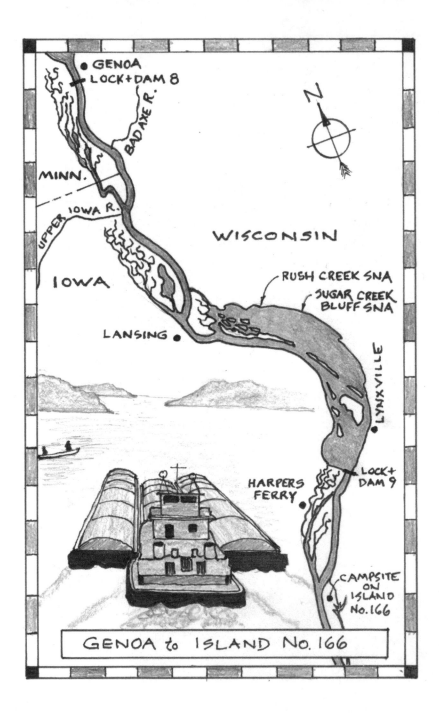

GENOA to ISLAND No. 166

In Their Own Pool

July the first. The day dawns cloudless and cool, and our tailwind still sleeps. Mostly, anyway. On the water by six, and into Lock & Dam 8 without a hitch, we're glad to be ahead of the big tow that's lumbering toward the lock from upriver. As we drop the eleven feet to the level of Pool 9, Bob asks the sleepy lockmaster about the best route through the backwater maze to Harpers Ferry, Iowa, some miles downstream of the dam. He shakes his head, tells us he's not sure where Harpers Ferry is, and apologetically explains, "On the river, pretty much everyone stays in their own pool."

And it turns out that he is right. A FWS study done in 2006 on boating habits in Pools 4 through 9 revealed that 87 percent of recreational boaters do stay in the pool into which they launch. It's the barge tows, the tournament fishermen, and the long-distance travelers in canoes and kayaks that lock through. Navigational pools are separated from each other by dams almost as effectively as natural lakes are by land, and the experience of being on a lake that some seek, combined with the extra effort required to lock through because of barge traffic, no doubt persuade many boaters to stay put.

Of course, not everyone stays in one pool. And for a certain breed, the lure of traveling the Mississippi under one's own power is strong. Written accounts of these adventures abound, and we've met a few people who made the journey. In the summer of 1936, soon after reading Eric

Sevareid's iconic *Canoeing with the Cree* and less than a month after the locks at Trempealeau and Fountain City were first put into operation, my Uncle Harry and his cousin Jim canoed the Mississippi from Jim's home in Winona, Minnesota, down to Hannibal, Missouri. My uncle told me with a wry smile that they didn't know they could lock through and portaged those first two dams. In Hannibal, they sold their canoe and camping gear and used the proceeds to take the train to Chicago and then home. Not the whole length of the big river, by any means, but an exciting summer adventure for a couple of teenagers. In 1975, Denny Caneff, now director of the River Alliance of Wisconsin, canoed with a friend the whole length of the river, from Lake Itasca, the Mississippi's northern Minnesota source, to the Gulf of Mexico. Caneff, who turned twenty-one on the trip, recalls the awe he felt knowing he was floating on the water that drains off almost half the land in the lower forty-eight states. John Sullivan, the water scientist and long-distance canoeist who lives in La Crosse, paddled the length of the river in two stages, from the headwaters to La Crosse in the spring of one year and from Lock & Dam 9 to the Gulf in the fall of the following year. "I did this last trip to make it to an Interstate Water Quality meeting at Fairport, Iowa—I figured I would paddle to my last meeting," said Sullivan. Sullivan has also paddled the length of the Minnesota, the Wisconsin, the Iowa, the Ohio, the Illinois, and even the big Missouri— state-named rivers that flow into the Mississippi, going solo on all but the Illinois.

Sullivan told me of the interesting ways that modern technology and social media have transformed long-distance paddling. Before beginning his trip to the Gulf, he learned of a Facebook group called the Mississippi River Paddlers. On the river, Sullivan used his cell phone and iPad, both powered by a portable solar charger with an external battery, to check the group's Facebook posts, post his own entries and questions, and stay in touch with fellow paddlers all down the river. In Memphis, a member of the group picked him up at the river and took him to their home, where he showered, ate dinner with the family, and stayed overnight. The next morning, he was back on the river.

"There's a network of people you don't even know," said Sullivan. "People we call 'river angels' will help you solve the problems that always come up. And the network constantly changes as you go downstream. Someone I reached through a Facebook contact took me to the Cape Girardeau post office to pick up my food drop." The paddlers share their stories, their advice, their time, their homes. This growing internet network seems to have led to a lot more people doing trips like this, Sullivan said, and he warned against people taking unnecessary risks on the river, assuming they will be saved by technology. Then he chuckled, "Can you imagine what Marquette and Joliet and other earlier explorers would have to say about today's modern technologies?"

Before he retired, Sullivan didn't leave his day job entirely behind when he headed out on river adventures. At work he focused on long-term water quality changes and problems in the Wisconsin reach of the Mississippi. And so, as he paddled down the Mississippi, he sampled water quality along the way, measuring dissolved oxygen, water transparency, water temperature, and conductivity—a measure of dissolved solids. Sullivan speculated about the potential of today's many long-distance paddlers to contribute to deeper knowledge of the river, as citizen scientists, trained to test the river water and report what they observe on their journeys to natural resource agencies that manage the river. He sees the growing group of long-distance paddlers as an untapped resource.

Soon after we leave the lock, we pass the coal-fired Dairyland Power Plant and the Boiling Water Reactor. The latter is an inactive nuclear power plant that has been in the process of being deconstructed since 1987. The twin stacks cast their looming industrial shadows over lush green riverbanks and a quiet river, populated only by a few fishermen in their small boats. Within a mile, though, as we wander the sandy shoreline during a stop, I sense only the natural persona of the river. An egret fishing in the shallows flies away, calling *kuk-kuk-kuk*, scolding us as it departs. Bob finds a nest of turtle eggs partly buried in the sand. We listen to the rustle of small creatures in the undergrowth. Back and forth between the cultural landscape and the natural landscape.

Floating along the main channel edge once again, I study the chart, and it occurs to me for the first time that we have been following, approximately anyway, the state line between Minnesota and Wisconsin, an invisible line that meanders with the channel, a line I only think about when looking at the river charts. As a wandering dashed line on the map dividing the channel, it does seem a bit more real, but close the chart book and it's invisible and forgotten. And now we're getting close to the equally invisible state line between Minnesota and Iowa, surveyed in 1849 by Captain Joseph J. Lee of the U.S. Topographic Engineer Corps, a line that runs straight, true, and imaginary along the parallel of 43 degrees 30 north latitude. Somewhere in the middle of the river channel ahead, just east of Island No. 135, the boundary lines of the three states meet, at a politically important yet physically invisible point, plotted by the intersection of a line drawn from mathematical concepts with a meandering line designating the middle of the ungovernable river channel. Sometimes the collision of the cultural world with the natural world seems quite absurd.

Even though physically invisible, boundary lines are no less powerful in defining our world, and each state has its own regulatory relationship with the ecosystems that lie within these boundaries. A river channel will shift and change over time, yet a river is widely accepted as a useful political boundary. This may be because of the practicality of letting nature choose the line. I muse about Joseph N. Nicollet's map, which shows only rivers. Rivers were the roads, the boundaries, and the reality of the presettlement land. Back then, all the important stuff happened along the rivers. When a political boundary is also an ecological boundary, there is implicit agreement with nature's design.

But when these three states were surveyed for settlement, government bureaucracy imposed a grid on the land, defining boundaries without regard to the shape of the land. This is the reason for the deeply familiar landscape grid we see when we fly over this land today, a grid that in our imaginations almost defines the land of the Upper Midwest. In his essay "The View from Man Mound," conservation biologist and historian Curt Meine writes about the survey: "In subdividing and bounding the land—legally, politically, economically, and imaginatively—it would reshape the biological diversity, ecosystems, and human communities of Wisconsin in profound ways." He argues that by imposing the grid, we reduced the importance of the watershed as the dominant reality by fragmenting and simplifying a complex and fragile ecosystem and speeded the ecological problems of the Driftless Area, the host of ecological problems that reached a crescendo in the early twentieth century. Speeded, not caused, he is careful to point out. Now we are involved in "refitting rectangular land parcels into watershed-shaped realities," backpedaling our way into nature's original map-making design.

Yet the wonderful nature of the river is that it has always defied the grid. All along the edges of this vast river valley, the shape of the intersection between the land and the river has shaped the way that towns and villages can fit into the landscape, not the other way around. When humans build on a river terrace rather than the floodplain, the natural landscape is, in Cronon's words, shaping their cultural landscape.

Lost in my thoughts about imaginary lines, I forget to look for the confluence with Wisconsin's Bad Axe River, flowing in through the backwater tangles on our left, and we float on past. If we had paddled just a short distance upstream on the Bad Axe, we would have found the Genoa National Fish Hatchery, where biologists raise channel catfish to stock the river with this iconic creature. But that's not all. The channel cat plays an integral part in the life of an endangered mussel named the winged mapleleaf, which the hatchery also raises. Bringing up mussels is an intricate process for human beings. Each September, on the lower

St. Croix River, at the only known mussel bed where the winged maple-leaf still reproduces in the Upper Mississippi valley, scuba divers collect female mussels that are carrying tiny mussel larvae, bi-valve babies called glochidia, and bring the mothers and babies back to the hatchery. Here's where the catfish comes in. Hatchery biologists prompt the female mussels to expel their glochidia, and these tiny floating organisms attach to the waiting fish's gills. And it has to be a catfish. If they don't attach to a catfish, the glochidia die. The catfish and its hitchhikers live in a hatchery tank for the winter. In the spring, having grown to the juvenile stage, about the size of the head of a pin, the tiny mussels drop off the gills to the bottom of the tank. In June, the biologists gather these juveniles and move the new cohort to their ancestral mussel bed home on the St. Croix. Those that survive have grown to the size of a marble by the following year. Those that thrive may live another thirty to forty years.

But life is uncertain when humans have altered the ecosystem.

Less than five hundred winged mapleleaf mussels live in that St. Croix bed, making it the most endangered mussel in the Upper Mississippi watershed. The hatchery at Genoa also raises Higgins eye pearly mussels, a bigger creature which hatchery manager Doug Aloisi says has a better survival rate than winged mapleleaf. Biologists plant Higgins eye juveniles in beds near Harpers Ferry, Iowa; in the East Channel at Prairie du Chien, Wisconsin; and in the Orion Mussel Bed on the Lower Wisconsin River.

If we were to paddle even further upstream on the Bad Axe, past the hatchery and up to its tributary, the North Fork of the Bad Axe, we would find good trout water. For much of the twentieth century, this was not true. Like most Driftless streams, the Bad Axe was damaged by past farming practices that led to the topsoil washing from ridge tops down the steep valley slopes and into the stream, destroying the floodplain, which is nature's best flood control.

When the river is connected to its floodplain, floodwaters can spill over the banks instead of being forced to rush straight downstream, as floodwater does when the river cannot reach the floodplain. Though the same amount of water flows in both situations, spreading into the flood plain reduces the energy of the flood and slows its downstream rush.

Even though agriculture has changed its ways, it takes years and lots of work to restore the floodplains. The Mississippi Valley Conservancy and Trout Unlimited have established conservation easements, primarily for trout habitat, on about nine hundred acres of land in the Bad Axe watershed, a holding called Eagle Eye State Natural Area, named for the prehistoric rock shelter that was discovered on the land. And over the last forty years, the Wisconsin DNR has used income from trout stamps to fund the work of reshaping and replanting the stream banks, gradually restoring the river's access to its floodplain. The test of their restoration came with the historic floods of 2007 and 2008. In areas with flood control dams but where the floodplain had not been restored, dams were badly damaged, unstable hillsides became catastrophic mudslides that carried houses downhill and washed out bridges and culverts. According to the DNR Bad Axe River Watershed Plan 2010, in reaches without floodplains to absorb the deluge, stream banks were devastated. Yet the many stream miles with restored floodplains were relatively undamaged.

Not too far downstream from the Bad Axe confluence, across the river from the site of the shameful Battle of Bad Axe where federal troops massacred the last of Chief Blackhawk's people at the end of the Blackhawk War, the mouth of the Upper Iowa River hides behind an island along the Iowa side. This Blufflands river originates in Minnesota and in its upper reaches swoops and dips along the borderline between Iowa and Minnesota for several miles before dropping decisively into Iowa where it meanders east for another eighty miles to the Mississippi.

Pool 9 on the Mississippi

In his guidebook *Paddling Iowa*, writer and paddler Nate Hoogeveen describes the swiftly flowing Upper Iowa as "ultra-scenic," riffling past "breathtaking" limestone bluffs topped with pine and balsam fir. It is "heavily spring-fed and the water clarity is excellent," a real beauty of a river. Where it meets the Mississippi, however, the Upper Iowa is straight as a drainage ditch, an anticlimax for paddlers after all the upstream beauty. We paddle the short distance upstream to see the confluence, an unremarkable meeting of waters. Yet having read Hoogeveen's glowing descriptions, I know there is so much more upstream. We will paddle the Upper Iowa someday.

Though the chart, still open on my knees, shows me that the Great River Road runs close to the river along the Mississippi's Wisconsin shore, wooded islands buffer the channel from the highway, and this

120

uninhabited reach of the river feels quite remote for a moment. Then, with a low warning growl, a barge tow moves around the bend ahead, the engines of the tug uttering their sustained rumble, the low waves of the wake crashing rhythmically onto the sand as it passes us. It's headed upstream and is soon out of sight. The quiet returns and we meet no more traffic downstream.

Until we reach Lansing. As we near the Iowa town, a dredging rig crane's engine roars, the big mechanical arm swings back and forth, moving sandy spoil from a barge and dumping it on one of the islands. Just as we pass the rig, another big tow comes around the bend, headed upstream, straight toward us. It's a veritable barge tow traffic jam. Not wanting another close encounter, we dart over to the Iowa shore, slide under the Blackhawk Bridge, and paddle hard up to one of the town landings, where we park the canoe and go foraging for groceries. It feels good to be on foot instead of sitting, and our tour of Lansing lasts longer than planned.

"Hey, how about something to eat?" says Bob.

Sidetracked at River's Edge restaurant, over a second breakfast of classic diner food—cheesy omelets and buttered white toast served with little plastic containers of grape jelly on the side—we eavesdrop on three women who are drinking coffee and planning an ice cream social. The loudest member of the group bemoans the fact that they can't get anyone to volunteer for the dunking booth.

"I wouldn't volunteer either," I whisper to Bob.

Back on the river, our stomachs full, groceries and a bag of ice from Moore's IGA stashed in the cooler, we float serenely downstream. I've heard there's a mussel bed near here, at a place known as Whiskey Rock, but it's not shown on the chart. And so my gaze goes upward to the bluffs. Goat prairies, those dry south and southwest-facing prairielands found almost exclusively in the Upper Mississippi River valley, are visible on the high bluffs, beyond the sloughs and the open water of Lake Winneshiek that separate us from the Wisconsin shore. Goat prairies, because only goats can keep their balance on the steep inclines. One after another, small treeless prairies front the march of the bluffs. These little grassland wonders are remnants of the prairies and oak savannas that once covered most of the Driftless. Despite being thin and dry, the soil on goat prairies supports short grasses like little bluestem, side-oats grama, and hairy grama (also known as mustache grass); and the bunchy growth habit of the grasses invites wildflowers to fill in the gaps, species like pasque flower, bastard toadflax, and harebell, whose populations are otherwise declining throughout the Midwest. Goat prairies like those in Rush Creek and Sugar Creek Bluff, both units of the Wisconsin State Natural Areas program, are little field museums that remind us what the vegetation of the Upper Midwest once looked like. And in the Driftless, soil building on the bluff tops is a wonderful thing.

In tribute to the prairie plant, Aldo Leopold wrote, "What is the most valuable part of the prairie? The fat black soil, the chernozem. Who built the chernozem? The black prairie was built by the prairie plants, a hundred distinctive species of grasses, herbs, and shrubs; by the prairie fungi, insects, and bacteria; by the prairie mammals and birds, all interlocked in one humming community of cooperations and competitions, one biota." From down here on the water, I can't see those grasses and flowers, of course, but they're there, quietly humming, plumping up the thin soil of the rocky bluff with their deep roots.

In the midst of this happy prairie interlude, the modern world returns, this time in the form of Alliant Energy's power plant, another huge coal burning facility at the foot of a high rocky bluff on the Iowa shore. *The beast in the beauty, again.* This is the third of its kind we have passed on the Mississippi, and each time, the massive structure has a starkly incongruous presence in a national wildlife refuge. Its sheer size forces me to wonder about it.

Power companies have historically built plants on big rivers like the Mississippi. One reason is the ease of delivering coal by river barge to plants like the one at Lansing. And perhaps building power plants on the river and delivering the coal by barge makes power generation less expensive for consumers, perhaps not. The more variables one introduces, the more unpredictable the results of the cost equation. This and other difficult-to-answer questions about the economics of barge transport as opposed to train transport are posed in an interactive exhibit in the National Mississippi River Museum in Dubuque, Iowa, an exhibit that lays out all the variables, not just the financial costs. And the individual museum visitor forms his own opinion.

Quite separate from the ambiguous economics and environmental impacts of coal delivery, power plants like this definitely and directly affect the river because they use river water to cool their generators. Another reason power plants are built on the river. Yet if handled wrong, this cooling process is destructive to the riverine ecosystem. The cooling systems for all three power plants we have passed on this journey— Alma, Wisconsin; Genoa, Wisconsin; and Lansing, Iowa—systems which are termed "once-through cooling," draw in river water to cool the generators and discharge the resulting hot water back into the river. According to the 2009 U.S. Energy Information Administration's Annual Electric Generator Report, the daily river water intake capacity of just these three plants combined is 757 million gallons per day. Though the actual intake varies seasonally and the plants don't always operate at full capacity, that's a lot of hot water. In comparison, a tributary river like the Upper Iowa contributes an average of only about 466 million gallons of water per day to the Mississippi.

"Heat is like any other pollutant," said Helen Sarakinos of the River Alliance of Wisconsin. "It is an impairment to water quality." Because heat is destructive to the river and its denizens, states that border the Mississippi have set temperature caps that hot water discharge to the river cannot exceed, limits that vary with the season, sometimes described as narrative standards. According to Rochelle Weiss of the Iowa Department of Natural Resources, the rules that govern this Lansing plant we are passing today are narrative standards. Simply put, these standards mean that discharge cannot heat the water more than five degrees Fahrenheit above the normal temperature of the river for that time of year, as listed in a table of monthly maximums.

Wisconsin once had this type of thermal discharge regulation as well, but in 1975 the Wisconsin Supreme Court nullified the standard because of how it was written. Rewriting the law took thirty-five years. According to Sarakinos, this remarkably long delay was due to several factors including Wisconsin DNR delays, opposition by utilities and municipalities, and a ruling by the court that the former narrative standards had to be replaced with numeric standards.

"[Wisconsin is] the first state in the country to develop numeric standards. Every other state had that five degree Fahrenheit change standard for rivers since no other state Supreme Court nullified it. That was part of the angst—there was no precedent," said Sarakinos. "Heat is hard for the DNR to permit. Heat does weird stuff; it dissipates in a way no other pollutant does."

For this reason, dischargers are given a "mixing zone" at the end of their discharge pipes where heat is allowed to further dissipate before they need to meet the water quality standard. Discharge water from a power plant is often so hot that water at the end of the pipe is termed by some as the "zone of immediate death" for aquatic organisms. The permitting process defines the extent of the mixing zone for every discharger as a function of the effluent temperature and the size and flow of the receiving water. According to Sarakinos, determining the base temperature of the discharge and the size of the allowable mixing zone were contentious issues in the Wisconsin debate. Those who advocated for a big mixing zone—this would have allowed them to discharge hotter water because the heat would dissipate before the temperature was taken—were the paper plants, the utilities, and the food canning facilities.

Wisconsin's recently adopted numeric standards apply to the Alma and Genoa plants. Permits for these facilities not only define the size of the mixing zone, but also define how hot the discharge can be by considering the base temperature of each specific water body as well as the specific time of year, because the temperatures that fish and other aquatic organisms require to thrive vary with the seasons.

Once-through cooling is an old technology. According to the Sierra Club, the Environmental Protection Agency (EPA) began in 2001 to require newly built plants to use what is called "closed-cycle cooling," where the water is cooled down to ambient river temperature before discharge. Converting to closed-cycle cooling can reduce total water withdrawals by about 95 percent, but the change is expensive and translates into higher utility rates. But closed-cycle cooling also dramatically reduces the number of aquatic organisms that are swept into the intake pipe of a once-through cooling system where they are boiled and ground to death in the system—collateral damage in the struggle between our economics and our ecosystems.

Down the river, we leave the power plant conundrum behind us, but not the beautiful bluffs of Iowa. Soon we pass the tall wooded face of Capoli Bluff, named by the French as Cap à L'Ail, or Garlic Promontory, and well known to river travelers. Catlin painted the distinctive half-dome bluff on his Mississippi travels. Were we to hike up the backside of the bluff, we would find a southwest-facing goat prairie much like the ones we saw upstream at Sugar Creek Bluff and Rush Creek.

The beauty of the Mississippi Blufflands, including the distinctive goat prairies, has lured American landscape painter Sara Lubinski, who has captured the shapes and textures of the valley landscape in her compelling oil paintings. Lubinski formerly worked as a botanist and the integrity in her paintings derives from her wide knowledge of native plants. The places she is drawn to paint are often conserved properties, like the goat prairie at Capoli Bluff, which she called "a fabulous example of preserved native species, like compass plant and seven foot high Indian grass." When I first saw her painting of Capoli Bluff, I was instinctively drawn to her depiction of the shape of the land, to its truth. She said that the way that she merges her science and her art recalls the awe of nature's grandeur that Thoreau, also a botanizer, shared with the land-scape painters of the Hudson River School, whose art she aspires to emulate. "Art has the power to connect us to our world in ways that a photograph cannot," said Lubinski, "and in my art people see what their own region is like through the eyes of a painter. They see places they know intimately and places they didn't even know existed." And seeing is the first step toward understanding.

After Capoli, river traffic diminishes and then, remarkably, disappears. Though it is an illusion, the islands, the sloughs, and the bluffs of the Mississippi feel wild and remote again, a haze of gentle green midsummer bluffs. A beautiful illusion. No talking, just quiet paddle strokes. I get lost in the rhythm of the paddle—the torso pivot, the reach, the catch, the pull. Release and repeat, and each time, a delicate line of water drops traces the path of the paddle on the bow wake. An eagle soars above us, climbing a thermal in lazy circles. If I had to choose a Mississippi pool to call my own, it would be this pool.

Too soon, it seems, we reach Lock & Dam 9, a little ways downstream of tiny Lynxville, Wisconsin. We float in the quiet water beside the lock's concrete retaining wall while first a southbound tow and then a northbound powerboat lock through. *That powerboat's an outlier—it's not staying in its own pool,* I think idly. As we wait, a northbound freight rumbles by. Bob studies the chart as we wait and tells me that the elusive town of Harpers Ferry lies, unseen, beyond the maze of islands to our right. I remember that there's supposed to be a mussel bed near there. *That's where the Higgins eye pearly mussel lives.* But we aren't going there.

Finally we are within the lock, and as the river water lowers us about ten feet, there's time enough for a chat with the lockmaster. Tom Caya tells us that his family has been in the Lynxville area since his father's grandfather, a French-Canadian named Michel Caya, moved here in 1846. He asks about our trip, eager to hear our story and to tell his.

Mississippi Lock

"You know," he says, "my great-grandfather Caya and his partner Louis La Force, they had the contract with the government to carry the mail between Fort Crawford in Prairie du Chien and Fort Snelling in St. Paul. They sometimes went by horseback, and the Indians referred to my great-grandfather as Long Knife, because he carried a machete-style knife on his belt. And other times they went by canoe."

"Delivering the mail by canoe? Amazing!" I say.

"No dams to lock through then, of course, and there must have been a lot more current then. It's close to two hundred miles, I think—they say it took them two weeks to do the whole trip, by horse or by canoe," he adds.

The lock gates are open now, and as we paddle out, I think about those intrepid mail carriers paddling upstream against the power of the

Island No. 166 on the Mississippi near Prairie du Chien, Wisconsin

undammed river's current, about the inevitable bad weather, about the wind that so often sweeps the length of Lake Pepin—and I'm grateful we are headed downstream on this powerful river.

"Good luck!" he calls, as we leave the final lock on our journey down the Mississippi.

We are now in Pool 10, as lovely, green, and quiet as its upstream sister. I may have to change my mind about which is my own pool. There's not another soul on the river, and as the wind gently dies, the surface of the water shimmers softly in the golden light of late afternoon.

We land at a likely camping spot on the floodplain along the Wisconsin side: a wide, flat sandy shoreline backed by a sparse forest of mostly silver maples, a single swamp white oak and scattered undergrowth, Island No. 166 on the chart. Bob fries steaks, potato slices, mushrooms, peppers, and onions over our little camp stove. As usual, we sit cross-legged on the sand to eat our dinner, watching the sun drop behind the tall bluffs of Iowa.

"It's less than ten miles to the confluence," says Bob, smiling.

"And our water bottles are almost empty," I reply, taking a small sip.

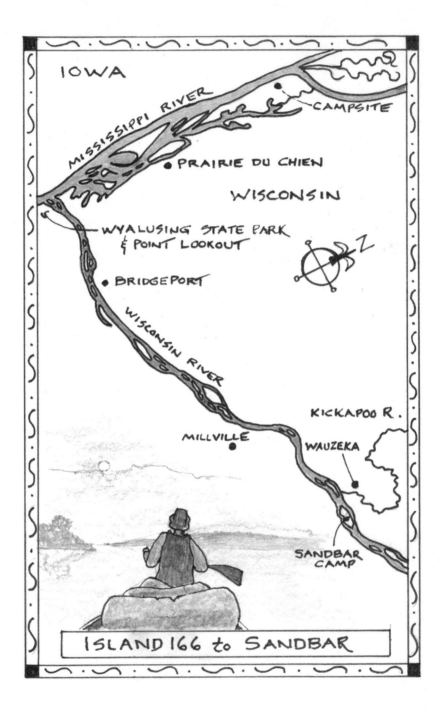

ISLAND 166 to SANDBAR

Take a Left at Wyalusing

July the second. Before the sun rises, fishermen are already on the water, quietly casting from small aluminum motorboats, drifting slowly in the current. We float past them, wordlessly easing our way into our last day on the Mississippi. Small songbirds are up and about as well and as their morning racket fills the silence, I am reminded that peregrine falcons nest on these bluffs and eagles nest in big dead trees on the floodplain. To a raptor, a songbird is just an amuse-bouche with wings. These avian predators make a better living by hunting ducklings and goslings, cannonballing out of the sky to snatch the young waterfowl from water or land. I scan the treetops hoping to spot an eagle's nest, but see none, and no airborne hunters are on the prowl.

We're just upstream of the mouth of Iowa's Yellow River, a lively stream that races swiftly through Effigy Mounds National Monument to its confluence with the Mississippi. But we never do see that junction. Downstream of us along the Iowa shoreline, a tugboat captain darts his powerful craft about. He revs the engines forward, then a hard reverse, then forward again, as he rearranges his collection of barges into proper lineups. We swing wide around the chaotic water and head through a narrow cut to reach the East Channel, a side road between the islands that lie along the Wisconsin shore at Prairie du Chien. Surely there's drinking water at the park on St. Feriole Island.

131

At the landing, Prairie du Chien doesn't feel historic, just a typical river town, its barren riverbanks and concrete boat landings a bit forlorn. But it is truly historic. In 1673 Father Marquette the Jesuit missionary and Louis Joliet the fur trader, the requisite duo for exploring the north woods in those days, were the first Europeans to see the Mississippi, yet Native Americans had already lived and farmed for centuries on the broad, flat river terrace where the town of Prairie du Chien now stands. Conveniently situated as it is near the confluence of the region's two major river routes, the Mississippi and the Wisconsin, the wide prairie was a favored trading and gathering center for tribal groups. In *Immortal River*, Fremling writes that long before Europeans arrived, traders at this riverine marketplace bought and sold an impressive array of goods: copper brought down the St. Croix and Mississippi from Lake Superior's Isle Royale, lead ore carried upriver from Illinois and Iowa, pipestone transported from southwestern Minnesota by way of the Minnesota and Mississippi rivers, obsidian and grizzly bear teeth brought from out west by way of the Missouri and Mississippi, alligator teeth from the Mississippi Delta, and whelk and conch shells from the Gulf of Mexico. During the Late Woodland period, people who lived here traveled down the Mississippi to trade at Cahokia, the largest city in prehistoric North America, which stood on the Illinois side of the Mississippi across from present-day St. Louis.

According to researchers at Wyalusing State Park, at least fourteen different tribes lived in the Prairie du Chien area or visited to trade, and as the land around the confluence was considered a neutral area, trading generally proceeded peaceably. This trade nexus expanded much more during the fur trade era. When the French first arrived in 1673, a large, well-established Fox village stood by the river, and the women of the tribe farmed the prairie to the east. Fur traders quickly established a trading post, and a multicultural town emerged on St. Feriole Island, where we are landing. Prairie du Chien later became the site of an historic 1825 treaty between the Sioux, Ojibwe, Sauk and Fox, Menominee,

Iowa, Ho-Chunk, Ottawa, and Potawatomi nations that established boundary lines around their respective hunting grounds, boundaries that the United States later used, with unintended irony, to force cession of the tribal lands to settlement.

In order to allot this corner of the world its proper significance, think about the time frame. When Marquette and Joliet arrived at the populous Fox village that stood at the intersection of the Mississippi and the Wisconsin rivers, the Pilgrims had landed at Plymouth Rock just over fifty years before, the young country that was forming had no identity, and the rebellion against England was years in the future. Yet this confluence, out here in the middle of the presumed wilderness, was already an important center of commerce. It's not exactly paddle-past country.

On a low-water day like today, Prairie du Chien seems well situated. But ever since Europeans moved in and built permanent dwellings, the city's location has created challenges. For centuries, the river's natural flooding cycles plagued neighborhoods and businesses built on low-lying St. Feriole Island, and during the historic flood of 1965 the Mississippi really outdid itself, cresting here at over twenty-five feet, its highest recorded level, completely inundating the place and ruining almost everything that had been built here. This deluge launched a dramatic change in Prairie du Chien's relationship with the river. Island residents wanted to rebuild and asked the Corps to construct dikes and floodwalls, but the Corps decided to fund moving them off the floodplain island instead, at about the same time the Corps was also relocating the town of Soldiers Grove, Wisconsin (a story for a later chapter). By the late 1970s, almost all the residents had left St. Feriole Island; and only a few buildings now remain along the empty streets. The historic mansion Villa Louis still stands at the north end of the island, built as it is atop a large prehistoric Indian mound; it is said that though the river sometimes fills the basement, the main floor has never been flooded. The mansion's modern visitor center is not located on the high ground of the mound but is instead perched on stilts. Part of nineteenth-century Fort Crawford had originally been built on the same mound, but most of the fort flooded so often and so disastrously that in 1830 the military moved the whole thing to higher ground.

Why do the Mississippi and other Driftless rivers flood so much? Flooding is simply part of the river's annual cycle. On a river like the Mississippi, floods flush, rejuvenate, and fertilize the riparian zone, re-arrange the sediment, recharge the groundwater, move fish to the back-waters to spawn and, in Fremling's words, to "feast in untapped pan-tries." It's a wild spring housecleaning. On a river like the Kickapoo, floods serve the same purpose, but they cause even more trouble because people have changed the landscape so much that the land around the river system can't absorb the runoff as well as it could before settlement arrived. The river by its nature is flow and change, never static, always moving, always in flux, a wild creature that won't be confined without putting up a ferocious fight.

Another question is one my father used to ask—rhetorically, and with vehemence, as he didn't like it that taxpayers bear the burden of these risky decisions. Why do people build in floodplains? In the case of early settlers at Prairie du Chien, living in the floodplain meant they were close to the river highway, to a convenient water supply and abun-dant fish, and to fertile floodplain ground for planting. With these amenities, who would not want to live by the river?

Today, people generally value waterfront property for the aesthetics. If the river is presumed likely to flood in a disastrous fashion only every one hundred years—the common, willful misinterpretation of the term hundred-years flood—the modern property owner's decision to build in a picturesque waterfront location can be seen as a reasonable gamble. Until the flood arrives, that is. Then the landowner must acknowledge that the term actually means that a flood of that magnitude has a 1 percent chance of arriving every year, not that there will be a hundred years between each huge flood. In settlement times, frequent flooding would have eventually forced the initially shortsighted property owner to move. Today, the individual expects engineers and government to solve the human problems caused by the natural event of a flood.

But another piece of the flooding question is that scientists tell us floods are worse now than when the land was uncultivated and undeveloped. Farming practices such as putting steep slopes under plow, ditching fields, tiling wetlands, and planting right up to the edge of streams; the sea of pavement that is the modern city; and the storm sewers that rush water off the streets and into the tributaries have all irreversibly altered the river's hydrological profile. Worst, we have disconnected many rivers from their floodplains. "Rivers adjust their shape to carry some mean flow. Fluvial geomorphologists argue about what is the channel-forming flood. But we know that the result is a channel that fits most of the time. Sometimes it would rather be in the skinny jeans, and sometimes the fat jeans. But is has to make do with the average jeans all the time," said Carrie Jennings. "It is time for a new pair of jeans. Really fat jeans, but know that they will flap around us the rest of the year after our new drainage systems squeeze the soil dry." If we don't give the river the space it needs, inhabited and farmed floodplains will be inundated. Simply put, floods are worse now because of the destructive things we have done and do each day to the land and to the rivers and we must adjust to that reality.

When the rivers are damaged, so are the mussels. In 1975, the Higgins eye pearly mussel, already on the Endangered Species List, was known to live here in the East Channel at Prairie du Chien, in huge prosperous beds, along with thirty other varieties of mussel. When Marian Havlik, a former nurse who became an expert on Mississippi River mussels and who was known all along the river as "that clam lady," found out that the Corps was planning to dredge the channel, she told them about the endangered mussel. They dredged anyway. Havlik said that afterwards, she found two hundred, mostly freshly dead, Higgins eye mussels in the dredge material. She went to federal officials, and ever after, the Corps did mussel surveys before dredging. The Higgins eye is Havlik's favorite mussel. "I like the colors inside—white to shades of orange and pink—and I like the heft of the species. It's a fairly big mussel," she said. "And at first the Higgins eye made a difference for the whole mussel population on the Mississippi. Federal and state agencies spent millions of dollars protecting it. Despite all the money, things have gone downhill. That's in part because of the zebra mussel and in part because of barge traffic, which churns the mussel beds. In the 1970s, there were thirty-four species in the East Channel. In a recent study, only seven were found." After forty years of studying and advocating for these humble creatures, Havlik is discouraged. The mussels are struggling.

Right now Bob and I are not looking for mussels but for water we can drink. Our quest leads us on an early morning walking tour of the island park. The restroom buildings are locked, there's not a hand pump anywhere, and not a soul around. Then, happily, a truck pulls up and a uniformed young man hops out. Though he says he probably shouldn't, he agrees to turn on the building's outdoor faucet, the handle of which has been inexplicably removed, leaving only a post. He uses a vise-grip to turn the post, and the water flows. This generous young man seems worried that he shouldn't be doing this, and I feel guilty for asking him. As soon as our bottles are full, Bob and I both thank him profusely and run back to the canoe, clutching our contraband.

Past the highway bridges, we stay along the Wisconsin shore, following the edge of an intricate delta of sandbars and tiny islands fuzzy with alder and sandbar willow thickets until we soon come to the unmistakable confluence with the Wisconsin River.

Time to turn left.

Bob and I climb out of the canoe and stand in the shallows at the mouth. I want to believe it looks the same as it did centuries before, that damming has not permanently altered the river beyond recognition. *Is this the river that Nicollet saw?* The massive, enduring bluffs of Wyalusing that tower above us are silent.

The confluence has gravity, actual sandy gravity. Under our feet, here at the mouth of the Wisconsin, the sandy sediment that covers the bedrock floor of the Mississippi gorge is three hundred feet deep, which means the gorge was once scoured that much deeper. And the blufftops are over five hundred feet above the water. This valley must have once looked like a little Grand Canyon. The deep layer of sediment on the riverbed gradually diminishes as the river flows downstream, and by the time the Mississippi reaches the Quad Cities, where the Rock River flows in, the riverbed is almost down to bedrock, swept clean of the weight of the glacial sand, and the big river has left the Driftless behind.

Did the idea of confluence hold significance for the prehistoric inhabitants of the area? Ancient Woodland Indian burial mounds in Wisconsin's Wyalusing State Park are on bluffs above the confluence. Across the river from Prairie du Chien, effigy mounds of birds and bears were built on bluff tops in Iowa's Effigy Mounds National Monument. There once were mounds on many of the bluff tops above confluences along the Upper Mississippi, though most are no longer there. In his essay "The View from Man Mound," Curt Meine notes that, "Lakes, streams, and wetlands were the most important features of the early maps. The geography of the Indian mounds reflects this. Almost all were located in gathering places near water." In order to travel long distances most efficiently, the tribes, the traders, and the explorers had to bow to the topographical realities of the Driftless landscape, where the river was the best conduit, and knowing the confluences was like knowing which turns to take on a system of roads.

It is at the confluence where the meaning of the river as highway, as trade route, as connection, is concentrated. Research shows that during the Hopewell period—500 BC to AD 500—people used rivers all over the Upper Midwest as organized transportation routes. After that, more Indians, and then a steady stream of missionaries, fur traders, adventurers, soldiers, settlers, and historians, traveled up and down the Mississippi and the Wisconsin to this place, just to be here. Nicollet unwillingly spent a miserable December here in 1838. Some wrote of their travels and most did not. A few became famous. For all these travelers the remote wooded confluence was a destination.

From this crossroads, a traveler could paddle north up the Mississippi, connect with the Minnesota River, then with the Red River of the North and the route to Hudson's Bay. Or the traveler could push just a little further up the Mississippi and paddle up the St. Croix, cross the portage at Solon Springs, head down the Bois Brule River and thence to the north shore of Lake Superior, the route to the famous Grand Portage and the vast fur trade country. One hundred sixteen miles up the Wisconsin, a two-mile portage into the Fox River links the Mississippi with the Great Lakes. To the south lie the confluences with the Missouri and the route west, and with the Ohio and points east. Or a traveler could head all the way down the Mississippi to the Gulf of Mexico. This confluence was a north woods version of Chicago's Union Station.

But the answer to my unspoken question is that of course the river and the land through which it flows have changed. The river is all about change—where and when it flows, when and where it chooses to flood—and the river continually changes the land through which it flows. About the undammed lower river Mark Twain wrote, "The Mississippi is remarkable in still another way—its disposition to make prodigious jumps by cutting through narrow necks of land, and thus straightening and shortening itself. More than once it has shortened itself thirty miles at a single jump!" In a sense, all that matters is what the river looks like today.

Looking up at Wyalusing again, I can see the curved manmade stone wall that bounds the park's Point Lookout, where on other visits we arrived by car, looked down at the confluence, and talked abstractly about paddling this trip. Now we're about to paddle up the Wisconsin, the river that flows for over four hundred miles from Lac Vieux Desert, its source in the far northeastern corner of the state, gathering the waters that flow from one-fifth of Wisconsin's land area. After seven days of paddling downstream, our muscles are warmed up and ready, yet we both harbor small secret doubts about whether we can do this. I remind myself that we're only planning to go seventy-eight miles. Bob does the numbers to reassure me: at low water levels like these, the Lower Wisconsin flows at an average of only two to three miles per hour. When we're on flat water, we can paddle all day at about four miles an hour, which means that at worst we will average as little as one mile an hour. Even if that were the best we could do, it would take us just over a week to travel to Arena and the connection to Black Earth Creek. If we do better, that's great.

We have already established that we aren't purists. That was clear when we started the trip in Faribault instead of at Cedar Lake and again when we accepted the ride from Lake City to Reads Landing. All along, we've held Plan B in quiet reserve: calling one of our sons to ask for a ride home. But that would mean ignominious defeat, and we're not going to even talk about that plan when we haven't even tried. So off we go.

Now here is a remarkable thing. All the way down the Mississippi, we had a tailwind. When we were headed southeast, the wind blew steadily out of the north-northwest. When we reached La Crosse and headed south, the cold north wind whooshed us down the river. Today, as we turn east-northeast to go up the Wisconsin, the wind has shifted again and is now blowing from the west-southwest at about nine miles per hour. *How can it be that the wind always follows us?* No answer. It definitely beats a headwind.

Up on the railroad bridge where long freight trains cross the Wisconsin on their way up and down the Mississippi, a crew works on the tracks. Soon after, we pass by a backwater pool where an elderly couple is fishing, dressed in matching gray coveralls, their johnboat anchored.

He hooks a smallish fish; she nets it. "Catfish," she says, quietly, and he casts again. They're a team.

The paddling is surprisingly similar to paddling downstream, just slower. According to the readings on Bob's GPS unit, we're traveling at two miles per hour. After a mile of steady paddling, he says we're keeping that pace. There's no need for an embarrassed plea for help. All my inner angst was for naught.

Alongside a wooded bank bordered by a narrow margin of sand we meet the avian counterpart of our laconic anglers. It's a wild introduction. In a sudden flurry of black and white feathers, a bald eagle rockets in on a shallow flight path, wings outstretched, flared talons thrust formidably before, and nails a hapless fish that is cruising near the surface of the river just upstream. Unfortunately for the eagle as well, however, this particular fish is too heavy for an eagle, which can only lift about four pounds. As we watch from a respectful distance, a brief tragicomic drama unfolds. The eagle and the fish struggle ferociously in the shallows, wings and tails flapping and flopping. Without releasing the fish, the eagle hops awkwardly through the shallows and onto the sand, dragging the wildly thrashing fish along the shoreline, dredging its catch in sand, lifting it just a little with each determined hop, its earnest efforts faintly absurd. The eagle pauses to reset its talons, one eye on the predators in the canoe, and then in a burst of wing flapping, briefly lifts off again, breakfast in tow. The fish—a long, fat shorthead redhorse—is indeed too big, however, and the pair sags heavily to the earth. This much failure seems to defeat the eagle, which extracts its talons and flaps away, leaving the exhausted, dying fish draped across a rock in the shade of an old cedar overhanging the shore, a scene that the eagle will no doubt revisit, possibly for lunch.

I regret that the Lower Wisconsin is mostly too turbid for us to see the fish swimming beneath us. But they are there. Eagles thrive on the Lower Wisconsin in part because it is home to the most fish species anywhere in the state, 98 of Wisconsin's 147 native species.

I'm no angler but my fascination with watching fish dates way back. The rivers and lakes of my childhood were typical southern Minnesota waters, murky places for the most part. The Zumbro and Cannon rivers often ran thick with eroded sediment. Only during an extended dry period was the river clear enough to see the bottom, and then only in the shallows, where I liked to wade and hunt for rocks. Cedar Lake would begin the year with crystal clarity, but by the end of June, suspended algae would tint its eutrophic (nutrient-rich) waters a pale chartreuse, and a thick belt of pond lilies, cattails, rushes, and coontail would ring the perimeter. In the intense heat of late July or early August, a spectacular algae bloom would usually coat the water, sometimes more than once, calling a temporary halt to our swimming.

I knew, but only because I had been told, that Cedar Lake is almost fifty feet deep at points, but when I swam or canoed on its surface, even when I was over what I knew to be the deepest point, this depth seemed abstract, hard to comprehend, impossible to visualize. Because I couldn't see down into those cloudy depths, I couldn't think about them. So for me, a lake was all about the surface. This changed when I was twelve years old and went for two weeks one summer to Camp Olson, a YMCA camp on Little Boy Lake, just south of Leech Lake in northern Minnesota. Deep in the forest on the west side of the camp's acreage were the Shurds, a chain of three small, deep, mysterious lakes where we campers sometimes canoed. I still remember the first time I looked over the gunwale of the canoe into one of the little lakes, staring down through the clear water and realizing that what I saw down there was the trunk of a large dead tree lying on boulders and that the large tree was so far down that it looked quite small. Yet through the lens of the still water I could see it clearly. A long thin fish, possibly a northern, slid along the tree trunk and out of sight. At first, I was gripped with the same fear that I always have in a high place, a weak-kneed fear of falling, this time down into the depths of the Shurds. But fascination quickly replaced the fear, and I stopped often to peer over the gunwale, wishing to see all that was down there, until the girl paddling in the bow told me the other kids had moved on to the next lake and we better catch up.

Though the Wisconsin is a shallow river on average, there are many depths where exotic creatures like paddlefish and gar make their homes. When it's deeper than about two feet, though, the water of the Wisconsin is too murky for my fish-spotting ambitions. I won't be able to pass the time by looking over the gunwale.

We cruise upstream at the satisfying pace of two miles an hour, soon passing under the bridge where the Great River Road crosses. Though we are now officially in Wisconsin's Driftless Area, where glaciers never ventured, geologists suspect that glacial ice once did move up the Wisconsin River, a little way at least. The evidence is here at Bridgeport, where Highway 60 comes in from the east, along the north side of the river. In *Roadside Geology of Wisconsin*, Robert Dott and John Attig write, "Wisconsin 60 is on a high bench with sandstone cliffs to the north and the river below it to the south. This bench, the Bridgeport terrace, is the dissected remnant of an outwash plain deposited by a river flowing eastward from a glacier that advanced from the west and blocked the mouth of the Wisconsin River. The exact time . . . was probably before 790,000 years ago." The mighty Wisconsin has not always flowed westward, and part of the Driftless was actually glaciated! This shifts what I thought I knew about the river. Layers of glacial time seem to appear in the bedrock outcrops as we pass the terrace and head toward the geologically true Driftless.

Upstream at the Millville landing, the Wisconsin is suddenly a busy, noisy place, an explosion of people playing in the river, the parking lot filled with cars, minivans, trucks, and trailers. Though the day has not yet acquired the intense heat of midsummer, everyone is swimming and splashing. A shirtless old man, already sunburnt, calls happily to us from his fishing boat, "Great day for it!" On the other side of the river, three teenagers slither like otters in and out of a small boat, chasing each other, hooting with laughter.

During the next few miles we work hard, still learning to read the water backwards. Around its many sandbars and islands, the river plaits a braided channel, and the flow changes from strand to strand of the braid. Where the strand is narrow, the current runs deeper and faster than average. Where the water spreads out over a broad shallow strand, the current slows. On our many downstream journeys on the Wisconsin, we tried to follow what we call the "fast lane," the serpentine line of the thalweg that meanders across the riverbed, swaying from side to side, skimming the outside of river bends, carving ever deeper into the sediment of those outside banks.

"One might think that this constant erosion would cause the river to become ever wider and shallower," explained Matt Diebel of Wisconsin DNR, "but at the same time, sediment is deposited on 'point bars' on inside banks, balancing the erosion. Because water is constantly transporting sediment downstream, the migration of a river's meanders tends to march downstream. Through this process, the location of a river channel in its floodplain is constantly shifting, while the dimensions—width, depth—of the channel remain approximately constant. This 'dynamic equilibrium' is one of the basic principles of fluvial geomorphology, which is the physical science of rivers." Ever changing, the river is constant.

Headed upstream we seek the slow water, the shallows. Sometimes we walk these shallows, towing the canoe with the bowline. It's a welcome break for our butts, but a slow slog. Mostly we focus on finding that elusive strand of river deep enough to paddle and yet slow enough to let us make good headway. There's no rest for upstream paddlers. If we stop paddling, we move backward, so we must try to keep an even steady pace, a pace we can sustain for hours, ever scouting the water ahead for the best route. It's satisfying work. We feel a kinship with the Native Americans and the voyageurs, able to travel both ways on the river, under their own power, truly using the river as a highway. We are voyageurs, voyageurs with cell phones.

Past the Millville landing, the Wisconsin is once again quiet and secluded, buffered from the outside world by high wooded bluffs. From its confluence with the Mississippi to the Prairie du Sac dam over ninety-two miles upstream, the river, its floodplain, and its bluffs are protected territory. This stewardship is rooted in the 1980s, when the environmental protection movement had gained significant traction.

According to David Aslakson, the Wisconsin DNR's lead planner for the project, it began in 1980, when Richard Chenoweth at the University of Wisconsin–Madison realized that the increasing level of blufftop and riverside development would eventually threaten the area's remarkable scenic beauty. Chenoweth and his colleague Bernard "Ben" Niemann went to people at the DNR and to politicians such as Spencer Black and Russ Feingold and told them that if something wasn't done, this beauty would be lost. The DNR and the politicians listened. In Aslakson's words, Chenoweth was "the burr under the saddle," the reason the project went ahead. The times were right: environmental issues were on everyone's minds then. And the way the project was developed—by building consensus, not by dictate—was right. In 1989, after almost a decade of planning by DNR, the state legislature created the Lower Wisconsin State Riverway—77,300 acres of riverine sandbars, islands, bluffs, and lowland forest—to protect this natural beauty from excessive development, and Governor Tommy Thompson signed it into law. The text of the legislative proposal characterized the Riverway in scenic terms: "one of the longest remaining free flowing stretches of river left in Wisconsin and possibly in the Midwest. The wooded bluffs, long vistas, hundreds of sandbars and islands and thousands of acres of lowland forest and open wetlands still appear largely free of man's impact." And the Riverway is about scenic beauty management of all the land, both public and private. In addition, the goal is to manage the natural resources, including endangered species, on state-owned land.

"It was a confluence of ideas, social changes, things happening on a landscape level," said Gary Birch, also a Riverway planner. "The baby boomers had grown up and everyone wanted to go back to the land, or in this case, to the river." The Lower Wisconsin is within convenient traveling distance of urban areas yet it feels like wilderness. The environmental ethic that emerged during the 1960s and '70s was still strong. It was the right time.

From beyond the trees, sandhill cranes sound their approval with prehistoric croaks, and I think to myself that this river might actually look much as it did when the first Native Americans lived here, when tribal groups gathered at Prairie du Chien to trade, when Marquette and Joliet arrived that June day in 1673. If it is true that we see essentially what they saw, it is a rare experience in this modern world.

That could change. The Lower Wisconsin Riverway faces unanticipated challenges as the boom in hydraulic fracturing for shale oil has led to a rapidly increasing demand for huge quantities of the sand that is a necessary part of the mining process. Lured by abundant high-quality sand deposits and willing landowners near Bridgeport, Pattison Sand Company of Clayton, Iowa, purchased sand mining rights on three hundred acres of land between Highway 60 and the Wisconsin River, just upstream of the bridge that carries the Great River Road. Two-thirds of the land in question adjoins the Riverway and one-third is on Riverway land. The company acted on a 1990s change in the Riverway statutes that allows nonmetallic mines to be permitted in the Riverway, "as long as the excavation and stockpiled material are not visible from the river." Intended to benefit landowners by allowing them to quarry for local road repair materials, the change in statute created a loophole that prevented state authorities from rejecting the sand mine proposal.

This is not a small issue. The conditional use permit issued by the Bridgeport town board would allow Pattison Sand Company to operate twenty-four hours a day, seven days a week, for up to sixty years. Which means that, at worst, a truck would enter or leave the site every six minutes. Even parts of the mine that are not on Riverway land would be quite close to the river and noise from mining operations and truck traffic—250 forty-ton trucks a day headed for Iowa on Highway 60—would be clearly audible to those on the river who go there for the solitude it offers. From Point Lookout at Wyalusing State Park we would clearly see this vast sand mine. Not what the Riverway planners had in mind. Residents worry that mining dust would reach the river, that drawing water from the river to reduce the dust would not be regulated, and that their property values would drop. Many observers worry that this operation would be a precedent for eroding protections guaranteed by the Riverway legislation. It's a messy business.

The approval process went like this: The Bridgeport town board approved the mining permits. The Wisconsin DNR approved the permits, including those for mining on Riverway land. After the town board approved the mining permits, however, members of the Riverway board learned that some members of the town board owned land on which the permits were being granted. A conflict-of-interest lawsuit ensued. When he learned that the DNR was forced to approve the permit for fifty acres of Riverway land because of the loophole, Mark Cupp, director of the Riverway board, was concerned that if the board refused to give final approval to the permits that affect Riverway lands, as was their right, state government might retaliate by reducing funding to the Riverway. The board, however, voted six to two to refuse the Riverway permit. Mining will happen, but not on Riverway land.

Late in the afternoon of this long hot summer day, we reach the mouth of the Kickapoo River, quietly flowing in close to the head of big Harris Island, and pause, resting in an eddy near the confluence.

Oh, the beautiful Kickapoo. Upstream of us flows both a lovely paddling river and a river that tells the story of the relationship between people and rivers of the Driftless in vivid terms. Books have been written about the Kickapoo and the people who live along this winding river, including an account of the long and contentious struggle over the dam that was started but never finished, chronicled in the local, personalized voice of Brad Steinmetz in *That Dam History*. In Lynne Heasley's fascinating book, *A Thousand Pieces of Paradise: Landscape and Property in the Kickapoo Valley*, she analyzes the epic battle of the La Farge dam in the larger context of the young environmental movement and the accompanying national debate, concluding that the key to its resolution was in acknowledging and respecting the sense of community in the Kickapoo valley, not in actions by the federal government.

Many stories about the river have to do with its habit of flooding disastrously and washing away houses in the bargain. Say these town names—Gays Mills and Soldiers Grove—and what quickly comes to mind are the news accounts of floods and disaster, stories about the moving of whole towns onto higher ground. The Kickapoo floods because of its nature as a Driftless river with a lot of quick-to-flood tributaries feeding it after heavy rains, and it floods even more because man has separated it from its floodplain sponges and has farmed and otherwise altered the steep valley lands so that they shed water rather than absorbing it. Land uses that most exacerbated the flooding have for the most part ended, but the floods keep coming. People who live in houses built in the flood zone and farmers who till the rich bottomland of the river valley and pasture their livestock there want to try to stop the floods because they don't want to or can't afford to move, or both. The river, of course, doesn't care what people want. It's an old story.

This fascinating river, the Lower Wisconsin's biggest tributary, begins in Monroe County and flows south to the Wisconsin through a winding valley that cuts deep into the rugged land that is the ancient remnant of the Paleozoic Plateau. Tall sandstone bluffs, with overhanging trees that cling to the bluffs and shade the river, line the river's middle reaches. These rocky outcrops are undercut, so as you paddle underneath them you can look up at the underside of the overhangs, where lichens, liverworts, and mosses grow, minerals paint the sandstone, and groundwater seeps from the crevices. Laminar flow lines tracing the direction of the water's erosive action over the millennia add sculptural beauty. On a summer weekend, the stretch between the towns of Ontario and La Farge is a busy place, with a steady stream of canoes and kayaks, many of them rentals, floating downstream through seemingly endless meanders, river bends that after a time become predictable, like the curves of a snake. And bridges, numbered not named. Bridges and bluffs, bridges and bluffs. What are not predictable are all the deadfalls, rocks, and overhanging branches the paddler encounters and dodges. Young agile paddlers have been known to grab one of these branches and hang from it as their paddling partner continues downstream, until another companion's canoe floats underneath, then dropping in.

The river runs through the Kickapoo Valley Reserve, 8,569 acres of state land between Wildcat Mountain State Park and the town of La Farge. Of this, 1,780 acres would have been flooded had the dam that was to be upstream of La Farge been completed. First proposed as a flood control measure in the wake of the Flood Control Act of 1936, construction of the dam was repeatedly delayed. When a more extensive project was conceived in the 1960s, a plan that would have yielded a much larger impoundment, the federal government forcibly purchased 149 valley farms, many from unwilling sellers, and the Corps began construction. But in 1975, Congress decided the project was costing too much, and research by the Institute for Environmental Studies at the University of Wisconsin–Madison made clear that the dam had the potential to do serious damage to the region's ecosystem. Though the partially built dam was never finished, the dam intake tower still stands on the site, in the words of Lynne Heasley, "a monument to an environmental nightmare averted."

In 2000, the federal government turned over control of 1,200 acres of the land to the Ho-Chunk Nation, the previous inhabitants of the valley, and control of the balance of the state-owned land to a citizens' group, the Kickapoo Valley Reserve Board; these two groups manage the land together as an area for public recreation and environmental education. The once-wild land is wild once more. And the river still floods.

Along the Kickapoo, the forested valley slopes and sandstone river bluffs shelter relict plant communities, leftovers from glacial times that are still alive in the Driftless because of the region's unique cool moist microclimate pockets, species that scientists believe repopulated the barren world left behind when the glaciers retreated. Some of these species live only in the Driftless, not anywhere else in the world, on moist sandstone cliffs and algific talus slopes. Which is to say that their homes are cool, damp, and rocky. Steep wooded north-facing slopes are kept even cooler by the fascinating air-conditioning properties of karst topography. In winter, subzero air pours into the fractures, fissures, and sinkholes, supercooling the bedrock as deep as forty feet. Spring rains seep into these icy rock cavities and freeze solid. When summer's heat finally thaws the bedrock, the ice becomes frigid water vapor and ice-cold water, both of which flow from openings in the bedrock. In the heat of midsummer, a blast of icy air may pour from these vents, startling a hiker. Ancient species of plants that had adapted to live in the peri-glacial climate still find the cool habitat they need to survive.

Riverway planner Gary Birch, a botanist by training, said he loves exploring the river valley to look for these botanical treasures. Here he finds rare birdseye primrose, northern monkshood, and Lapland azalea, the only rhododendron native to Wisconsin. "These ancient species still grow in the Kickapoo valley. Remnants and scraps of the rich, rich forests of the Kickapoo valley were preserved because the slopes are so steep and are a good indication of the rich biological diversity that was once here," said Birch.

Ancient varieties of land snails live on as well. Who would have guessed that creatures this small could persist through a glacial age? Graced by us humans with fanciful names like obese thorn, toothless column, carved glyph, bristled slitmouth, white-lip dagger, winged snaggletooth, and cherrystone drop, these oft-forgotten and sometimes maligned macroinvertebrates live their quiet lives throughout the cool moist forests of the Driftless. Their lowly task is to glide over the forest floor, clearing it of rotting debris. Tiny barometers of the health of the land, they begin to die out when the habitat that is their home is under siege.

And now it seems possible that chipmunks were chilling in the Driftless during the Late Pleistocene as well, just waiting for the ice to go away so they could expand their range. When biologists Kevin Rowe and Ken Paige at the University of Illinois studied the mitochondrial DNA of the eastern chipmunk, they found evidence that most of the eastern chipmunks in Illinois and Wisconsin are descendants of a population that spent the last ice age in the refugium of the Driftless. Long before the humans arrived, there were chipmunks. Which suggests the possibility that the climate was not as harsh as has been assumed.

According to John Long, an Indian interpreter and trader who in 1791 compiled a vocabulary of Indian words, the Ojibwa name for squirrel was *chetamon*. When Europeans arrived, the chipmunk population must have been substantial. The name they evolved for this striped little ground squirrel was *chitmunk* and eventually chipmunk. And thus we find North Chipmunk Coulee and South Chipmunk Coulee, small streams that drain into the Mississippi bottomland just south of La Crosse, named for what seem to have been the earliest mammalian inhabitants of the post-glacial Driftless.

When Norwegian and Bohemian settlers arrived in the Kickapoo Valley in the nineteenth century, they found—along with chipmunks, snails, and flowers—a vast network of small streams, fed by icy groundwater and filled with cold-loving brook trout. These streams flow down steep narrow valleys that the early French explorers named coulees, into the Kickapoo and other Driftless rivers. DNR fisheries biologist Jordan Weeks said that over the years, agricultural practices unsuited to the fragile ecosystem of the Driftless gradually changed the flow of the coulee streams. Rainfall ceased to infiltrate the soil and recharge the groundwater, and began to run down the surface of the slopes instead. Weeks explained that it was this warmer surface water that flowed in the streams instead of the cold groundwater. The trout disappeared.

"It took a three-pronged approach to bring them back: stream channel restoration by the DNR fisheries program improved habitat, improved watershed land management increased groundwater flow by increasing infiltration of rain, and stocking gradually brought back the trout," said DNR aquatic ecologist Matt Diebel. And now trout fill the streams: between 2,500 and 6,000 trout per stream mile.

Weeks said this successful change had a lot to do with the work of longtime Fisheries stream supervisor Dave Vetrano. In the early 1980s, after observing that wild trout live much longer than the hatchery-raised trout that the DNR then used for stocking Driftless streams, Vetrano quietly experimented with raising some trout that were born to be wild, trout with the genetic makeup that made them scatter when they saw people instead of just sitting there waiting to be caught. After he released these wild ones in streams where populations were skimpy, trout numbers increased dramatically. Vetrano then told the department what he had been up to and apologized for working in secret. And the "Wild Trout" program is now the model for trout stream management.

"We don't have to stock trout anymore," said Weeks. "They do it all on their own." And anglers travel from far away to cast their lines here. Weeks cited a 2008 economic study by Madison-based NorthStar Economics that included anglers who visited the Blufflands of southeast Minnesota and northwest Iowa as well as the Driftless Area of southwest Wisconsin. The study showed that trout fishing brings about $1.1 billion a year in economic benefits to the Driftless Area.

Timber Coulee, one of the most productive trout streams in the Driftless, is tributary to Coon Creek, which flows into the Mississippi at Stoddard. Many remember that in the 1930s Coon Valley was the poster child for the disastrous effects of the old farming practices. In "Coon Valley Days," her essay on the history of the Coon Creek watershed, Renae Anderson writes, "It took only seventy years, from the time of the first infusion of white settlers to the 1930s, for traditional farming methods to reduce the land around Coon Creek from pristine to the brink of agricultural uselessness." Photographs from that time show gullies eroded to almost forty feet deep. Hugh Hammond Bennett of the United States Department of Agriculture (USDA) and Wisconsin's legendary Aldo Leopold played pivotal roles in the soil conservation project that brought the land back from the brink, introducing the contour strip farming that slows runoff and defines modern Driftless agriculture. It was all about respecting the contours of the land, not subjugating them.

In his essay "The View From Man Mound," Curt Meine notes that the Coon Valley restoration project defied the grid that nineteenth century land surveys had imposed on the Driftless, replacing that relentless geometry with "watershed-shaped realities." Thinking like a watershed instead of like an urban planner required first the catastrophe, then a huge shift in human habits and perception of the land. By the time I was old enough to notice the landscape of the Driftless, contour plowing was the norm.

Even so, the work of restoring streams altered by agriculture continues, Weeks said at the rate of about one stream mile each summer, a relatively slow pace given the thousands of stream miles in the Driftless. Along streams like Timber Coulee, North Fork of the Bad Axe, Seas Branch, Mormon Coulee, crews "peel back the banks" where the loess soil that washed down from the overgrazed ridge tops has built up artificially high, vertical sides along the streams. "The crews re-grade the banks to a two-to-one slope and get them grassed up to stop the erosion. In the streambed, they install root wads (a tree stump with the roots still attached), rock weirs, and wooden structures called LUNKERS, Dave

Vetrano's invention," said Weeks. "They shelter fish and stabilize the banks." LUNKERS is the acronym for the whimsically named Little Underwater Neighborhood Keepers Encompassing Rheotaxic Salmonids. Weeks said Vetrano also likes to tell of when he found the carcass of a 1950s Ford in a streambed, where a farmer had dumped it to keep the banks from eroding. Living inside the rusting car was a twenty-inch brown trout.

Along an as-yet-undisclosed reach of the Kickapoo River, a major restoration project is underway. Abbie Church of the Mississippi Valley Conservancy (MVC) said that the farmland that will be restored is "a poster child for poor agricultural practices" and that one gully on the property is already four to five feet deep, a sad echo of the 1930s environmental catastrophe in the Driftless. As the land is the site of several existing homes, the property will be a working farm rather than put into conservation reserve. Using a new understanding of the relationship between upland bird habitat and careful grazing practices, the team will create a system that works for both, a system of rotational grazing, crop rotation, contour and buffer strips that protect the river from agricultural runoff. Together with their partners the Kickapoo Grazing Initiative and the Wallace Center Pasture Project, MVC will restore sixteen hundred acres of land.

We've just left the eddy at the mouth of the Kickapoo. In seven hours, we've traveled about sixteen miles up the Wisconsin—averaging a respectable 2.25 miles per hour—and it's time to look for a place to spend the night. We choose a nice sandbar—reasonably high above the water, wide, handsome, and as yet uninhabited by tents. Intermittent faint traffic noises from Highway 60, beyond the trees to the north, remind us that it's only a mile up the Kickapoo to the little village of Wauzeka (population 711), but on the river we feel far from everything.

On a branch of a nearby tree, two bald eagles perch side by side watching us pitch our tent. Later, we sit cross-legged on the sand, side by side as well, eating our supper of tuna and rice and watching the river roll past. A flat-bottomed metal johnboat edges out of the greenery at the mouth of the Kickapoo, and the elderly fellow at the tiller motors his craft upstream, slowly. He waves but doesn't speak, and we wave back. The evening frog choir ramps up the music a notch. And the river flows.

I've long been in the habit of watching the water levels on the Wisconsin when we camp. The river can rise as much as three feet during the night, either after heavy rain or when water is released from the dam at Prairie du Sac. Once long ago, while camped on a large but rather low-lying sandbar near Arena, we went to sleep with the river at least a hundred feet away and woke to find it lapping at the tent door; fortunately we had dragged the canoe even higher than the tent. It's a common story, and some campers on this river take the extra precaution of tying their canoe to the tent. But because it's not going to rain tonight, and because the persistent drought has left upstream water levels lower than average, the river is quite unlikely to rise tonight. Only out of curiosity, then, I mark the evening waterline by pushing a row of sticks into the mudflat to track any change during the night. Bob chuckles at my fussy ways.

It's easy to settle into the familiar routine of camping on a Wisconsin sandbar. Sand in our food, the green glow of our flashlight-lit tent at evening, our dirty clothes draped over a clothesline strung above us in the tent, sand on the tent floor and in our sleeping bags, soft bed of sand under the tent floor cushioning our weary bodies, the low steady hum of nighttime insects and the murmur of the river. It always surprises me how little we really need to be happy and comfortable in life. At the end of a day on the river, I don't even look for a book to read in bed. Sleep comes quickly, before it's dark.

Soft voices in the warm velvet dusk. I resurface from half-sleep, sit up, and look through the tent's screen door. A group of teenagers, by their voices, slowly motor down the river in two small boats, outboards barely putt-putting along. One boat grounds gently on a submerged sandbar. Soft crunch. Several of the kids jump out to push. More quiet talk.

"You can camp anywhere you want to."

"Jeremy, are you in the boat?"

Both boats drift past.

"Hey, that's a big ass sandbar. Let's camp there."

Soft laughter.

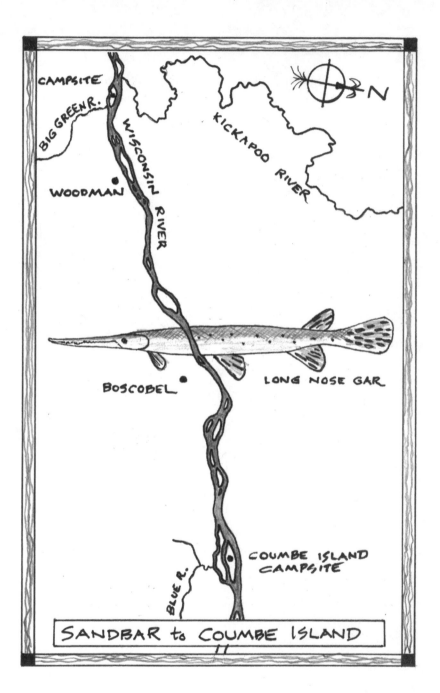

CAMPSITE

BIG GREEN R.

WISCONSIN RIVER

KICKAPOO RIVER

WOODMAN

LONG NOSE GAR

BOSCOBEL

COUMBE ISLAND CAMPSITE

BLUE R.

N

SANDBAR to COUMBE ISLAND

Up the Lower Wisconsin

July the third. We wake to dense fog, rendering the river and everything around it invisible. Bird song magically fills the soft, cool, moist air, seeming to flow out of the mist. The sandbar willow thickets behind our tent are alive with the dawn rustling of wings, energetic chirping and song, unfamiliar melodies blending with old favorites: wren, meadowlark, sparrow, catbird, robin. This is bird country. North of the river along the Kickapoo, the floodplain forest of the Wauzeka Bottoms State Natural Area covers almost eight hundred acres. Almost two thousand acres of marshy river bottoms, sloughs, and prairie of the Woodman Wildlife Area, just upstream and south of the river, are habitat for some rare warblers—Kentucky, prothonotary, and cerulean—as well as an amazing array of other birds, both migratory and nesting. And all seem to be singing melodiously around our tent this morning. I crawl out of the tent to attend the concert.

As the fog begins to thin, it is clear that there was no change in the river level overnight, and despite the damp air, the sand is dry. The miasma still conceals the tents of the youngsters camping on the "big-ass sandbar" next door, however, and not a sound emanates from over there. In less than the time it takes us to break camp, the rising July sun burns away the fog to reveal our neighbors' tents, still zipped and quiet, despite the efforts of the noisy birds seemingly bent on waking the world. As we launch, three kids emerge sleepily from their tents, and I wave goodbye to our fellow river travelers.

Back on the water, lingering patches of mist float like mysterious veils over the riverine world. A lineup of six turtles, motionless, watch us pass from their perches on a partially submerged log; they also hope for the sun to burn off the fog. Near the confluence with the Big Green River, the Woodman boat landing hides just upstream on that tributary, and we pass a white house, partly concealed by the foliage but still visible, a reminder that almost half of Lower Wisconsin land is still privately owned.

When the Riverway came into being, the DNR owned 22,600 of the 77,300 acres designated by the legislation. Now the state owns close to 48,000 acres, if you include the permanent public hunting easements—more than double the initial land holdings. On the private land that remains, zoning rules require manmade structures—new ones—to be inconspicuous, painted in earth tones, invisible from the river during the leaf-on conditions. The imposition of zoning rules like this rankled, and still rankles, some landowners and it's easy to guess why this old house is still painted white.

I talked with Riverway planner David Aslakson about landowner participation in planning the Riverway. Aslakson feels that the planning team transcended politics, giving everyone a voice. He said that he insisted, as coordinator, that they must not let anyone believe they weren't part of the planning process, that there was ample citizen input, that the process was "not done in the dark of night but in bright sunlight." In pursuit of this goal, he attended every one of over four hundred public meetings held over a period of six years, meetings that gradually built a common vision for the Riverway.

But the tension was there nevertheless. Aslakson tells the story of one town meeting, held in the autumn, close to Halloween. "I arrived after dark, and we met in a combination bar, grill, and funeral home. When I walked into the building, right inside was a casket with a stuffed effigy of me inside, complete with my big black beard and glasses, and a sign that read *DNR Chairman*. I said to them, 'You know, it looks just like me.' They laughed, though uncomfortably, and one said, 'We thought you'd like it.' Driving home after the meeting, which was mostly civil, I still watched for headlights behind me, all the way to Spring Green. But understand that that was the one and only time in those six years that I ever felt even an implied threat."

Landowners opposed to the project felt their constitutional rights were being violated. Some organized under the name Private Landowners of Wisconsin (PLOW). Though Dale Schultz, a newly elected state representative at the time, initially supported PLOW, he gradually shifted to support the Riverway.

Aslakson and others on the planning team traveled the Lower Wisconsin by car, by canoe, by airboat, and by plane. They asked the landowners, other interested citizens and their governmental representatives, as well as interested organizations, what they wanted from the project, what they recommended. They included the nude beach at Mazomanie because a citizen spoke up, wanting the sunbathers to be represented as well, in part to protect them from harassment. *Newsweek* magazine wrote then that the Riverway was the most publicly discussed project ever. And a 2009 survey of valley citizens by a group of geography students at the University of Wisconsin–Madison revealed that even twenty years later, though most landowners embrace the project, some are still unhappy.

The Boscobel landing where we stop for lunch is tucked into an inlet downstream of the highway bridge and out of the current, which seems to have grown quite swift. The gradient of the Lower Wisconsin is steepest along this reach, though not by much, so the river feels a little pushier. Yet I think we only notice this because we're paddling upstream. And whether the current speed is increasing or our paddling strength is waning, we're ready for a break and some food. A few quick strong paddle strokes and we're into the inlet, free of the current's grasp.

A man and his preteen son stop at our picnic table to talk. "I've always wanted one of those canoes," he says eagerly, pointing to our long narrow Kevlar hull. "Where are you going?"

As I begin to tell him, he excitedly mentions Eric Sevareid and his book *Canoeing with the Cree*, the famous account of teenager Sevareid's upstream canoe trip with his friend Walter from St. Paul to Hudson Bay, the book that launched so many more canoe journeys. This fellow, clearly inspired by reading Sevareid, tells us that he once lived along the Minnesota River in New Ulm, Minnesota, and knows what it's like to paddle a river like the Minnesota, downstream anyway, and has always wondered what paddling upstream would be like. "Someday," he says with earnest determination. Now he takes his son to the Boundary Waters and on day trips down the Wisconsin, exciting adventures for a boy growing up in suburban Chicago.

After lunch, the current feels ever stronger. "I can examine every leaf on every bush and tree . . . in detail," says Bob with some amusement in his voice. We paddle close to the riverbank, slowly creeping upstream, trying to achieve a Zen-like relationship with the current, to relinquish our usual impatience and goal setting. The current is what it is. There is no other way to paddle upstream.

Traveling close to the bank: when we're there, we feel most connected to the river community. Two turtles sunning on a rock watch us with blank reptilian stares, a river otter slide on a muddy bank marks the presence of those elusive creatures, clouds of dragonflies float past, the blurry beat of their wings sounding an audible buzz, and birds sing in the riparian tangles.

And today we meet many, many, many canoeists. It's the Friday of the July Fourth weekend, and the river is getting into party mode. A couple with two lively children on board asks how far it is to Boscobel; they urgently need to make a bathroom stop. I suggest a sandbar. Several other paddlers laugh when they see us and yell that we're going the wrong way. Some are more curious about our trip but there's rarely time to explain as we pass midstream. Bob just calls, "We're headed for Arena!" Which we are.

In yet another canoe, two young children sit in the middle, one occasionally hanging over the gunwale to dabble his fingers in the water. Neither child is wearing a life jacket. My inner parent reacts and I want to ask them why they are taking chances with their children's lives. I don't, but wish I had. The placid surface of the Wisconsin belies a powerful, tricky, unpredictable current that can easily overpower an inexperienced swimmer.

Some travelers pass in small fishing boats. The Lower Wisconsin supports a good warm-water fishery, and anglers seeking sport fish catch smallmouth bass, walleye, sauger, channel catfish, flathead catfish, and northern pike, though the DNR warns that elevated levels of PCBs and mercury have been found in some game fish samples taken from parts of the Lower Wisconsin River. And there are also panfish, including bluegills, crappie, white bass, and rock bass.

Those fish that anglers shouldn't and usually don't go after—the lower layer of the river—are the little known, the endangered, and the threatened. Some live deep and often secret lives. One of these denizens, the paddlefish, is also a long-distance traveler; individuals tagged and tracked by the USGS Paddlefish Study Project have journeyed down the Chippewa River, down the Mississippi, and then up the Lower Wisconsin to the Prairie du Sac dam. The longnose gar, another old fish with a long nose, prowls the Wisconsin as well. Another species with an ancient pedigree is the shovelnose sturgeon, also known as a sand sturgeon or hackleback. A small sturgeon with the same bony plates that give the larger sturgeon its gnarly prehistoric look, it's a popular sport fish. But fishermen lured by the high price of caviar also go after the eggs, and illegal fishing has endangered this old fish's future. The little-known blue sucker is a threatened species in Wisconsin. According to Wisconsin DNR ichthyologist John Lyons, the blue sucker prefers cruising the depths of large rivers with strong currents, migrating in the spring to shallow rocky areas to spawn, and thrives only in the least-modified and highest quality waters, like the Lower Wisconsin, where it does particularly well, though it is found in the Upper Mississippi as well.

The health of any riverine fishery depends not only on clean water but also on free passage for the resident finny inhabitants, many of which need to migrate in order to spawn and thrive. Since its construction in 1915, the Alliant Energy dam at Prairie du Sac has been a barrier to this important seasonal migration of fish such as shovelnose sturgeon and paddlefish and thus has reduced their numbers. According to Wisconsin DNR aquatic ecologist Matt Diebel, fish focus on the turbulence below a dam and congregate there, striving to move further upstream, but in vain. Anglers know this and fish the tailrace. When the Federal Energy Regulatory Commission (FERC), which regulates this hydroelectric dam, issued the most recent permit in 2002, they mandated a fish passage.

Unfortunately, the Lower Wisconsin may also be vulnerable to the notorious species of Asian carp, or jumping carp, aliens that have invaded the Mississippi and Illinois rivers in alarming numbers. An angler caught a grass carp near the Prairie du Sac dam, and the DNA of silver carp has been detected in the river. Thus far, however, no one has found evidence of the jumping carp upstream of the dam and everyone wants to keep it that way; this is one situation where a dam can be of some benefit to a river. Though there is no evidence yet that these carp are actually breeding in the Lower Wisconsin, a conventional fish passage or ladder would allow any fish that can jump to move upstream. Add to this the fact that viral hemorrhagic septicemia, a fatal fish illness, has been afflicting fish in the lower river, and it's clear why anglers upstream have been anxious about letting those fish move in.

An unexpected solution has been proposed to resolve this dilemma: a doorman and an elevator. During the spawning season, when the proposed fish elevator would operate, fisheries staff would open a downstream door to let a group of fish enter. But only the desirable fish—like shovelnose and lake sturgeon, paddlefish and blue suckers—would be allowed to ride the elevator. At the top floor, the operator would open the door and release them, free to travel upstream to their preferred spawning grounds. Carp would be detained, no doubt indefinitely.

A few miles up from Boscobel, we're making better time against the current, though still working on that Zen thing. It helps when I see a great blue heron in the shallows of a slough, or an eagle soaring overhead. It's another clear, hot day. When I take off my hat, dip it in the river and don it again—quickly, so as not to break the paddling cadence—the cool river water trickles through my hair and down the back of my neck. It's a lovely feeling.

Despite our many trips down the Lower Wisconsin, on this journey we feel the need for a map. It's something about changing the direction we're traveling, the way we remember things. Everything looks different. So we photocopied the maps from Svob's *Paddling Southern Wisconsin* and packed them in a ziplock bag that rides on the bow. I like tracking the wooded islands and pass the time by reading their names aloud as we pass their tangled shorelines: Feather Island, Patterson Island, Little Island, Big Island.

Another thing I learned from Mike Svob is that the river valley is wider here, that the bluffs have now retreated from the river on both sides. This is surely an unexpected pattern in a river valley, which usually widens as it nears the confluence. Geologists say that when the torrents of water from the melting Laurentide ice sheet carved the modern Wisconsin valley, the flood cut readily through the soft Cambrian sandstone—the Wonewoc, Tunnel City, and Jordan layers—that underlies the soil at Prairie du Sac and for a number of miles downstream. The harder Prairie du Chien dolomite bedrock that dominates closer to the Mississippi put up more of a fight. Thus the valley tapers from about four miles wide near Prairie du Sac, to two miles wide at Muscoda, and only half a mile wide at Bridgeport.

Just short of the Blue River landing, Bob announces that we've paddled twenty miles today and that's enough. We stop on the north side of Coumbe Island, a densely wooded island that is two miles long, big enough to be mistaken for the riverbank on the south side of the river. A bit upstream, near the Port Andrew boat landing on the north bank, DNR biologist David Heath says there is a large mussel bed, but we're too tired tonight to pay a visit to the mollusks. Our chosen camping spot is the downstream end of a long stretch of sandbar, which we share with another couple, one tent at each end. This sandbar is part of a mini-braided channel of water and sand, separated from the island and from smaller sandbars by shallow streams.

Take a moment to consider the Wisconsin River sandbar, shifty creature that it is, and easily manipulated at the whims of the ever-changing river. We landlubbers generally feel that the ground beneath us, even sandy ground, has some kind of permanence. We don't expect it to move. And on many sandbars grass, willow thickets, and even small trees are further evidence that the ground will not be departing any time soon. At low water stages, as we are now experiencing, the sandbar flourishes and grows in height, width, and length as the water recedes. But were the river to rise over a foot, a change that can happen during a spring freshet or after only a day or two of heavy rain, in part because of releases from the dam at Prairie du Sac, the sandbar on which we stand could be inundated, its silica granules swept downstream in the flood, randomly scattered to future locations known only to the river, in its secretive ways. It is thus that the sandbar migrates downstream.

Even without such floods, the sandbar changes daily in small ways, its margin nibbled away by the quiet power of the current as it flows around the tapered shallow upstream head of the bar and along its flanks. At the tail end of the bar, the current deposits the sand it carries into the downstream eddy and often scours a deep hole there swirling with a recirculating current. The sand at this end can be as loose and unstable as quicksand, subject to sudden collapse into the eddy. The tail of the sandbar is a dangerous place.

Seen from above, the river at low water is a maze of sandbars; at high water, their shadowy shapes are faintly visible under the surface. It is easy to imagine how a sandbar becomes a semi-permanent island over a series of dry years, with swiftly growing networks of roots capturing and holding the shifty sand, keeping it in place until the trees are large enough to call it more than a sandbar and eventually, if luck will have it over the years, one of the islands. And yet a big enough flood can take even an island.

Despite the impermanence of the sandbar, river travelers love to camp on the invitingly soft open expanse of a large bar, the color of pale ale in the sunshine. Small villages of tents, grills, volleyball nets, and beach umbrellas spring up in the late afternoon.

Occasionally, a sandbar has been the site of a delightfully improbable event called "Dinner and a Canoe." Waiting on the sandbar when the lucky paddlers arrived was a circle of tiki torches around a table set with candles. At sunset, the caterers arrived by canoe, lit the torches and candles, served a gourmet dinner—all locally raised foods, all home cooked—and then disappeared in their canoes into the night. The very first time the canoe rental company held this sandbar extravaganza it was deemed a success: "The guy proposed to his girlfriend on a sandbar. She accepted, of course," said Ryan Schmudlach, who invented this wonderful event and with his wife Amy owns the Wisconsin Canoe Company in Spring Green. Unfortunately for romantic canoeists, the logistics proved far too daunting and it lasted only a few seasons.

There's a festive air to claiming a sandbar as your own sandy island in the wide Wisconsin. The perfect sandbar is one that is open enough that the breeze blows away the mosquitoes, but with enough thickets at one end to provide shelter for a temporary latrine. The sandbar toilet is just a cat hole, scraped at best only six inches down, deep enough to cover the contents but shallow enough to allow quick decomposition. People who are used to river camping pack out their used toilet paper and often their waste with their garbage. Though this may sound disturbing, it is surprisingly easy to do if one dedicates a large zip lock bag for the purpose. A useful product called Wag Bag includes an odor neutralizing powder and "a decay catalyst that breaks down solid waste."

When one considers how many canoeists camp on the river, the problem of untreated human waste on the sandbars becomes formidable. Mark Cupp, director of the Lower Wisconsin State Riverway Board, told me that this is one of the big challenges the river faces. "We have to educate the public to respect this resource," he said, "and it's not easy."

Scott Teuber, owner of a canoe rental company based in Boscobel, lamented that often after a weekend, shrubs are festooned with toilet paper on one sandbar after another. Though toilet paper degrades fairly quickly, and he said tests show that the water quality is fine, he longs for the DNR to establish firm, enforceable policy about the issue. Many campers already understand. Ryan Schmudlach said, "We try to get people to take care of the river. A lot of groups come out with more garbage than they brought in."

On the topic of the dark side of the sandbar, there's a bit more to tell. In *The Wisconsin, River of a Thousand Isles*, August Derleth writes that the "Wisconsin's sand has for decades been a bogey for the boys who haunt the old swimming holes along the river." He recalls that "the excitables" told of a girl being swallowed up by a Wisconsin River sandbar, slipping into the sand and drowning, dragged down by what people said was quicksand. Though he dismissed the tale, knowing that the truth was that she drowned because her chosen sandbar had become unstable and she slipped into the current, not because she was swallowed up, Derleth did capture the sentiments of those who lived along the river in the early twentieth century and were leery of its impermanent

Wisconsin River sand bar

shifting sands. Derleth himself paid no attention to the warnings and wrote that he often swam with his friends in the river, continuing this habit for decades.

On summer weekends like this, even when the weather is cool, this river playground is the place to be. With this summer's low water, the inevitable consequence of extended drought, campers find that sandbars big enough for camping are plentiful and spacious. At high water the sandbar count drops precipitously and competition for the good camping spots can be fierce.

During the Riverway planning process in the 1980s, Gary Birch and others conducting the study counted canoes from a small plane that flew low over the river the length of the Lower Wisconsin and divided the Lower Wisconsin into three segments, according to the amount of recreational use. About 68 percent of canoeists used the stretch of the river from Prairie du Sac to Spring Green; 20 percent used the Spring Green to Boscobel reach, and only 12 percent canoed from Boscobel to the Mississippi.

Today's paddlers, at least those who rent their craft, seem to follow the same pattern. Ryan Schmudlach said that more and more renters choose to canoe the Prairie du Sac to Spring Green run, including those who come back year after year. He rents to one group of six guys in their late seventies and early eighties who do an annual trip. "They tell me they still feel awe and wonder on the river," said Schmudlach. Another group rents eight canoes for ten people, fills the extras with firewood and coolers full of beer, and tows them. Although almost 40 percent of his renters are from the Chicago area, he said that he sees a number of visitors from European countries. During a single week in the summer of 2013, he rented canoes to a group from Germany, a family from the Netherlands, a group of young men from the United Kingdom who were holding a bachelor party on the river, and a French family that brings their grandmother to canoe the Lower Wisconsin every year.

Tomorrow morning, the first confluence we will pass is with the Blue River, just upstream of the bridge, though technically this juncture is the opening to Cross Slough, into which the Blue flows. In late August of 1835, on his way downstream to the Mississippi, adventurer George William Featherstonehaugh stopped right about where we are now, though perhaps on the riverbank at that confluence rather than on a sandbar. In his account in *A Canoe Voyage Up the Minnay Sotor*, he wrote, "About half-past nine we stopped at the Rivière Bleu to breakfast." A connection in place seems to bridge the passage of time, at least in the imagination.

I have never explored the Blue, but a young conservationist named Abbie Church told me that about eighteen miles upstream from the confluence, the Mississippi Valley Conservancy (MVC) has over one hundred acres of land in conservation easement. Working with Trout Unlimited, the landowners stabilized about a mile of stream banks, on a reach that is known as good trout water. Their restoration work proved its worth during subsequent floods—the banks survived high water that tore up nearby unrestored stream banks. The uplands are thriving as well. Church said that during a casual survey they found amazing diversity—271 species, including relict species like naturally occurring white pines, descendants of ice age populations. "All you do is walk to the north-facing slopes on this property and you're in a whole different world of species," said Church.

Back here on the Wisconsin, as we set up our little sandbar camp, the river rocks with noise, both manmade and natural. Traffic hums on Highway 60 to the north, on Highway 133 to the south, and on the county bridge that crosses the river. Fishermen in motorboats buzz past. A large flock of sandhill cranes flies purposefully overhead, headed to farm fields to browse for their evening meal, telling the world of their hunger with warbling croaks. Cows bellow to be milked. Dogs bark. The cacophony reaches a crescendo with the rat-a-tat-tat of a distant round of firecrackers.

But by the time our supper is ready, the sun is going down and with it the noise. Our neighbors, who have pitched their dome tent and flipped over their canoe—a maroon Spirit II, just like the one we left at home—pick up folding sand chairs and wade to another little sandbar for a better view of the sun setting behind the bluffs. We eat standing up, devouring two bowls each—tortellini mixed with canned chicken, onions, and rehydrated peas and carrots—then quickly fall asleep, long before the sky is dark.

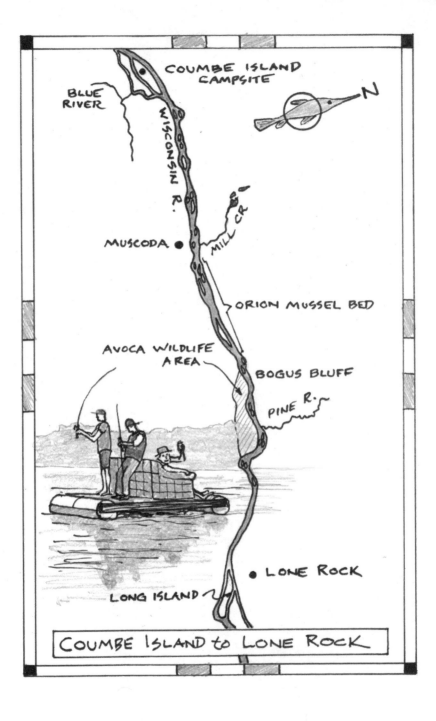

COUMBE ISLAND CAMPSITE

BLUE RIVER

WISCONSIN R.

MILL CR.

MUSCODA

ORION MUSSEL BED

AVOCA WILDLIFE AREA

BOGUS BLUFF

PINE R.

LONE ROCK

LONG ISLAND

N

COUMBE ISLAND to LONE ROCK

Fourth of July

On the morning of our nation's birthday, the rattling voices of sand-hill cranes sound again, echoing mysteriously in the pale light of early dawn. The door of our tent fly is open and through the screen I once again see nothing but cool white fog, as though the world outside the walls of our little green tent disappeared during the night. More croaking fills the air. *The sandhills are heading off to work*, I think sleepily. *We should probably get up too*. But it's cool outside and Bob is still asleep. Burrowing deeper into my sleeping bag, I doze instead.

When we finally crawl out of the tent, only a light misty veil remains and that quickly dissipates as we get ready to go. We're on the river again, warming up our tired muscles with slow, steady paddle strokes. As we pass the tail end of Steamboat Island, behind which hides the mouth of the trout stream Byrds Creek, I can't help but think about those steamboats that once plied the Lower Wisconsin. They carried passengers, including those on the Fashionable Tour, and they carried mail, grain, and lumbermen's supplies—anything that needed transport and that they could load. The twin-stack steamer *Ellen Hardy* drew only sixteen inches, according to historian Richard D. Durbin, which explains how this 132-ton boat navigated the frequent and shifting shallows. This morning, working hard in my still sleepy state to read the river, I'm grateful that I'm not a steamboat captain. Our little canoe is enough.

And then, at the head of Steamboat Island, a strange apparition appears upstream. Three young men are standing on a raft in the middle of the river, gracefully casting their fishing rods. As we call a greeting, they grin and one announces proudly that they built the raft just this morning. It's a platform of discarded plywood, resting precariously on six steel barrels that are strapped together. In addition, perched atop this small rickety vessel, are a large, filthy plaid sofa—on which one of the intrepid shipwrights now reclines—two coolers, and a big spray-painted sign that reads "Gilligan's Island." These fellows built their ship before dawn, launched it at Muscoda, and are headed for Boscobel, eleven miles downstream from where we meet them.

"Are you catching anything?"

"Not yet, but we will. The fishing's great along here."

"What'll you do with the raft when you get to Boscobel?"

"Just leave it at the landing. Let someone else use it."

Other Huck Finns will no doubt be delighted to abscond with this raft, though that's not always the case with stuff left along the river. Under the leadership of Tim Zumm, the Friends of the Lower Wisconsin (FLOW) spend time every year cleaning up after people who dump stuff in the river and on the shoreline. At a program about the Lower Wisconsin at Canoecopia, the annual celebration of all things paddling held in Madison each March, I listened to Zumm tell about a group of volunteers and DNR staffers who hauled more than five tons of steel post, copper wire and cable from the river bed near the beach at Mazomanie, where it had lain since the 1930s, slowly sinking into the sand. This particular project started in 2003, when they dragged out a lot of the mess. But there was more. By waiting until the low water of a drought exposed the tips of this hazardous manmade debris, and by using the power of a fisheries backhoe, provided by conservation warden David Youngquist, they dragged the last of the junk, the final remains of what was probably once a power line or telegraph line, from the river's sandy bottom. Bill Gauger of Gauger Salvage in Arena donated dumpsters to collect the scrap, and sold the steel for almost five hundred dollars, covering his expenses. Another time, members of FLOW pulled tangles of steel from the river near Ferry Bluff. Zumm told the audience that there is far less large trash in the river now, thanks to the volunteers. A tireless advocate for the Lower Wisconsin, Zumm followed his trash-picking story with a brief pitch for Rhythm of the River Festival, an annual environmental fundraiser held in Spring Green, and finished his talk with instructions on How to Clean Up a River: 1. You go into the river. 2. You pick up a piece of junk and put it in the truck. 3. You go back again.

Just past the bridge at Muscoda, we pull into the Victora Riverside landing. Aluminum rental canoes are stacked in great piles on the grass and lashed in tall tiers on canoe trailers. Paddlers are landing, launching, waiting to launch, and just milling about, watching the river. A tall man, probably in his thirties, strides down the concrete slope, a long slender racing canoe slung effortlessly over his shoulder, a paddle in one hand. In a smooth, practiced move, he drops his narrow craft into the shallow water, slides in, and begins paddling upstream with the powerful efficient strokes of an experienced racer. A little girl wearing her pink lifejacket stands on the ramp, silently watching him disappear around the bend. Muscoda's Wisconsin River Canoe and Kayak Race is just two weeks away, and our paddler is no doubt training hard to compete with racers from Iowa, Illinois, Michigan, Minnesota, and of course Wisconsin: the Big Five Challenge. On the longest stretch of the race, the twenty-one miles from the bridge near Spring Green down to this landing in Muscoda, the top canoeists finish in only two and a half hours, over eight miles an hour on a river that's hard to read. This guy looks like he's a contender.

As we fill our water bottles at the outdoor faucet, Bob and I chat with Steve and Brandy, young people who live in Chicago and are visiting the river with friends, tenting at the adjoining campground for the Fourth of July weekend. They aren't sure whether they'll paddle today; the weather's still cool and gray and they enjoy the spectator sport of watching paddlers launch and land. Brandy says they love being on the Wisconsin.

"Do you know where there's a grocery store?" asks Bob.

"The closest one is almost a mile away," replies Steve. "There's a convenience store closer but it doesn't have much. We'll give you a ride to the grocery," he adds. "We're not busy."

Bob returns with three full bags slung over his arms and a big smile on his face. Our cooler replenished through the kindness of strangers, we head upstream, though not nearly as swiftly as that lone racer. And the Wisconsin is even more crowded now. No longer does the river seem the secluded and almost wild place we traveled two days ago.

It used to be true that the river between Prairie du Sac and Lone Rock was the most popular paddling route. Almost every summer weekend, canoe campers would float downstream on this reach, often in makeshift barges, constructed by lashing up to four canoes together, loaded with camping equipment, coolers full of beer, firewood, and battery-powered boomboxes, cranked up to high volume. Mark Cupp of the Lower Wisconsin State Riverway Board told me that kind of river party has waned and he is glad. Canoe rental business owner Scott Teuber said he now urges people to choose the reach of the river between Spring Green and Boscobel. They both want to find the fine balance point between people enjoying the river and too many people using and sometimes abusing it.

Teuber said he feels that many people who live here in southern Wisconsin don't know much about the Lower Wisconsin River. "People who drive over the river don't really see it," he said. "Perhaps because a lot of them live so close by and don't see the point of visiting something local. They don't realize what's here—the sandbar camping; the wide, shallow river; the bluffs."

Along the north bank, the houses of the tiny town of Orion are visible and we head that way, weaving our path among fishermen buzzing about in small motorboats, a steady stream of canoeists drifting past, some holiday celebrators floating downstream on inner tubes and rubber rafts. Campers and picnickers festoon the sandbars.

Oblivious to all this busyness, an unusual state natural area lies, quiet and invisible, on the river bottom along the north shore. We follow the several miles of wooded shoreline along which the Orion Mussel Bed State Natural Area stretches, past the mouth of Indian Creek, partly concealed by a fallen tree, past the boat landing, upstream toward tall Bogus Bluff and its rocky outcroppings. Peering occasionally into the murky water, I see no mussels, though I want to. In my imagination their mollusk bodies are arranged on the gravel riverbed like the stars in my favorite winter constellation, perhaps with three oblong lilliput mussels in a row forming the familiar hunter's belt, their unassuming brown shells concealing the iridescent star-like inner beauty of their nacre.

Yet the future of Orion is uncertain. "The Orion mussel bed has been clearly declining since 1988, when we started monitoring it, though this may have been going on for much longer," said Wisconsin DNR biologist David Heath. "We have mussel records for the state that go back to 1820, and though the northern half of the state is holding its own, the southern half shows drastic declines all over, probably because of more development down here. On the Lower Wisconsin, it may be due to water quality and fluctuating water levels as well. Because the river gets higher peak flow more often now, the gravel and rock substrate that the mussels live on is disturbed more often. And with more low water times, the beds dry up and the mussels die." Because of these stresses, Heath added, there's very little reproduction, way below replacement levels. Of the approximately twenty-eight mussel beds that lie along the Lower Wisconsin, Orion is one of the most important. Other significant beds are located at Bridgeport, Port Andrew, Lone Rock, Sweet Island and Peck's Landing, and Mazomanie Flats. Yet all are declining.

We leave Bogus Bluff on a diagonal heading toward the south side of the river and soon reach the shore of the Riverway's Avoca Unit, more than 5,700 acres of wetlands, bottomland hardwood forest, tall-grass prairie, and oak savanna sprawling along ten miles of shoreline over the valley's wide sandy outwash terrace. As the river begins its big bend toward the south, the shoreline is low and heavily wooded. But not with elms.

"When the Riverway was being designed, all the American elms were dying of Dutch elm disease—those beautiful big trees aren't there anymore," said Riverway planner Gary Birch. Other species are gone as well.

Before dams were built on the Wisconsin, the river always flooded in the spring, often shifting its channel during those turbulent spring freshets. By late summer, the flow was low and the river was shallow. Trees in the bottoms were accustomed to lots and lots of spring flooding. Brad Hutnik, Wisconsin DNR forest ecologist and silviculturist, explained that these historical spring floods helped certain trees flourish. Cottonwood, black willow, and river birch, trees that drop their seeds in the spring, took advantage of the open soil that follows the spring freshet to get established.

As the river adapted to the effect of the dams, changes during the annual flow cycle diminished. "Seasonally, the river doesn't go nearly as high or as low," said Hutnik, "so some trees aren't as common as they used to be." Other species, such as hackberry and bitternut hickory, are taking their places. In an effort to anticipate future shifts in tree populations that may come with climate change, foresters have experimented with planting southern species such as sycamore near Bridgeport, in an area where they will do well if the climate warms. "We still have healthy forests," he added. "And we know that man is not separate from the ecosystem. We try to emulate the natural process in our management of the state land, but nothing is pristine. There have been people here for a long time, and the Native Americans made their own changes, like regular burning." But in contrast to rivers that are farmed right up to the riverbank, Hutnik said, "The Lower Wisconsin is kind of an aberration. Because of its wide bottomland, dry, sandy nature, and flooding, row crops have never been able to get very close to this river."

We're around the bend and headed southeast now, passing the open land of the Avoca Prairie. No more houses anywhere in sight. The prairie terrain is a mix of upland and wetland, a quietly beautiful place where we have hiked several times. From the parking area at the end of Hay Lane, an access road off Highway 133, it takes only about twenty minutes to cross the shallow flow of a slough named Avoca Lake and walk the trail all the way to the river, generally in the company of singing birds and various unidentified rustlings in the grass. On scattered upland rises, oak savannas punctuate the floodplain. The Avoca Prairie is one of the largest tall-grass prairies east of the Mississippi. The Riverway designers decided at some point that there should be a road through the prairie to the river, and Hay Lane was installed. Unfortunately, truck wheels and boots carried in the seeds of invasive reed canary grass, which is nearly impossible to control. According to Birch, "We had one of the richest prairies in the country, and we blew it."

Today, as we paddle up to the same shoreline where we have hiked, the riverscape appears familiar yet disconcertingly different, seen through the backwards-looking lens created by approaching a known scene from a different direction. Raised bands of sand running parallel to the river-bank and alternating with narrower bands of shallow water inscribe the sandbar terrain close to the riverbank. At high water, all this sand would be under water and invisible. Low water makes landing easy.

Despite the reed canary grass, an unfortunate fact of modern eco-systems, we are struck by the fact that the landscape seems to appear pretty much as it must have looked to Native Americans before Euro-peans arrived in the Lower Wisconsin valley. We look in every direction and see no apparent trace of modern man's effects on the land. The inter-mittent and distant hum of traffic on Highway 133 is audible, and jet contrails occasionally cross the sky, but the land itself endures, seemingly unchanged.

It is not a hot day, but the sun is high and intensely bright in the cloudless sky, lighting the river in classic shimmering midsummer style, relaxing all who travel the Wisconsin today. The five miles to Lone

Rock pass quietly. At the low-slung Wisconsin & Southern railroad bridge, a swirl of current around the concrete piers we pass between grasps at the hull, threatening to twist it sideways, jolting us from the midafternoon torpor into which we have slipped. We correct our course.

And we realize that we're dog-tired. There's a spot along Long Island that looks like a good campsite, with the added bonus of a clear view of the bridge at Lone Rock. This old bridge is a beauty. Bob, an engineer by profession, tells me it's a steel through-truss bridge. I just like its shape, so familiar to one who grew up in southeastern Minnesota in the 1950s and '60s. Three gracefully arched spans, built with steel that resembles the pieces in an erector set, tie the hills of the south shoreline to low-lying and wooded Long Island, which divides the river both up- and downstream of the crossing. Seen from downstream on the river, the geometric patterns of the bridge structure, interlocking steel triangles of various sizes, form the arched trusses. The name through-truss means that the traffic drives *through* a boxy tunnel, the sides of which are the truss walls, the steel under the roadbed, and the steel cross bracing that forms the roof of the box. Against the panorama of the meandering river, sprawling sandbars, and green hills, this old bridge seems an organic addition to the scene, and its arches seem even to echo the curved shape of the hilltops. A smaller, less impressive steel bridge, out of sight from our sandbar, crosses the narrow channel that runs between the island and the north bank of the river.

Another even smaller bridge beyond that one crosses a slough named Long Lake, which connects to the wildlife area known as Bakken's Pond, a maze of lovely off-channel water on the north side of the river, a flowage created by the DNR and known to them as Bakken's Pond Wildlife Area. To the northern pike, smallmouth bass, and panfish, it is home, the place where they spawn. These waters all are part of the watershed of Bear Creek, which runs for twenty-seven miles down a narrow valley through the bluffs north of Lone Rock and flows into the Wisconsin about three miles back down the river from here. From north of Lone

Rock, Highway 130 follows the Bear up into the Driftless hills to its headwaters. A good trout stream in its upstream half, the Bear is fed by cold-water tributaries such as Little Bear Creek and Marble Creek, and Little Bear and Marble are fed by springs in the hills north of Lone Rock. Everything that happens back in the hills, on the Bear and on its feeder streams, and down in the valley, in the sloughs and in the flood-plain lakes, ends up in the Wisconsin. It's all connected.

There's also a mussel bed around here somewhere, but as I don't know the exact location, we're not even going to think about looking for those ever-elusive mussels.

Various other canoeists, also ready to stop for the night, begin homesteading on adjoining sandbars. A group of boisterous young guys sets up their encampment of six tents, a raucous process that seems to require a lot of beer. As we cook our evening meal, their good-natured antics provide dinner entertainment. Audience and players meet on the sandbar stage.

As the sun sets, we celebrate our twenty-two mile day, our nation's birthday, and the everlasting beauty of this river by eating most of a package of Oreos for dessert.

And then the fireworks begin. From our tent, where we have retired for the night, we watch sleepily and happily. On the sandbar next door, firecrackers explode in rapid succession, and bottle rockets light the dusky shadows of the wide river valley. Our energetic young neighbors are now dark shadowy figures running through the shallows waving sparklers, splashing, whooping and laughing. Fireworks are officially forbidden on the Lower Wisconsin, but at this moment, drowsily watching stars streak through the night sky, we don't care.

It's the Fourth of July on the mighty Wisconsin.

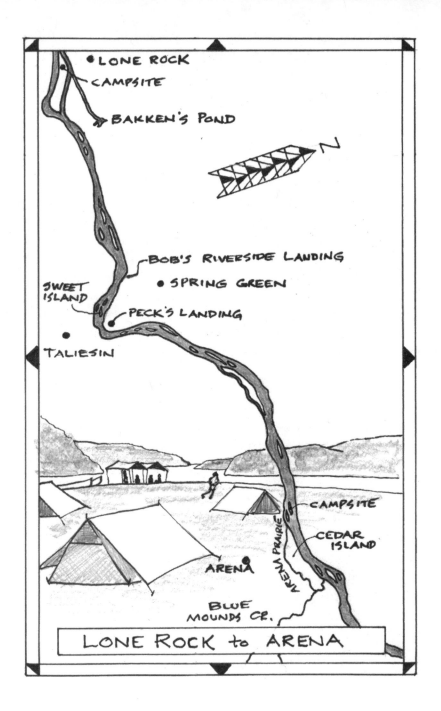

LONE ROCK to ARENA

Out of the Fog

July the fifth. Fog again. Even after the sun is up, the air is still so gauzy with moisture that the Lone Rock bridge is invisible. Our sandbar, its margin still saturated with recently departed river water, is bordered by a wide bank of dark sand. The river dropped during the night, it looks like at least five inches. I ponder how this change to our sandbar is connected to the dam upstream at Prairie du Sac as we stand in the cool fog, eating muesli and yogurt, staring upstream, shivering a little, waiting for the landscape to emerge from behind the veil.

As we eat, the ghostly outlines of the steel bridge emerge, ever so quietly and indistinctly, backlit by the rising sun. The only sound we hear is the murmur of the river and muted bird song, until the machine-gun chatter of a pileated woodpecker assaulting a tree abruptly echoes through the quiet river valley. In the aftermath of the Fourth, no one else is on the water yet, and the tents of the party boys on the adjoining sandbar are zipped up tight.

Though mist still hangs over the water, the rhythm of the river calls and we head upstream toward the bridge. On our right, the channel clings tightly to the layered stone bluff face, where road builders had to carve out a ledge for Highway 130. At the boat landing upstream of the bridge, a pair of wild turkey hens struts along the sandy margin at the mouth of Otter Creek, herding a clutch of ten fluffy little poults. Out

Wisconsin River near Lone Rock

in the channel, a small flock of canoeists floats past and waves to us, their arms tracing ghostly movements in the heavy air.

For almost an hour, we paddle through wispy clouds, and then the fog is gone. And under a clear sky, the day heats up in a pleasant way. Paddling the quiet edge of the serpentine thalweg when we can find it, wading the sandy shallows when no passage is visible, watching startled birds take flight from the low brushy banks of small islands, wading, paddling—the morning passes quickly. We're feeling strong, and surprisingly soon, we see the first Spring Green landing just upstream, partly concealed by trees.

"We averaged two and a half miles per hour this morning," Bob calls over his shoulder with a grin. "Want to get a burger at Bob's?"

"It's not even eleven."

"But I'm hungry. Breakfast was a long time ago."

Getting over to the landing involves finding our way around a massive sandbar flanked by a pod of smaller bars, a whale with her calves. This is a task that becomes more complicated and strenuous than it should be. Finally we resort to having me tow the canoe. Up the hill, the diner has just opened for lunch and it's already crowded. Formerly known as Bob's Riverside Landing, the business at this landing is now called Wisconsin Riverside Resort. The same family has owned it for almost a half-century and the younger generation just changed the name. We like this place, in part because it's a low-key family business, in part because of the former name, and in part because of the view from the diner. We carry our burger baskets to a table by the window.

On the beach far below us, our slim white canoe rests gracefully on the sand—as graceful as a canoe completely stuffed with gear can look—paddles propped up and ready to grab, life jackets at the ready. A child runs past and disappears; no one else is in sight. Beyond the beach, the Wisconsin spreads its wide watery self, peaceful bands of pale blue water and golden sand, punctuated by the bright midsummer green of small islands and shoreline. Beyond the water, the rounded wooded hills of the Driftless, the bluffs that bound the wide river valley, frame the scene in deepest green. The burger tastes wonderful.

At the table next to us, a group of fishermen drink beer and grouse about their lack of success this morning. I turn around to talk with them.

"Hi. Do you know why the river dropped so much last night?"

"It's all about dam closure and release," says the one closest to me. "They close it just to keep the water high on Lake Wisconsin, for the people up there. That means we don't get enough down here. It shouldn't be this low, not even with the drought and all."

"Why do they do that?"

"They're not about to let the lake levels drop. It's always been this way."

Wisconsin River near Spring Green

The dam upstream at Prairie du Sac is owned by Alliant Energy and regulated by the Federal Energy Regulatory Commission (FERC). According to Mark Cupp, director of the Riverway board, it became a "run-of-the-river" hydroelectric facility in 1990, which means that the levels below and above the dam must vary proportionately, with the downstream varying within one foot of the upstream variation. Theoretically.

Does the FERC license allow Alliant to maintain higher than proportionate levels upstream, for the sake of the property owners on Lake Wisconsin? The simple answer seems to be yes. Lake Wisconsin is fifteen miles long, heavily developed and heavily used, and that creates pressure on Alliant to favor the impoundment. When there is a drought, keeping water levels pretty much the same in Lake Wisconsin means that levels on the lower river drop even lower than a proportionate decrease would dictate, though the flow to the lower river cannot drop below a defined minimum. For water on the Lower Wisconsin to drop abnormally low is one of the many prices we pay when we dam our rivers.

Full of burgers, fries, and sodas, we depart Bob's. It soon seems that either we're sluggish from the digestive demands or perhaps the current is now flowing faster, but the journey to the Highway 23 bridge, just over a mile, feels unreasonably slow, especially compared with this morning's blazing pace.

At the bridge, the channel narrows as the river flows around a sharp bend, bounded on the south by an imposing rock bluff that runs right down to the water. As we paddle doggedly along the limestone face of that bluff, our canoe advances upstream so slowly that I am able to closely examine and even count the leaves of each liverwort and lichen growing out of the shaded rock crevices. *Remember the Zen thing.*

Partway up the bluff above us, out of our sight from this angle, County Highway C cruises along a narrow road cut. We're also below the Frank Lloyd Wright Visitor Center, where the dining room overlooks the river. Wright's home Taliesin is in the hills just south of the river, and his architectural style, deeply rooted in the landscape of the Driftless, echoes the shapes and forms of these bluff faces, their out-croppings, and the low, rounded hills that rise above them, an organic expression of this land where the architect grew up, the materials and shapes derived from the landscape, and at times from the riverscape. Wright built with Cambrian sandstones and dolomites quarried from the hills of the Driftless and mixed Wisconsin River sand into his plaster.

On the opposite shore is Peck's Landing, the canoe access where great numbers of canoeists have now parked their boats and are milling about like water bugs in the shallows by the big sandbar adjoining the landing. Peck's Landing has long been a crossing, located as it is at a narrowing of the channel. According to Richard Durbin in *The Wisconsin River: An Odyssey Through Time and Space*, it was here that an enter-prising fellow named Alvah Culver ran a flat-bottomed scow ferry across the river in 1840, from the mouth of Mill Creek at the Tower Hill State Park canoe landing to approximately the site of the canoe landing. Durbin writes that the ferry service changed ownership at least five times before the first bridge, a drawbridge resting on a massive turntable, was built in 1887, followed by an iron bridge in 1906, an army surplus Bailey bridge in 1948, and in 1966 the concrete structure that now bridges the river, carrying the road that leads to Spring Green.

The village of Spring Green was built above the river valley's flood plain, but not by much. When the Baraboo ice dam that held back Glacial Lake Wisconsin broke for the final time, about fourteen thousand years ago, the torrent raged down the Lower Wisconsin River valley to the Mississippi in a sudden and spectacular flood that geologists Dott and Attig write "likely happened in just a few days or weeks" and was over a hundred times the present size of the river, carving the old valley much deeper. Erosion of glacial deposits in the upper river's watershed refilled the valley with up to 150 feet of sand and small pebbles in places. As the flow diminished to become the modern river, it carved a much smaller channel in the sediment of the wide valley, leaving a meandering trail of sandy terraces along its banks, above the flood plain but below the level of the high valley walls. Spring Green, like many towns in the valley, is built on such a terrace. To the north of the river near the village, groundwater flows from an aquifer and emerges from upland springs. The same aquifer feeds a network of sloughs—Hill Slough, Cynthia Slough, Hutter Slough, Norton Slough—that weave a watery web on the terrace, a web that connects to the river, especially during flooding. These backwaters, which lie all along the Lower Wisconsin, are important threads in the fabric of the riverine ecosystem.

At Spring Green's River Valley High School, science teacher Joel Block weaves lessons from the river into his conservation science and biology classes. These kids, juniors and seniors in high school, are already tuned into the river's offerings. Many spend their summers fishing the backwaters and their fall weekends hunting on the floodplain. "The sloughs are the place that a lot of them spend more time than on the main river, though they like to go tubing in the summer," said Block. "Hunting for waterfowl in the marshes and sloughs and on Long Lake is big for them." In class, Block talks with them about the connection between the river and the forest, about the wetland community of plants and animals, about the ecology of fishes that live in the Wisconsin. Lessons are sometimes outdoors, in the school forest near the river or at the river landing. When they take a trip to Peck's Landing, the students fish and Block teaches them about what they have caught.

"The river is important to the kids, and they value and respect it," said Block, who has himself canoed the river from Spring Green to the confluence.

"If we can get kids outside, those who live here will value the Riverway. The Riverway is an educational opportunity, a living laboratory," said Mark Cupp.

The lower layers of the river, the less visible threads of the intricate tapestry, can be found in those sloughs that Block's students know so well. These quiet, off-channel lakes are homes for species of fish most of us haven't heard of, fish with fanciful names and unexpected ways—purple pirate perch that have their anus located right under their gills, starhead topminnows that will jump out on the bank to escape a pursuing bass and then jump back into the water when it leaves. And fish that don't like fast currents, like bluegills and largemouth bass, spawn in the sloughs. Unless the river is high, these small shallow floodplain lakes that lie between the river and Spring Green are fed almost entirely by the groundwater of the aquifer along the side of the river valley, also the source of the river's baseflow.

The sloughs have long been clear-water refuges for their finny inhabitants, but in the last decade nitrate levels in the water have crept up to a point that threatens the fish and feeds dense algal blooms on the once clear ponds. Nitrates are also increasing in private wells, and fish aren't the only ones hurt by nitrates—babies who drink water high in nitrates can suffer from "blue baby syndrome." Aquatic biologist Dave Marshall, recently retired from the DNR, feels that the nitrates are coming from agricultural fields on the river terrace. Because the farmer must add nutrients to this sandy infertile soil in order to grow a crop, many truckloads of liquid manure and tanks of anhydrous ammonia are spread on a field during the growing season. Nutrients that are not used by the crops percolate down through the porous sandy soil into the groundwater. Marshall suggests that establishing buffer zones planted with deep-rooted plants—the roots of prairie grasses like big bluestem and switch grass go down twelve to fifteen feet—may reverse the trend of excess nutrients in the sloughs, an idea supported by research at Iowa State University, but it is up to landowners to decide whether to install these buffers. He also feels that sloughs with excess nitrates, and in some cases, excess phosphorus as well, should be placed on the Wisconsin's Impaired Waters list.

Now here's an interesting paradox. In the high rocky bluffs north of Spring Green, those icy springs bubble from the vast subterranean aquifer to feed the little tributaries of Bear Creek and the floodplain lakes and sloughs of the Wisconsin. Very occasionally, this groundwater even floods low-lying areas of the town. Yet on the south faces of these bluffs the land is so sandy and infertile and temperatures get so hot that prickly pear cactus grows there among the sand dunes. Years ago, Bob and I hiked there with a Nature Conservancy group led by a guide named Gigi who explained that Spring Green Preserve is a little desert microclimate, populated by lizards, snakes, pocket gophers, and open-country birds like dickcissel and lark sparrow. There are black widow spiders and wolf spiders here, and cicadas, tiger beetles, and predatory wasps. Clumps of native sand-prairie plants—silky prairie-clover and yellow evening primrose, false heather, three-awn grass, and rare prairie fame-flower, plains snake-cotton, Venus's looking-glass, and dwarf dandelion—are scattered across the sand. Sand barrens like this, a fascinating anomaly in the Driftless topography, are not unique to Spring Green. Scattered all along the Lower Wisconsin, at Arena, Gotham, Blue River, and Woodman, are other remnants of sand barrens, a reminder that glacial meltwater had long ago filled this valley with sand, from bluff to bluff.

Two more miles upstream of Peck's Landing, we discover that crews are still working on the new bridge for Highway 14 and the river is a chaotic construction zone. We're paddling harder than ever, yet are traveling slower than at any other time on this river, less than one mile per hour. It feels as though a surge of swifter current, or a narrowing of the channel, is pushing us back downstream. Under the blazing midday sun, somewhat overheated and cranky, I clutch my paddle grip tightly as we maneuver between sandbars and construction equipment in the river, obstacles that swirl the current in confusing patterns.

I want to look one last time at the old bridge, a handsome steel through-truss bridge with eight curved arches painted a classic bridge green, a structure that has carried traffic since 1949. But the heavy, graceless span of its concrete replacement blocks its shape from our view until the moment we are in between the two, trying to find the best route through the maze and focusing on the river. This fall, the old bridge will be torn down and forgotten as traffic moves to the new.

The push of the current and the swirling eddies ease upstream of the bridge, and we return to our relaxed paddling rhythm. Now chaos of a different variety reigns at the boat landing upstream of the old bridge. As we paddle past, canoeists and motor boaters are jockeying about, all trying to use the ramp first. Cars, trucks, and boats on trailers fill the parking area, as do piles of aluminum canoes, some dumped in the middle of the ramp. "The landings are where trouble happens on the Lower Wisconsin," said Mark Cupp, director of the Riverway board. "There are so many more people on the river, and inconsiderate people— both canoeists and motor boaters—bump heads at the landings. Some canoeists refuse to move their rental canoes off the ramp because they feel that they paid the canoe livery to do that, so the guy with the boat on a trailer who can't use the ramp jumps out of his pickup truck and gets angry and the conflict begins." In one sense, the conflicts are a problem begging for a solution. In another, they signify that people value their time on the Riverway but really need to learn some manners.

Speaking of which, as we paddle under a second Wisconsin & Southern railroad bridge, a jet ski roars by, pulling an inflatable raft. Three preteen kids wearing swim goggles cling to the raft, screaming ecstatically, continuously, in unison, as they bounce over the water. As he abruptly crosses our path, throwing off a big wake for us to slam into, the driver smiles and waves.

Upstream of the tracks, Bob suggests that we detour into a back channel between an island and the riverbank. Several small camping trailers parked along the shore are empty and quiet. Here the river is just deep enough to float our canoe, the water is coppery clear and minnows dart away as we approach. I think of a small northern Minnesota river we once paddled, where it was like this, the mesmerizing movie of a sandy riverbed sliding past under the canoe, everything visible, fish, rocks, waterlogged branches, shells. Here now are dozens of lovely big mussels—live ones—resting quietly in the water along the edge of a sandbar, their hieroglyphic tracks etched in the sand tracing their paths to the water, the mussels I've been longing to see.

So many varieties of mussels live in the Lower Wisconsin, and the folksy names of these bivalves are as delightfully evocative as those of snails along the Kickapoo. One can imagine their gnarly shells without even seeing them. The imagery is sometimes pedal: elktoe, Wabash pigtoe, Ohio River pigtoe, fawnsfoot, deertoe, squawfoot, creek heel-splitter, white heelsplitter, and pink heelsplitter. Sometimes it's facial: Higgins eye, sheepnose, and monkeyface. Sometimes the names are festering: purple pimpleback, wartyback, threehorn wartyback. Sometimes they're delicate: fragile papershell, pink papershell, paper pond-shell. Simply descriptive can also serve: mucket, fat mucket (as in buckets and buckets of muckets), giant floater, flat floater, cylinder, yellow sandshell, rockshell, spike, threeridge, fluted-shell, black sandshell, plain pocketbook, mapleleaf, and hickorynut. And some names are fanciful: lilliput, pistolgrip, salamander mussel, and butterfly. The long list of names, reading like catalog verse, testifies to the species' past diversity and fragile hopes for the future. The mussels that already lie on the bottom of the river, wherever there are the layers of gravel and rock that are their preferred housing, will probably live out their long reclusive lives. But if conditions change and they are unable to reproduce, some say they could be gone from the Wisconsin within several decades.

These relatively sedentary creatures depend on certain fish to expand their ranges. This isn't a handshake deal. The female mussel tricks its chosen fish, often by extruding and wiggling the ruffled edge of its mantle, the mollusk version of a fan dance. When the fish moves in close to nab what looks like prey, the mussel quickly sprays a cloud of nearly microscopic mussel larvae right into the fish's face. The tiny hitchhikers swiftly attach themselves to the gills or eyes of the fish. When the startled fish darts away, they hang on tight, riding their fish to a new mussel bed, and if all goes well, to a long life as well. Some live several decades and in a few cases, a century or more. You can find out how old a mussel is without asking; just count the ridges on the shell, each of which represents a winter resting period, as you would count the rings on a tree stump.

Looming over the Lower Wisconsin's population of artfully named yet reclusive bivalves is the knowledge that the dreaded zebra mussel has invaded this reach of the river. Were the small striped alien with the razor-sharp shell to gain a foothold, the future of the river's native mussels would be even more uncertain. Zebra mussels attach to just about anything, including other mussels, and grow so prolifically, typically several hundred on a single native mussel and sometimes thousands, that they starve the native mussel by limiting its movement and reproduction. On a less existential level, these rapidly reproducing menaces can also clog manmade devices such as water intake pipes, turbines, and other equipment. And with a multitude of sharp-edged shells on sandbars and in shallows, it would no longer be safe for us bipeds to walk barefoot.

Beyond our back-channel byway, we meet more of the high, noble bluffs that grace the Lower Wisconsin. Here the cliffs crowd dramatically close to the river's edge and the valley is even more beautiful than it was downstream—awe-inspiring in fact. The shape of the land here and the wide sweep of the river valley, textured with pale gold sandbars and wooded islands, flanked by an undulating band of wooded hills, evoke the grandeur of the entire Driftless—the softened ruggedness that millennia of erosion and vegetal growth have wrought on the ancient bedrock of the Paleozoic Plateau that was the raw material for this creation. I always feel this way on the Wisconsin, and even more so on a day like today.

As it is for many, this reach of the Wisconsin is our favorite. It is Sunday afternoon, the peak moment of the long holiday weekend. On this hot July day under a clear blue sky, the river shimmers crystalline blue in the sunshine. Who would not want to be playing in the waters of the Wisconsin today? And it is true that more people than ever are out on the river now. They float in canoes and kayaks, recline on inflatable rafts, drape themselves over inner tubes as they drift downstream on the current, slowly weaving their way between the islands. They play on the sandbars and fish the sloughs. River rats, every one.

When the planning for the Riverway was in its infancy, the designers knew they had to document how people used the river, to convince the legislature it was important to preserve the aesthetics of this river valley. This led to a whole lot of DNR employees being out on the river during a whole lot of the spring, summer, and fall, counting river rats.

"In the early 1980s, there were thousands of people on the river every weekend. People were just flocking to the river then," said Gary Birch. "And we'd go out and count the people, most summer weekends for two years." The pilot of an aircraft that Birch called "a teeny, weeny plane" would stuff Birch and his colleague Tom Watkins into the little cockpit with him, take off from Truax Field, and fly the whole length of the Riverway. They had removed the doors of the plane so they all could see better, and the pilot took the plane pretty low, only about five hundred feet up. "We'd each have a counter in each hand: one for the canoeists, one for people on tubes, one for the fishermen, one for the pleasure boaters. And we'd be just clicking like crazy the whole way down the river," said Birch. "Between Sauk City and Spring Green, where most people were, he'd have to fly in a curlicue so we could get them all. We did these flights maybe fifty times over a period of two years."

"Once a pair of pilots in A-10s [a military plane], who took off from Truax when we did and knew what we were doing, decided to give us a surprise," added Birch. "We were only five hundred feet up and they both flew right under us. Oh my goodness."

Birch and Watkins counted on land as well, recruiting everyone in the DNR offices to camp out on the weekends at boat landings, where they counted and asked people about why they were going to the river. Birch remembers going to the well-known nudist beach upstream at Mazomanie. Fully clothed, equipped with binoculars and clipboard, he stood at the edge of the beach, counting. An unclothed sunbather walked up to him, smiled, and said, "You know, you don't really need those binoculars, you can just go right out there."

"I was so naïve," laughed Birch.

At the outreach meetings the planning team presented their ideas to the community members and explained their vision. Birch said that members of Private Landowners of Wisconsin (PLOW) attended most meetings. "I remember hearing over and over again from them that if you do this, you'll just attract those 'city maggots,'" he said. "But PLOW members eventually realized that the majority of people in the valley liked the project and gave up their campaign."

On the water, the long afternoon floats by in a haze of July heat. The west wind blows its hot breath on my back, helpfully pushing our little boat upstream like a leaf on the water. The river has carried us to the north side of the wide valley and upstream crouches the bluff called Sleeping Lion. To the south, the green of bottomland forest and sloughs borders the land called Arena Prairie. We're looking for a spot downstream of the Arena landing, a spot that now draws near. If we were to continue paddling upriver for another six miles or so, we would find a canoe landing at the mouth of Honey Creek. And rising up from the mouth of Honey Creek on the north side of the river are Ferry Bluff and its next-door neighbor Cactus Bluff, big stony high-rises with glorious views of the Wisconsin River valley.

I remember one early fall day when Bob and I hiked the steep trails to the tops of these bluffs, when the sky was cloudless and the air clear, in that way that a brisk autumn day can be, brightly presaging the cold to come. From the Cactus Bluff lookout, three hundred feet above the river, we saw the long rounded outline of Blue Mound rising above the southwest horizon, over fifteen miles away. From Ferry Bluff, one hundred feet higher, we saw the hills of the Baraboo Range to the north. And below us flowed the beautiful Wisconsin, spreading to the east and to the southwest, its sandbars, islands, floodplain forests, and sloughs laid out as though on a map. Being up there was the closest I've been to my desire to be a bird, soaring over the Wisconsin.

A few days after, on another cold clear afternoon, I remember standing atop the lookout tower at Blue Mound and looking toward the Wisconsin River valley, to the outline of Ferry Bluff and beyond it the Baraboo Range. Aspiring birds, once again. To the west we could see Belmont Mound, Platte Mound, and Sinsinawa Mound—scattered hills capped with Silurian dolomite, remnants of the great flat Paleozoic Plateau, the ancient seabed that once covered the Driftless. Military Ridge, the height of land that marches west toward the mouth of the Wisconsin at Wyalusing, divides the southern Driftless into the Wisconsin River watershed and the Rock River watershed.

"Back then, if you wanted to get from here to the Mississippi by water, you went down the Wisconsin. If by land, you went along Military Ridge," said Bob. "Either way, you avoided all the corduroy, all the up and down of the Driftless hills." From up there, it was clear that the Driftless is a corduroy land.

In a Driftless valley south of Military Ridge, the East Branch of the Pecatonica River begins its journey southward toward its eventual confluence with the Rock River. (On Nicollet's map the river is named the Pikatonoky.) Before settlers arrived to farm the land, the valley through which it flows was covered in grassland and oak savanna, as was most of the Driftless. After years of grazing, logging, and plowing, much of the rich soil that had once crowned the ridges had washed down into the valley floor and lay deep over the floodplain, in high stream banks with raw crumbling faces, easily eroded by every rise in the river. In place of the deep-rooted grasses that had once laced the floodplain soils together, fast-growing trees like box elders lined the stream's edge, their roots exposed by the constant erosion. The formerly damp valley had been tiled to drain off groundwater and was planted in corn. There was some evidence that farmers had straightened the formerly meandering channel. It was a typical twentieth-century Driftless stream.

The good part of this story began nearby, over fifty years ago. After receiving a donation of three acres of prairie land, the Nature Conservancy began a prairie grassland project, now called the Military Ridge Prairie Heritage Area, a project that now encompasses over fifty thousand acres. Over 4,460 of those acres are permanently protected land, including sixty remnants of original prairie, windows into the Driftless that once was.

In 2006, hydro-ecologist Robert Hansis, working with TNC and the Prairie Enthusiasts, decided to build on this work, this time in the stream department. Hansis designed a stream restoration project along a 2,700-foot stretch of the East Branch of the Pecatonica. Rather than leaving the high banks in place and simply covering them with riprap, the usual method of protecting highly erodible banks, Hansis wanted to try something new, to restore the stream geomorphologically. This means that he sculpted the banks and the ground surface of the valley into their presettlement contours, a change that reconnected the small stream to its wide floodplain. This meant removing twelve thousand cubic yards of topsoil from the floodplain, an expensive task. Fortunately, the team found a local excavator who hauled those twelve thousand cubic yards of good black dirt back to their provenance and put them to good use in the area.

On a cold gray day in November, we walked the damp valley with Hansis. "I wanted to create conditions where the stream can do its own work," said Hansis, "a healthy, dynamic floodplain." It turned out that restoring the stream's access to its floodplain—nature's original design—was indeed quite effective in reducing flood damage. He told us that during the big floods of 2007 and 2008, very little soil was washed downstream. By capturing floodwaters that formerly raced downstream, the floodplain recharges the groundwater aquifers, filters pollutants and sediment from the water, and slowly releases the excess. Regular testing of nutrients, sediment, organisms, temperature, and other variables in both the stream and the floodplain show great improvement. Hansis pointed up the valley slope to limestone outcrops where the cold groundwater feeding the East Branch of the Pecatonica originates and to a series of small, clear ponds, created during the restoration and fed by the abundant groundwater. Hansis said that the number and variety of frogs and toads living and breeding on the wet floodplain has increased greatly. "On a summer night, the amazing amount of frog sound gives you a sense of how many there are now," he said. Along the flat floodplain, prairie cordgrass and bluejoint grass, and plant species that love keeping their feet wet, like brown fox sedge, fountain sedge, hairy-fruited sedge, have replaced the invasive species. In 2008, Hansis led the restoration of another segment of stream with similar success. The results of his experiments, documented in several graduate student theses, created a model for the restoration of Driftless streams.

In one sense it seems straightforward. If we just reshape the land and replant the grasses that once held the land together, the streams will be healthy again. But even when a stream segment is restored, it is only one piece of a vast, intricate, interconnected system. As Hansis tells me, whatever happens upstream can undo the restoration. And thousands of miles of streams have been divorced from their floodplains. It will take time and resolve. To paraphrase Anne Lamott, it'll have to be done stream by stream.

About four o'clock in the afternoon, we reach the tail end of Cedar Island, long and wide, nestled into the right bank of the Wisconsin downstream of the Arena landing. Between the island and the shoreline flows a narrow channel.

Years before, on a blazing hot summer weekend, we camped with friends on a sandbar somewhere near here. In the late afternoon, we mostly lolled about camp, somnolent with the heat. Except for our friend Dave, an avid trout fisherman who decided to explore on foot. It turned out that our campsite was close by the outlet of a small cold creek, its mouth blocked by tangles of fallen trees. While the rest of us sat around, Dave waded into the mouth of that creek with joy in his

heart and a fishing rod in his hand, and spent at least an hour stalking
the trout that he hoped were there. When he returned to camp, it was
to lead all the rest of us, adults and children, over to the mouth of that
creek. We complied, and as we waded along the shallow edge of the
Wisconsin toward the creek, the water was warm and turbid. But when
I stepped into the clear creek water just a few feet above where it flowed
into the big river, it felt shockingly cold, ice cream-on-teeth cold. In
the heat of that afternoon, it was wonderful. There was a deep pool
upstream of the mouth, scoured by the rush of the creek water on the
sandy creek bed just before it hit the flow of the Wisconsin. I accidentally
slipped into the icy water up to my waist and gasped for breath.

Though he caught no trout that day, Dave did land a northern, a
bass, and some panfish, all fish that live in the Wisconsin and move into
the confluence to feed. Later that day, Dave told us that he often catches
trout at the mouth of a stream, where they like to hang out. "A lot of
different fish, including trout, will congregate at a confluence because
there is lots of food coming down the faster stream," he said. "Trout will
wait there for a long time, moving into the current to feed and out of the
current to rest." That the trout also love a confluence was a wonderful
revelation to me.

Today, it isn't easy to find the mouth of that cold creek again. The
chameleon shape of the Wisconsin sandbar may be the reason, as the
sandbar is always, always changing. So instead of searching for the confluence, we look for a proper place to camp, choosing a spot on a high
sandbar facing the back channel with scattered thickets of willow on
vast expanses of open sand, so hot in the afternoon sun that it is hard to
walk barefoot. That we cannot see the main channel from here makes
our camp feel secluded, somehow wilder than our wide-open tenting
grounds of the last few days. On the wet mud flats that abut the sandbar
on the shore side, trails of sandhill crane tracks, each footprint shaped
like the letter T, form intricate patterns of line and curves and loops
frequently punctuated by dried droppings.

And as it turns out, we are indeed camped at the confluence, or perhaps more accurately, at one of several points where Blue Mounds Creek drains into the Wisconsin. By studying the shoreline, Bob concludes that one branch of Blue Mounds Creek flows into the Wisconsin under a tangle of undergrowth that is just across the back channel from our camp. To confirm this, we paddle across the narrow channel and step out of the canoe into the water. It is clear and icy. We have discovered Blue Mounds Creek.

Back in camp, we bathe in the Wisconsin, lying full length on our backs on the sandy bottom of the shallows. My hair floats on the surface, Medusa-like, as I slowly cool off and relax. Later we dine on oranges, bananas, gouda cheese and Wasabrod and toast our arrival at the confluence with cups of ice water from the bottom of the cooler and the last of the Oreos. Bob suggests that when we get to Madison in two days that we spend the night at the Edgewater Hotel on Lake Mendota.

"We can paddle right up to the dock," he says, laughing.

I agree, delighted with his somewhat outrageous idea of staying at a posh hotel on a canoe trip.

Two sandhill cranes cross the mouth of the creek, pausing to look our way. A few quick running steps and they are launched. They depart over the trees, bodies glowing softly golden in the evening light, long wings silhouetted against the sky, and that distinctive wingbeat tempo— slow on the downstroke, quick up, another slow roll and quick snap— and then they're gone. The sun drops behind the bluffs and the world slowly cools. I listen to the distant cranes call to each other intermittently through the evening, not thinking of anything in particular. Then, out of the blue, I recall our long-ago-abandoned portage wheels and feel a mild sense of dread.

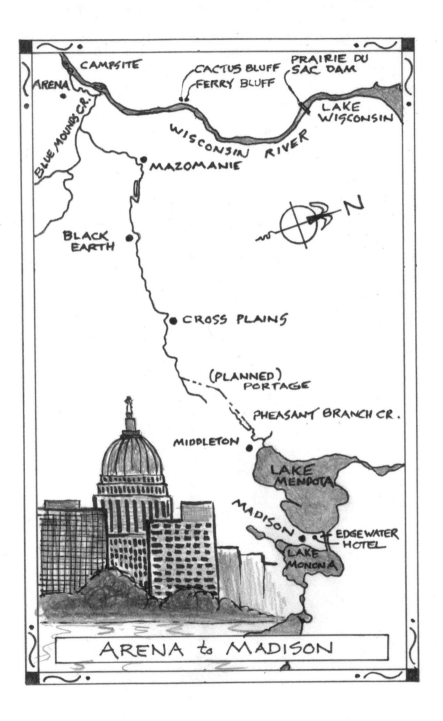

ARENA to MADISON

Defeated by the Bottoms

July the sixth. There is a tipping point in some journeys, a point beyond which we expend more energy on getting home as soon as possible than on paying attention to the places through which we travel. It is the point at which, in fact, the only thing that really matters to us is returning home. Bob and I are at that point right now, though we don't know it yet. That point will explode in our faces later this morning.

Right now it is dawn and we are optimistic and full of energy. I have set aside my worries about the portage wheels. We are on the next leg of the journey and it's both exciting and intimidating. We have never paddled Blue Mounds Creek or its tributary Black Earth Creek, and we don't have a detailed map. Because of the interminable drought, water levels are so low that at least one channel of Blue Mounds may be impassable. And we have no idea what other obstacles lie ahead in the low swampy bottomland between the Wisconsin and the bridge at Blynn Road where we saw that the Black Earth was passable three weeks ago.

One might ask why we didn't think about these things before we started the journey, and that would be a reasonable question. Perhaps because the total distance we will paddle on Black Earth Creek is only about twenty-two miles, and perhaps because we didn't have time to properly explore the route by paddling it downstream, we only did a cursory scouting by car, using a map of the Black Earth Creek watershed. We didn't think much about the stretch on Blue Mounds Creek that connects to the Wisconsin. After all, it is less than two miles, as the crow flies, from its confluence with the Black Earth to the Wisconsin River. How long and how hard could that stretch of the journey be? However, when that trout stream meets Blue Mounds Creek, their combined waters meander in a leisurely and quite circuitous fashion through the flat wooded bottomland that borders the Wisconsin, often paralleling the river, twisting and turning, dividing and diverging several times before joining the Wisconsin at three different points. Because we have not paddled the creek, we don't know which route is best passable by canoe. So last night we guessed. And now we are here and don't know what we're doing.

Standing at the confluence at dawn, in the icy water of the creek, we begin to realize that traveling up this stream won't be easy. As far upstream as I can see, fallen trees crisscross its narrow channel, which means we have to portage even before we start paddling. Dragging our loaded canoe through waist-high reed canary grass laced with brambles and fallen branches, and weaving around tight clumps of trees, we inch our way up the creek.

"I don't like this," says Bob, with a slight growl in his voice.

"I think it'll clear out once we get further upstream," I reply cheerfully, but I don't really mean it. *We can do this.*

After what seems like an interminable battle with the riparian thickets, we come to a place where we can slide the canoe into the stream. Success! Shortly thereafter, however, we meet what can best be described as a thick yellow blanket draped over the creek, a quilt of algae at least four inches deep that spreads from bank to bank, firm and dense enough for a small bird to walk on. Dead branches that have dropped from the overhanging trees protrude from the mat like alligators waiting to chomp onto our paddles.

Nevertheless, we forge ahead. Using the bow of our canoe and the thrust of our paddles to part the viscous yellow mass, we move about twenty feet upstream. Around a bend, the branches of a deadfall again block the creek. This time we climb out of the canoe and wade in the cold, waist-deep water, pushing aside the algal mats, dragging the boat through the tangle that crosses the stream, and continue upstream. At times the creek is so shallow that its sandy bottom is exposed and we drag the boat along.

Two hours later and less than two miles up the creek from the Wisconsin, we are exhausted, and the unbelievably winding channel of Blue Mounds Creek is still a nearly impassable swamp. We have no idea how many miles of meandering struggle we face before we reach Black Earth Creek. Other than brief exchanges about how to get around the obstacles, we haven't talked about a plan yet.

This is the tipping point.

"We have to turn around now," says Bob. "We don't have any idea how much longer it'll be like this."

"I don't want to quit," I reply. "Once we get to Black Earth Creek, we know it will be clear."

"But we don't know how far that is, and I just don't want to do this anymore," he says, adamantly. "If we turn around now, we can get back to the river, paddle up to the Arena landing, and call Matt to give us a ride to Middleton."

"You mean skip the whole Black Earth Creek part of the trip? No way. I want to keep going." I am getting obstinate.

"Well, I don't and I won't."

By now our voices are loud and angry. We stop yelling for a moment and simply glare at each other. I don't want to be defeated by this passive-aggressive little stream. Then I remember, again, that the portage wheels lie twisted and useless in a trash can in Alma. Even if we finally emerge from this jungle alive and paddle all the way up to Cross Plains, we will still need a ride, because the portage from there to the closest reach of Pheasant Branch Creek is over ten miles. We can't do that without the wheels, and we don't want to ask Matt for more than one rescue. Judging from how low this creek is, I suspect that Pheasant

Branch won't be passable either. The bugs are biting viciously. I beat an uncharacteristically hasty retreat.

"Alright, we'll turn around."

We've spent twelve days canoeing together without getting even close to an argument, until now. It stuns us both how quickly the conflict sparks and grows. But without any discussion of my capitulation, we begin the return trip down the creek, battling our way back to the Wisconsin.

It is almost eleven in the morning when we pull the canoe up on the sand at the Arena landing, fingers crossed that we'll find a cell phone signal there. Three bars. Bob calls Matt, who by good fortune is working at home today and agrees to shuttle his bedraggled, unwashed, crabby parents to Pheasant Branch Creek, the next leg of the journey. While we wait for him to arrive, Bob dials the Edgewater Hotel and reserves us a room for tonight.

"We'll be arriving by canoe," he says.

A long pause.

"Yes, by canoe."

Another pause.

"We can store it in the parking garage? Great!"

Pause.

"Oh, thank you!"

He hangs up and grins at me.

"Since it's Monday night, they're giving us a really good rate for a really nice room."

A quiet truce.

Driving along the River Road into the village of Arena, leaving behind the bluffs that line the north side of the Wisconsin and heading across the valley's flat terrace that spreads from this side of the river to beyond Highway 14, we pass and cross stretches of the stagnant backwater stream that we had planned to paddle. Everywhere, it is filled with fallen trees and algae and looks more like a pestilent swamp than a creek. But between the towns of Mazomanie and Cross Plains, its tributary Black Earth Creek runs close to the road several times, and I can see that it is clearly passable. It's a beautiful, clear, swiftly flowing stream that runs through a green, bucolic valley. Though we have never paddled the Black Earth and won't today, we do know the stream. Bob has fished for trout in its waters, and we have hiked together along its banks, where jewelweed and black-eyed Susans grow. *We could have paddled this.* But I keep my mouth shut. And I will later learn from paddler John Sullivan, who canoed the creek downstream on a trip from Madison to La Crosse, that Black Earth Creek itself is quite a challenge, frequently blocked by cattle-crossing fences, blockaded low bridges, deadfalls and debris dams. He took out just upstream of the confluence with Blue Mounds Creek and portaged the final couple of miles to the Wisconsin.

For many years, Black Earth Creek has been a popular Driftless Area trout stream. And for over twenty years, the Black Earth Creek Watershed Association (BECWA) first led by Steve Born has been trying to keep it a healthy trout stream. As a watershed group, BECWA is a clear winner. Over 90 percent of the landowners in the watershed support the group's vision and actions. Citizens in the small communities—Cross Plains, Black Earth, and Mazomanie—that lie along its banks are fiercely protective of their stream. But it was not always so. In the early years, working to establish a watershed-wide base of support for the group, Born enlisted the help of mediator Howard Bellman. Observing the squabbling citizens—developers, farmers, environmentalists, fishermen, and urbanites—Bellman is said to have commented, "You're nothing more than a dysfunctional family." He added that people identify with a village, town, or personal interest, not with an ecosystem. One supervisor from the town of Cross Plains said, "It's just too bad we can't do what we want with our own land." Which I believe goes to the heart of the problem. Whether they want to be or not, rural residents are part of communities, and communities need to reach a civil consensus on land use. In her research for *A Thousand Pieces of Paradise*, Lynne Heasley reached these same conclusions.

Under Bellman's guidance, the dysfunction diminished. "I've seen drastic changes in the way the communities and people view the creek," said Pete Jopke, longtime resident of the watershed and water resources planner for Dane County. "And I think there's been a cultural shift since the 2002 fish kill," added Jopke, referring to a devastating manure runoff event that killed thousands of trout. "There's less dairy in the watershed now, and we have an early detection system that is triggered when oxygen levels in the creek drop, telling us there's a problem. We've formed a good neighbor group, and communication is better than ever. Conservation-wise, the group's a poster child."

Despite the wrangling and infighting, it is clear that this is a well-loved watershed. Working with landowners, the Natural Heritage Land Trust has protected seven hundred of the valley's twenty thousand acres through land purchases and conservation easements. Agricultural buffers, which Jopke estimates protect about 90 percent of the creek's trout fishery, are permanent easements, wide margins of land along the edge of the stream where vegetation is allowed to grow wild. Deep-rooted native plant growth reduces erosion of the creek banks and helps shield the creek and its finny inhabitants from the destructive effects of agricultural runoff.

Long ago, the stretch of the creek that runs through the village of Cross Plains was straightened to meet the needs of a mill dam in town. The dam disappeared some time ago, but the creek stayed unnaturally straight until the village decided to restore the natural meanders of the creek along this short stretch between Highway 14 and the railroad tracks. The rebuilt reach is complete with critter habitat: lunkers, root wads, vortex weirs, and deflectors, everything a trout could wish for. And along with the restoration, the village added two pedestrian bridges and rebuilt the segment of Ice Age Scenic Trail that runs along the creek in Zander Park.

On land that was opened to the public by local farmer Fred Wolf, a mile of Black Earth Creek has been restored to its presettlement meanders and contours. The Natural Heritage Land Trust and Dane County hold the forty-five-acre conservation easement and led the restoration of a part of the stream that had been straightened and dammed over 150 years ago. The silt and mud have washed downstream, and this reach of creek now winds and riffles over the gravelly bottom favored by trout. Gently sloping banks have reconnected the creek to its floodplain. One of the best parts of this story is that crews removed the only dam left on the creek, a low-head structure that diverted water into an impoundment called Lake Marion. Black Earth Creek now flows freely its full length.

The first segment of a Good Neighbor Trail that will eventually connect Mazomanie and Middleton runs along the creek, a three-mile stretch connecting Mazomanie to Wisconsin Heights High School, the valley's consolidated high school. Students can walk, bike, or ride snowmobiles to school, connecting them to the creek along the way. The late fall day that I hiked part of the trail, the stream project was so promising. Yet at the same time, the New Zealand mud snail, a particularly aggressive invasive creature that competes for food and space with the trout, had just been found in the creek for the first time.

Just east of Cross Plains, we drive over the barely detectable height of land between the Black Earth Creek and the Yahara River watersheds. We have finished crossing the Driftless.

Admittedly, these last twenty miles were by car, not canoe, but we have crossed it, and it is clear we could have done the entire journey under our own power, had we been more prepared and more patient. As it is with a confluence, the edge of a watershed feels like a momentous place, but this one is almost invisible, except to the eye of the geologist. Yet today I see it because I'm looking. A meandering boundary, a low ridge of sand and gravel bulldozed in and left behind by the last glacier, defines the edge. It's called the Johnstown Moraine. Along that moraine runs a part of the Ice Age Trail, a long hiking trail that traces the further-most reach of the Green Bay lobe of the recent glacier, the glacier that departed Wisconsin eleven thousand years ago.

We are now in the land that was smoothed flat by that last glacier, and we are now in the Rock River watershed. From here, water flows not to the Wisconsin River but through the Yahara chain—Taychopera to the Ho-Chunk tribe—four lake beads strung on the strand of the winding river, downstream to the Rock. From there the waters join the Mississippi near Rock Island, Illinois, the southern tip of the long Upper Mississippi Wildlife Refuge.

Though the moraine is easily missed unless one is looking for it, leaving the Driftless is a topographical shift that most people notice. In the Driftless, heavily forested hills dominate the landscape, suggesting a land less influenced by people than by nature, a land displaced in space and time from the decisively urban landscape only a few miles away in Madison. Over the sinuous line of the Johnstown Moraine, the world is suddenly flat. And on that flatness, people have reshaped the natural landscape into a cultural landscape, to revisit Cronon's premise: "By using the landscape, giving names to it, and calling it home, people selected the features that matter the most to them, and drew their mental maps accordingly. Once they had labeled those maps in a particular way . . . natural and cultural landscapes began to shade into and reshape one another."

In the Driftless, it seems that people have been less successful in reshaping the natural landscape than they have outside the Driftless. There the natural world pushed back more than it did outside, and in some senses, the Driftless landscape prevailed. Driftless towns are small, farming the rugged land is difficult, and Driftless roads follow the contours of the landscape and run through the river valleys, rarely conforming to the straight lines of the grid.

In the low land along Airport Road, the arrow-straight road that would have been our portage route had we not wrecked our wheels, is where our next little stream heads up. We find that the North Fork of

Pheasant Branch Creek, which was still flowing four weeks ago, is now a nearly dry ditch. Moving on to the other side of the beltline highway, to Century Avenue in Middleton, we find some water in the creek bed, an alarmingly small amount, and decide to follow the creek into the conservancy marshland anyway. About a mile in, the creek doubles back and empties into Lake Mendota, known in Nicollet's day as 4th Lake, and labeled thus on his map.

Matt helps us unload and hurries back to work. Soon after we launch, we realize that Pheasant Branch is far too low to paddle, and piles of dead branches and tangles of urban trash, including a battered plastic wading pool, intermittently block the narrow channel. After slogging downstream for a half mile anyway, grumbling at each other once again, we reach a unanimous agreement. We will reslog that half mile and carry everything along one of the conservancy hiking trails— about a quarter mile—to the point where the creek has returned from the Conservancy, just before it flows into the lake. We had not thought of this simple solution before because we were so bad-tempered.

Paddling out into big Mendota, I feel exhausted, from the long morning of slogging creeks, from the long portage, and from the long argument. Happily, the lake is relatively quiet. Even with all the fetch afforded by over fifteen square miles of open water, the gentle west-northwest wind doesn't seem to be kicking up waves . . . yet. Still, it's a big lake, which we know from experience can change quickly, and with our low-slung canoe loaded above the gunwale with gear, we will follow the shoreline rather than head straight across to the hotel.

Decision time. Do we go right and follow the south lakeshore, past the Shorewood neighborhood, around the curve of Frautschi Point and the long slender spit of wooded land called Picnic Point, past the University of Wisconsin's limnology building and Memorial Terrace, to the hotel pier?

Or do we go left, the much longer northerly route, past Governor Nelson State Park, past the inlet where the little Yahara River flows in from the DeForest area, past Cherokee Marsh, past Governor's Island,

Maple Bluff and the governor's mansion, past the outlet of the Yahara River at the Tenney Park locks?

Going left will shelter us best from nearly all of the west-northwest wind that blows only lightly now but could easily rise as the afternoon progresses. If we head right, the journey will be half the distance.

Our decision has everything to do with the aforementioned tipping point. Because we're homeward bound and are thinking of nothing else, we go right. And for a time the paddling is easy, our watery path delightfully clear of obstacles. With each paddle stroke, our crabbiness dissolves a little more, and soon we are laughing about how cool it will be to stay at the Edgewater tonight.

Near Marshall Park, however, the wind begins to rise, and rapidly. It's time to get serious about the paddling, as a following wind can be even more treacherous than a headwind. And as we trace the curve of the lakeshore into a southeast heading, the gusts become a crosswind, a nastier opponent. Even worse, motor boaters are buzzing about, their wakes hashing the waves into liquid chaos. Soon whitecaps dot Mendota and we are dodging the crests of unpredictably choppy waves, occasionally plunging into a trough, knuckles white on the paddle grips, struggling to find the rhythm of the waves, to follow a safe line along the shore. Whitecaps break over the gunwale and puddle around our feet. Along the shore ahead, three boys play in the frisky water, leaping from an official looking pier and swimming to shore in the breaking waves. I look down at my feet; we have taken on over an inch of water, and we're only half way to the hotel. *We should have given Matt most of the gear.*

Ahead are Frautschi Point and Picnic Point, where the full force of the wind blowing across the open lake will slam us before we can duck into the lee of University Bay. Another unanimous decision. We slide the canoe along the downwind side of the pier, grateful for a safe place to land.

"Where are we?" Bob calls to the boys.

"Shorewood Boat House," yells one, as he leaps off the pier again, an agile little otter in the waves.

Safe on shore, we could wait out the wind. But instead, we indulge our impatient natures once again and further compromise the already questionable authenticity of the voyage by calling for help, for the second time in one day. Our friend Pat, who lives nearby, arrives in her station wagon, a bemused grin on her face.

"How is it that you two experienced paddlers can't handle Lake Mendota?" she ribs us. "You paddle all those wild northern rivers and then you're beaten by your home lake?"

"Well, when the lake tries to swamp the canoe, it's time to land," I say, struggling out of my smelly paddling shirt so that I can pull on a less pungent garment. "We could hang out here at the Shorewood Boathouse, I suppose, and leave at night when the wind has died," I add. "Or could you give us a ride to the Edgewater?"

She can't stop laughing.

Strewn about our fancy hotel lodgings—a suite with a view of the lake, two televisions, and two bathrooms, one for each of us—our big red waterproof paddling pack and filthy clothes do not belong. We're definitely out of place in this hotel, and we love it. It takes at least an hour of bathing, scrubbing, shampooing, and shaving to remove the ground-in layers of Wisconsin River grime. As I did in the river, I float with only my nose out of the water, submerged this time in a warm soapy bath. Once restored, I dress in the clean shorts and t-shirt that have quietly traveled with us, hidden away unused in a corner of the pack. Yet the grittiness of Wisconsin River sand lingers in my well-worn sandals, and its familiarity is sweet. We walk hand in hand to State Street for dinner at Nadia's Restaurant and Grapevine Lounge. Almost home.

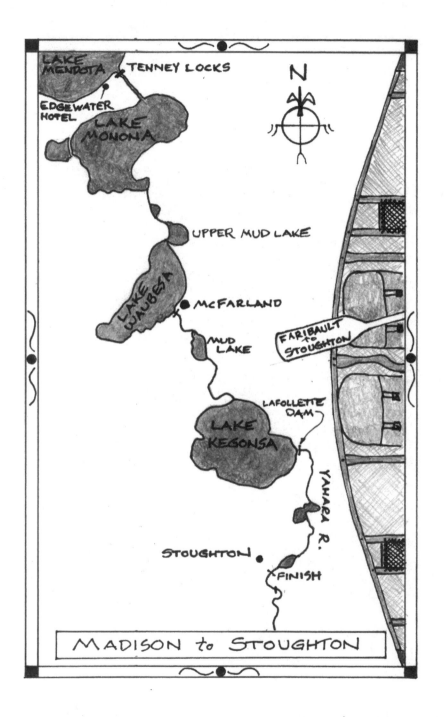

LAKE MENDOTA

TENNEY LOCKS

N

EDGEWATER HOTEL

LAKE MONONA

UPPER MUD LAKE

LAKE WAUBESA

McFARLAND

MUD LAKE

FARIBAULT to STOUGHTON

LAFOLLETTE DAM

LAKE KEGONSA

YAHARA R.

STOUGHTON

FINISH

MADISON to STOUGHTON

River Home Yahara

July the seventh. As the day dawns, Bob calls me out of a deep sleep to come over to the window. Lake Mendota is glassy smooth. It is barely light, and four members of the university men's rowing crew already skim across the mirror-like surface in four long slender solo shells, bodies leaning forward then smoothly pulling back, oars moving like metronomes. Two coaches and a driver motor alongside. Though we can't hear him through the sealed windowpane of our room, we can see the bullhorn one coach holds to his mouth and know he is barking commands to the scullers.

"Wow, they are out early," I say, adding blearily. "Do you want to leave now?"

"Sure, let's get on the water. I'd like to see them up close."

Bob and I once went to rowing camp. Our friend Steve was headed out east to spend a week rowing—or more precisely, sculling—those skinny little boats, and he asked us if we wanted to go. This was his second year at camp, so we figured it must be good. Bob and I love boats of all kinds, and summer camp on a lake for grownups sounded like a good adventure, so we said yes. Which means we ended up sculling long skinny solo shells down a long skinny lake called Big Hosmer Pond, deep in the Lowell Mountains of Vermont, every day for a week. Camp ended with a big race down the lake. Learning to keep the shell, no wider than the sculler's hips, from tipping over was the first challenge: never take the sculls out of the water unless you're in motion. Next was learning to keep the shell upright while also pulling on the long sculls and periodically glancing backward to stay on course. We learned to reach far forward to make the catch and to generate much of the power for the stroke by pushing back with the legs on the pull. By the end of the week, we both felt reasonably comfortable in these uber-tippy craft, and the added sense of balance on water that is required to scull without dumping improved the kind of paddling we do at home. Steve loves to quote the Rat in Kenneth Graham's *Wind in the Willows*, who famously muses, "there is nothing—absolutely nothing—half so much worth doing as simply messing about in boats."

After a quick breakfast, we hustle down to the parking garage to fetch our little canoe and portage it and the gear around the hotel to the pier. The guys are still out there, streaking across the water almost silently, except for the coach, and he isn't as loud as we expected. In minutes, we too are on the water, watching the crew fly by as we paddle slowly toward the locks, headed home.

It's early on a Tuesday morning, and the Tenney Locks, entrance to the Yahara River that is the river road to our home, are closed for business. Locked, so to speak. We portage around the blockade.

The Tenney Locks allow the DNR to control the water level of Lake Mendota. For years there's been a protracted and contentious political battle between those who want the lake's ecosystem to come first and those who want property owners to have predictable and favorable levels for their piers and marinas. Before the first dam was built in 1849, the lake was at least four and a half feet lower than it is now, some sources say up to seven feet lower. The river meandered then, across a low marshy isthmus to Lake Monona, several hundred feet to the east of where it now does. As the city grew, the wetlands were filled and a straight channel was dredged for the wandering Yahara.

Downstream, the lineup of fishermen standing on the banks quietly cast their lines into the Yahara, not bothering to look up as we pass.

They are used to canoeists. Of the six bridges we float under on this short reach of river, the one at East Washington Avenue is the one that I would call attractive, even magnificent, a Prairie style structure with a sign that tells us where we are. Though the river is totally urbanized here, banked by walls of stone and concrete topped by iron railings, the scene is architecturally impressive.

In the urban landscape, the river and the lake have a lot to put up with. Every rain flushes dirty storm water, road salt, and more into the waters. "The main water quality issue for this watershed is urban runoff of nutrients, solids, organic contaminants, heavy metals, oils and grease," is the assessment of the Dane County State of the Waters Report (2008), an unpleasant reality. People reshape the shorelines, altering and destroying the homes of the river's denizens in order to line Lake Mendota and the three other lakes in the chain with their houses. Seen in contrast with the more lightly developed Cannon River valley, the many miles of undeveloped bottomland along the Mississippi River pools, and buffered banks of Black Earth Creek, the Madison lakes are clearly more a cultural than a natural landscape. It's not just that we're out of the Driftless. People place a higher value on the lakeshore than they do on the riverbank, and that's where they want to build their homes. In parts of Wisconsin where there are no natural lakes, people often prefer to live on a river impoundment that resembles a lake rather than on a free-flowing river. It is safe to say that Madison, the city on the isthmus, the city of four lakes, was platted here because the lakes are here.

Floating into Lake Monona, shown on Nicollet's map as 3rd Lake, we begin the counter-clockwise circuit. Though the water is quiet enough today that we could easily cut straight across, we choose the scenic route: gliding past the Monona Terrace and Law Park, where the state capitol building, built on a drumlin hill, is a regal backdrop; past a weed harvester, a massive machine that clatters and munches through thick belts of aquatic vegetation, its operator working the shallow west end of the lake where the causeway crosses. We float past Olin Park, and the mouth of the channel that drains little Lake Wingra, and past Turville Bay, around the curve to Squaw Bay. Here the river regroups, flowing slowly and ponderously through a dense thicket of barely submersed greenery as it leaves the lake. Another weed cutter cranks slowly along this shore, dumping its soggy harvest—invasive water plants called Eurasian watermilfoil and curly-leaf pondweed—onto the flat platform in back.

Beds of aquatic vegetation are not new to these lakes. In 1887, Reuben Gold Thwaites wrote in *Historic Waterways* about "close-grown patches of reeds and lily-pads, encumbered by thick masses of green scum," native plants that grew here where the Yahara leaves Lake Monona. It is the nature of lakes like these to have what we call "weeds" growing in the shallow water. Fish like weeds; that is, if they are the right weeds and in the right concentrations. Even if the county is able to beat back the persistent algae growth, the water will become clearer and more weeds will grow.

Algae blooms are also a persistent and yet more disturbing plague on Lake Monona, fed by nutrients that flow in with urban storm water and from agricultural land in the headwaters and tributaries. People throughout the watershed are working hard to reduce those nutrients, and researchers are now exploring ways to reduce the algae in other ways as well. Algae grow by absorbing the nutrients, and tiny floating animals called zooplankton eat the nutritious algae. The largest and hungriest of these zooplankton is *Daphnia pulicaria*. Stephen Carpenter and Richard Lathrop of the University of Wisconsin–Madison have shown that *Daphnia pulicaria* is an "effective grazer" on algae and "causes large improvements in water quality." Which means that larger herds of grazing Daphnia are needed. This may be accomplished by spurring changes in the lake's food chain, according to Matt Diebel of the DNR. Small fish, like bluegill, eat Daphnia, so it may be helpful to reduce the lake's population of small fish. Increasing the populations of their predators—large fish like muskie, northern, and walleye—through stocking and changes in fishing regulations could help reduce the numbers of Daphnia-devouring fish, and the more that the big predators eat the little fish, the more Daphnia that will survive to graze on the algae. Sadly, however, the invasive spiny water flea, which feeds voraciously on Daphnia, has been found in Mendota and as it has no predators will reproduce unchecked.

The Yahara slides past houses, piers, and marinas, and beneath three more bridges, including the busy Beltline Highway, before flowing into Upper Mud Lake, which is surrounded by a large wetland. At the west end of the cattails, though we can't see them from here, are the facilities and settling ponds of the Nine Springs sewage treatment plant, operated by Madison Metropolitan Sewerage District (MMSD). In 1887, Thwaites wrote of canoeing on "the crystal water" of the Yahara chain. But that was written at about the same time that Madison first began dumping raw sewage into Lake Monona, when residents had not yet felt the full effects of this unfortunate practice. Madison's sewage flowed downstream untreated and unabated until the stench from the Yahara lakes and river became unbearable. In the late 1920s, public outrage led to the formation of MMSD, a treatment plant near the east-side Oscar Mayer plant and later, the Nine Springs plant. But the nutrients in the effluent still flowed into the Yahara system, and the resulting algae and plant growth became an increasing source of distress to communities on the lakes. In the 1950s, the district began pumping its wastewater through five miles of pipeline and a newly dug channel into Badfish Creek, a small tributary of the Yahara. Because the Badfish confluence is downstream of the lakes, landowners who lived around the lakes approved. Those along Badfish Creek did not. In recent decades, however, MMSD has made two substantial changes—ultraviolet light replaced chlorine disinfection, which created toxic byproducts, and modern biological filters and extraction processes now remove phosphorus from the waste-water. The waters of the Badfish now run relatively clear and forty-two species of fish, including brown trout, swim in the stream.

At the south end of the little lake we paddle under an aged railroad bridge supported by creosoted wooden pilings and through a narrow outlet into 2nd Lake, Lake Waubesa. Like Monona, the lake is filled with Eurasian watermilfoil and algae, and paddling through the thickly matted beds is discouragingly slow. Portaging the small dam at the outlet, we cross Highway 51, a road that runs between Madison and our home.

Past the canoe landing at Indian Mound Conservation Park in the village of McFarland, the shoreline quickly evolves into a lovely marsh-land, dragonflies hovering and darting above the cattails, and the river opens into tranquil little Mud Lake. A kingfisher screeches notice of our invasion, and a yellow-headed blackbird wings through the cattails. There is no sign of the village. Behind the tree-lined, marshy shore is a wildlife refuge, Marsh Woods Park, where an expanse of open grassland is bounded by an upland woodlot of old growth trees. From out here on the lake, the dense vegetation of refuge conceals the village behind a veil of green and allows river travelers a sense of remoteness. Bordering the shoreline, a cattail margin expands around us as we leave the lake.

We float toward the iron bridge at Dyreson Road, a structure that looks as though it is from another time, and that's because it is. A pinned Pratt through-truss bridge, built in 1897 by Milwaukee Bridge and Iron Works, it is now being repaired for only the second time in its long life, this time by the historically and environmentally minded citizens of the town of Dunn. Some years ago, I rode across this bridge on a bicycle circuit of Lake Kegonsa and remember thinking then that it seemed an appealing anachronism. This place has been a river ford for thousands of years. According to the Dane County Environmental Council's 2007 Water Trail Guide, it is "one of very few places on the Yahara River system that is narrow enough and with firm footing suitable for conve-nient crossing by horses and humans." Archeologists from the University of Wisconsin have found evidence along the river that Paleo-Indians were in this area more than eleven thousand years ago, when humans were first moving into the area at the end of the most recent ice age. And through the shallow green water, we can just make out the faint outline of a V-shaped fish weir—a rock dam designed to trap fish for netting and spearing. The Dane County Environmental Council alleges the weir has probably been in the river bottom since prehistoric times and the Ho-Chunk tribe used it as recently as the late nineteenth century.

According to the Water Trail Guide, federal surveyors mapped southern Wisconsin Territory between 1833 and 1835, and the Madison area was mapped from south to north in 1834. When Joseph Nicollet compiled and drew his map of the water routes further west, published in 1843, he would have used these brand-new surveys to complete the Wisconsin Territory section, an area that he had not personally explored. Though he labeled the nearby Sugar River on his map, Nicollet left our river unnamed. In 1844, naturalist and writer Increase Lapham called it the Catfish River. It wasn't until 1855 that the state legislature approved the names Mendota, Monona, Waubesa, Kegonsa, and Yahara, which were suggested by Frank Hudson, a surveyor and student of tribal lore, and Lyman Draper, secretary of the State Historical Society, to reflect the heritage of the watershed's original inhabitants.

Though we thought the weeds were thick in the upstream lakes, it is clear that Lake Kegonsa, formerly 1st Lake, is in a class of its own. At the river's mouth, a vast multihued algal mat, material blown in and concentrated here by the south wind, sprawls over this corner of the lake. Thick tangles of yellow filamentous algae, like those we battled on Blue Mounds Creek, blanket the water. Large dark brown clumps gather in their own unattractive flotillas. Patches of blue-green algae bloom like oil slicks. It's an ugly sight. Blue-green algae can be toxic, to dogs in particular and to humans as well, causing gastrointestinal and respiratory issues or even liver failure.

"This is unbelievably disgusting," mutters Bob.

"I'm trying not to splash it in my face," I reply.

At once saddened by the state of our lake and angry that humans choose to foul their own nests this way, we paddle cautiously through the stuff, with thick strands of the yellow algal mats dripping from our paddle blades, following the most direct route to Williams Point, the point of land that lies between us and the spot where the river departs Kegonsa.

To our left, though we cannot see it, is the mouth of Door Creek. It doesn't look like much, but this little stream causes big problems for the lake. A group of University of Wisconsin graduate students in Water Resource Management just finished studying the creek and its nutrient management challenges. The Door Creek watershed is thirty square miles of heavily farmed land, about a fourth of the land that drains directly into Lake Kegonsa, the remainder coming from the upper lakes. And almost a fourth of this land is drain-tiled, which accelerates the movement of nutrients into the lake. In 2009, farmers made regular applications of Metrogro—phosphorus-rich biosolids, distilled from Madison Metropolitan Sewerage District sewage sludge—to thirteen hundred acres of the little stream's watershed, resulting in increased phosphorus being stored in the soil and released into the creek. Erosion that results from the rolling character of the land combined with the prevalent practice of fall tilling adds excess sediment to the creek.

In addition to these agricultural stresses, the village of McFarland continues to develop more land in the watershed, and the nutrients from storm water runoff pour into the creek. On the other side of this nutrient equation, the large wetland that surrounds the final reach of the creek has the potential, if restored, to absorb some of the phosphorus before it can feed the algae. In fact, 9 percent of the watershed is wetlands. Much of Door Creek is channelized and bermed to reduce erosion, an alteration of the natural creek channel that helps during heavy rains, when phosphorus flow is highest.

The students recommend protecting and restoring wetlands in the watershed; retaining the berms, at least temporarily; promoting no-till farming and non-row crops on sloping land; further limiting the Metrogro applications; and adding buffer strips along the creek. And the team concluded that, if these recommendations were implemented, they would improve the water quality of Door Creek. Because most of the phosphorus in Lake Kegonsa comes from the upstream lakes, however, not from Door Creek, the students added that making these same changes in the watersheds of the upstream lakes would make it "possible to drastically improve the condition of the entire lake ecosystem." Perhaps the damage can be undone.

When the last glacier moved in, it covered the land that is now Madison and the Yahara river valley with ice more than a thousand feet deep. As the ice melted off the land where the lakes of Madison now lie, Glacial Lake Yahara took its place, draining first to the southwest and west, through the Sugar River and Black Earth Creek. Glacial Lake Yahara shrank until it filled only a basin bounded by the moraine that now divides the Yahara River and Black Earth watersheds to the west and by the retreating glacier to the northeast. The lake then found a new outlet to the south, through the glacial debris covering what is now the river valley. As the water moved downstream and the lake level dropped, a chain of smaller river-linked lakes appeared.

This giant frozen earthsmoother and its meltwater carved and polished the contours of our river system, shaped the gentle slope of the land, swept in glacial erratic boulders, sculpted sand and gravel into streamlined teardrop drumlins, and left us abundant marshlands. The peaty nature of the soil in the Yahara valley comes from the marshes, those organic sponges and cleansers of water. From the nineteenth century until the present, we tried so hard to drain those marshes, and it is only now that we have learned to appreciate and protect those that remain and long for those that are lost to return.

Yesterday we left the Driftless, where high wooded uplands and steep valleys define the shape of the world, where roads curve along river valleys, where the river route is often the most direct. It's a land of ancient bedrock layers, of the hidden world of karst, where icy groundwater flows and seeps through an intricate network of limestone fissures, following secret paths through the rocky underpinnings of the land, emerging at random moments, pouring down the coulee in a rush of icy narrow stream, surprising the hiker with gusts of icy breath. The oldest rivers carved deep pathways, time travelers slicing through the bedrock layer cake, trails of geologic and human history, forming a refuge where relicts from before the glacial age still live. Though ice never buried the Driftless, the massive glacier that covered the land all around it filled the riverbeds of its drainage channels through the Driftless with a deluge of glacial sand and gravel, and glacial winds coated the bare hills and valleys with deep layers of loess, the rich soil of the Driftless. While movement of sediment is clearly a key aspect of the natural history of the Driftless, farming the rugged land vastly accelerated the cycle of erosion along steep tributary streams and deposition along valley bottoms that continues today.

Today we came home to this gentle undulating Yahara landscape of lake, marsh, slow river, drumlin. Here, a glacial age that seems relatively recent in geologic time carved the physical shape of the land, with ice that transformed rocky hills and steep valleys into soft low-lying contours. It was this flattened world, frosted with sediment spread by the departing glacier, that greeted its human inhabitants and invited the settlement that shapes and is shaped by the natural landscape. Cultural pressures from extensive agriculture and development and the slower flow of the river over the glacial landscape together yield a different central challenge for the rivers here than for rivers in the Driftless: an excess of nutrients rather than of sediment.

Paddling the Yahara today, we feel that excess and it darkens our view of the future. Yet it would be simplistic and inaccurate to say this trip is about identifying environmental issues, a task that is simply the byproduct of being in today's natural world and paying attention. Instead, it's about feeling and knowing the rivers and the land through which they flow, the landscape that is our well-known world, just a little more deeply, the details and the whole. Knowing it as it is, not what it was or what it could be. It's looking at the familiar from a different angle, the up-close angle formed by sitting in the bow of a canoe, immersed in the river's reality.

I think of the lines from T. S. Eliot's *Little Gidding*: "We shall not cease from exploration / And the end of all our exploring / Will be to arrive where we started / And know the place for the first time." Eliot's words speak to me of the way we connect to the earth. Each journey out and each return home reveals the new in familiar places, the details of which we did not see before, imparting lessons we had yet to learn. After spending those days floating between rugged old hills, this flat-land river valley of ours feels so gentle, so subdued, so newly formed, and the contrast with the ancient Driftless valleys so sharp.

By canoe, our journey across the Driftless from home to home has taken twelve days. A flight from Faribault to Stoughton in a small plane, soaring over the corduroy land like a migratory bird, would take about two and a half hours. When we drive the familiar interstate route, it takes four and a half hours. Were we to walk home instead, following the back roads and traveling at the rate of eighteen miles a day, our hike would take fifteen days. In the days when there were no roads and we would have trekked the high plateau land through Minnesota to the Mississippi, dipping through steep tributary valleys along the way, and then following Military Ridge across the rugged Driftless, it is hard to know how many days we would have had to walk; we probably would have canoed instead. Ten years ago, Bob and our children rode their bicycles from Trempealeau to Stoughton, on long straight biking trails that once were railroad lines and then up and down the steep, winding back roads, crossing the Driftless in three days. On each distinctly different path across the intricate landscape of the Driftless, the traveler finds a different world, its details and beauty unique to the route.

We've finished crossing our lake. As with the upstream lakes, a low dam controls the outflow of the Yahara from Lake Kegonsa to maintain the water levels. Surprisingly, considering this summer's low water, the lock is wide open today. We're grateful that we needn't climb out of the canoe into this mucky mess to portage. Instead we slip smoothly through on the flat water without thinking about why. The algae slips through as well and follows us downriver, keeping us company as the Yahara meanders south between the cattails, wanders through the quiet place where we spot wild swans and yellow-headed blackbirds, across the wide shallow wetland where the channel is often hard to find and where our small town's annual spring canoe race starts, under the low bridge at Highway N, past the little island where our boys once loved to camp, down the river to Stoughton. As the blocky shapes of the buildings atop hospital hill, the dark horizontal line of the railroad bridge, and the low wooded rise of the hill on the opposite bank of the river appear in the distance, I am no longer thinking about the algae. Almost there.

"You know, we didn't see a single other canoe, the whole way down from Madison," says Bob as we paddle under the railroad bridge.

"Nope. And we never did eat lunch," I reply. "Let's hurry!"

At Division Street Park, our son Greg waits on the riverbank. Together, we portage up the hill to our home.

In this quiet fashion, our journey ends. We have traveled home by river, and in doing so have experienced the connectedness that the rivers offer, the physical reality of the riverine network that our ancestors used by necessity, a way to travel from one place to another that keeps us immersed in the natural world rather than detached from it, participants rather than observers at the window of a train or car. As we paddled past the confluences of rivers we had formerly canoed as visitors rather than river travelers, we became acutely aware of distances between rivers, their relationships to each other, discovering that we had a new sense of what it would mean to canoe down the Cannon, down the Mississippi and up the Zumbro, for example, not abstract knowledge derived from studying a map but a physical sense that would allow us to say with some authority how long such a canoe trip would take, what it would feel like, what difficulties we would face, what pleasures it would offer. I found that we like traveling the river from point to point even better than we like visiting the river on the usual kind of canoe trip where we return to our starting point, and the former also satisfies that goal-oriented part of our natures. And yet, though it was a struggle, we grudgingly learned that it is best for river travelers to be patient, to accept the conditions that the river and nature set forth, as the river and nature generally call the shots.

Sifting through the many mental images I gathered over the past twelve days, I am surprised by some that linger vividly in my mind's eye: the long, low line of a lock and dam ahead, slowly coming into focus as we close the distance; the flash of a goldfinch in a riverside willow thicket; the bleakness of a bermed and rock-clad riverbank; the startling beauty of a white steeple rising from the greenery of a Mississippi river town; the intimidating stony hulks of Barn Bluff, Frontenac, and Wyalusing; our first glimpse of each secretive wooded confluence; the wild overwhelming tumult that is a train roaring down the river valley; the ominous power of a barge tow. I recall with lasting fondness the riffles of the Cannon, the flight of the pelicans, the grand movie that is the Mississippi River valley bluffs, and the soft golden sand of the Wisconsin. In the end, I realize that I felt, rather than observed, the sudden absence of the Driftless following our departure from that compellingly rugged landscape, a passage we had made so many times over the years but which I had never experienced with such clarity and such a powerful sense of connection.

References

Anderson, Renae. "Coon Valley Days." *Wisconsin Academy Review* 48, no. 2 (Spring 2002): 42–48.

Anfinson, John O. *The River We Have Wrought: A History of the Upper Mississippi.* Minneapolis: University of Minnesota Press, 2003.

Becker, George C. *Fishes of Wisconsin.* Madison: University of Wisconsin Press, 1983.

Berry, Wendell. *The Unforeseen Wilderness.* 1971. San Francisco: North Point Press, 1991.

Born, Steve, Jeff Mayers, Andy Morton, and Bill Sonzogni. *Exploring Wisconsin Trout Streams: The Angler's Guide.* 2nd ed. Madison: University of Wisconsin Press, 2014.

Bray, Edmund C., and Martha Coleman Bray. *Joseph N. Nicollet on the Plains and Prairies.* St. Paul: Minnesota Historical Society Press, 1976.

Catlin, George. *Letters and Notes on the Manners, Customs, and Conditions of the North American Indians, Vol. II.* 1841. Minneapolis: Ross and Haines, 1965.

Cronon, William. *Nature's Metropolis: Chicago and the Great West.* New York: W. W. Norton, 1991.

Derleth, August. *The Wisconsin: River of a Thousand Isles.* 1942. Madison: University of Wisconsin Press, 1985.

Dott, Robert H., Jr., and John W. Attig. *Roadside Geology of Wisconsin.* Missoula, MT: Mountain Press Publishing Company, 2004.

Durbin, Richard D. *The Wisconsin River: An Odyssey Through Time and Space.* Cross Plains, WI: Spring Freshet Press, 1997.

Featherstonhaugh, George W. *A Canoe Voyage Up the Minnay Sotor.* 1847. St. Paul: Minnesota Historical Society Press, 1970.

Fremling, Calvin R. *Immortal River: The Upper Mississippi in Ancient and Modern Times.* Madison: University of Wisconsin Press, 2005.

Grahame, Kenneth. *The Wind in the Willows.* 1908. New York: Lemon Tree Press, 1982.

Heasely, Lynne. *A Thousand Pieces of Paradise.* Madison: University of Wisconsin Press, 2005.

Hoogeveen, Nate. *Paddling Iowa.* Black Earth, WI: Trails Books, 2004.

Leopold, Aldo. *Round River: From the Journals of Aldo Leopold.* Edited by Luna B. Leopold. Minocqua, WI: NorthWord Press, 1991.

Meine, Curt. "The View from Man Mound." From *The Vanishing Present: Wisconsin's Changing Lands, Waters, and Wildlife.* Chicago: University of Chicago Press, 2008.

Miller, Michael A., Katie Songer, and Ron Dolen. *Field Guide to Wisconsin Streams: Plants, Fishes, Invertebrates, Amphibians, and Reptiles.* Madison: University of Wisconsin Press, 2014.

Sietman, Bernard E. *Field Guide to the Freshwater Mussels of Minnesota.* St. Paul: Minnesota Department of Natural Resources, 2003.

Svob, Mike. *Paddling Southern Wisconsin: 82 Great Trips by Canoe and Kayak.* Black Earth, WI: Trails Books, 2001.

Thwaites, Reuben Gold. *Historic Waterways: Six Hundred Miles of Canoeing Down the Rock, Fox and Wisconsin Rivers.* Chicago: A. C. McClurg and Company, 1888.

Twain, Mark. *Life on the Mississippi.* 1883. New York: Signet, 1980.

Waters, Thomas F. *The Streams and Rivers of Minnesota.* Minneapolis: University of Minnesota Press, 1977.

Index of River Names